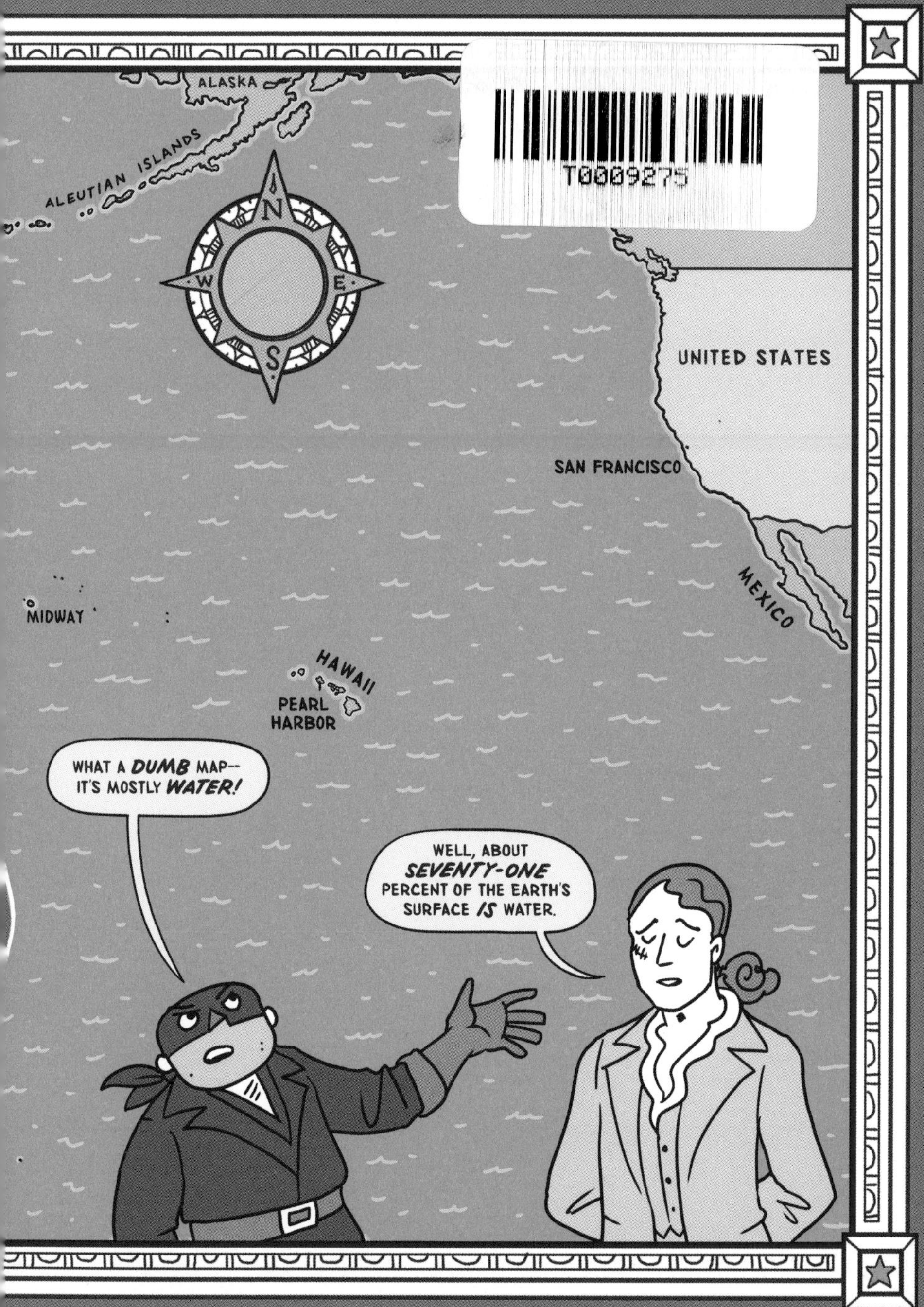
ALASKA
ALEUTIAN ISLANDS
N
W
E
S
UNITED STATES
SAN FRANCISCO
MEXICO
MIDWAY
HAWAII
PEARL HARBOR
WHAT A DUMB MAP-- IT'S MOSTLY WATER!
WELL, ABOUT SEVENTY-ONE PERCENT OF THE EARTH'S SURFACE IS WATER.

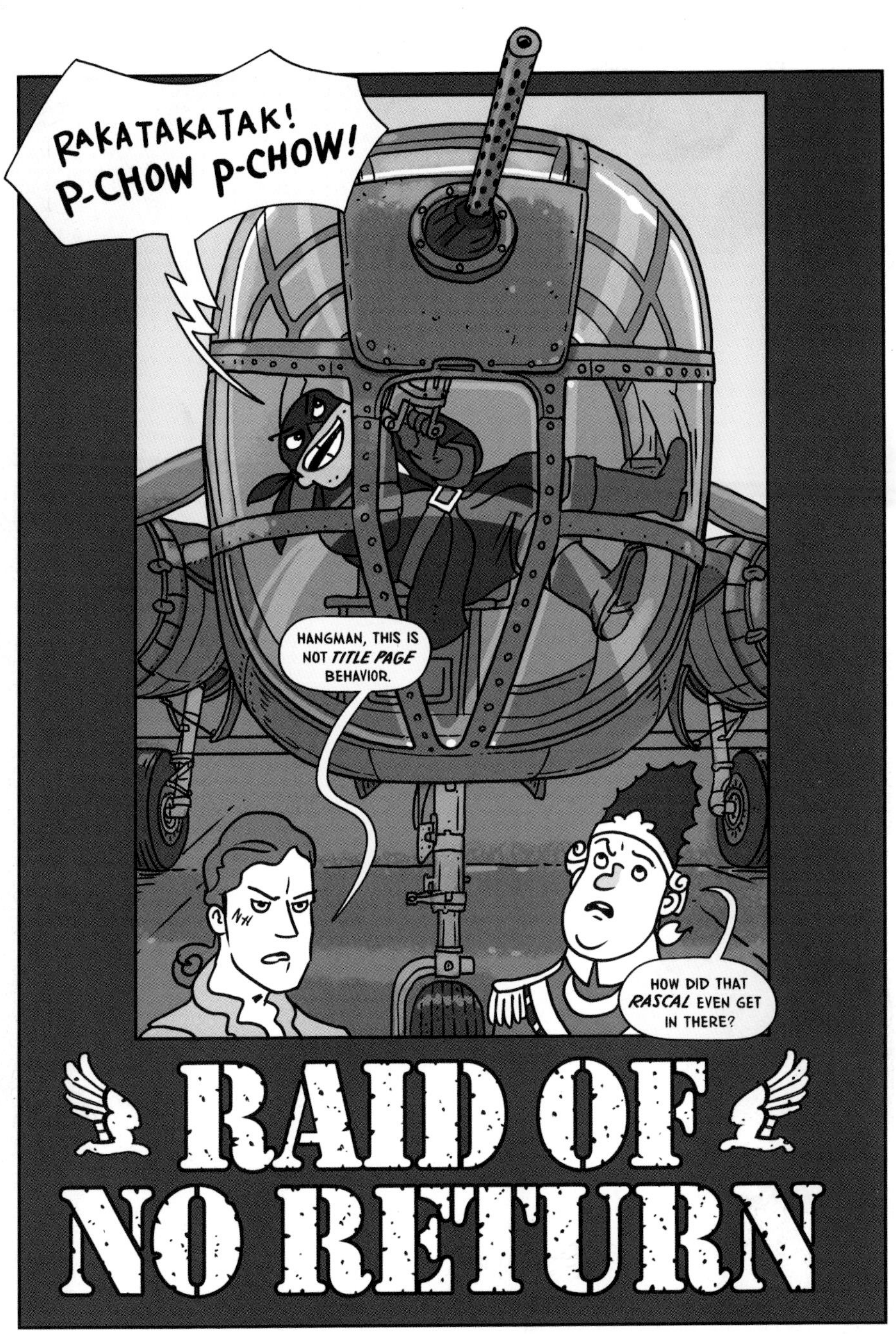

RAKATAKATAK! P-CHOW P-CHOW!
HANGMAN, THIS IS NOT *TITLE PAGE* BEHAVIOR.
HOW DID THAT *RASCAL* EVEN GET IN THERE?

RAID OF NO RETURN

AMULET BOOKS, NEW YORK

CATALOGING-IN-PUBLICATION DATA HAS BEEN APPLIED FOR AND MAY BE OBTAINED FROM THE LIBRARY OF CONGRESS.

ISBN 978-1-4197-2556-2

TEXT AND ILLUSTRATIONS COPYRIGHT © 2017 NATHAN HALE
BOOK DESIGN BY NATHAN HALE AND CHAD W. BECKERMAN

PRINTED AND BOUND IN MALAYSIA
1 4

ABRAMS The Art of Books
195 Broadway, New York, NY 10007
abramsbooks.com

FOR COLONEL
RICHARD E. COLE
THE LAST RAIDER

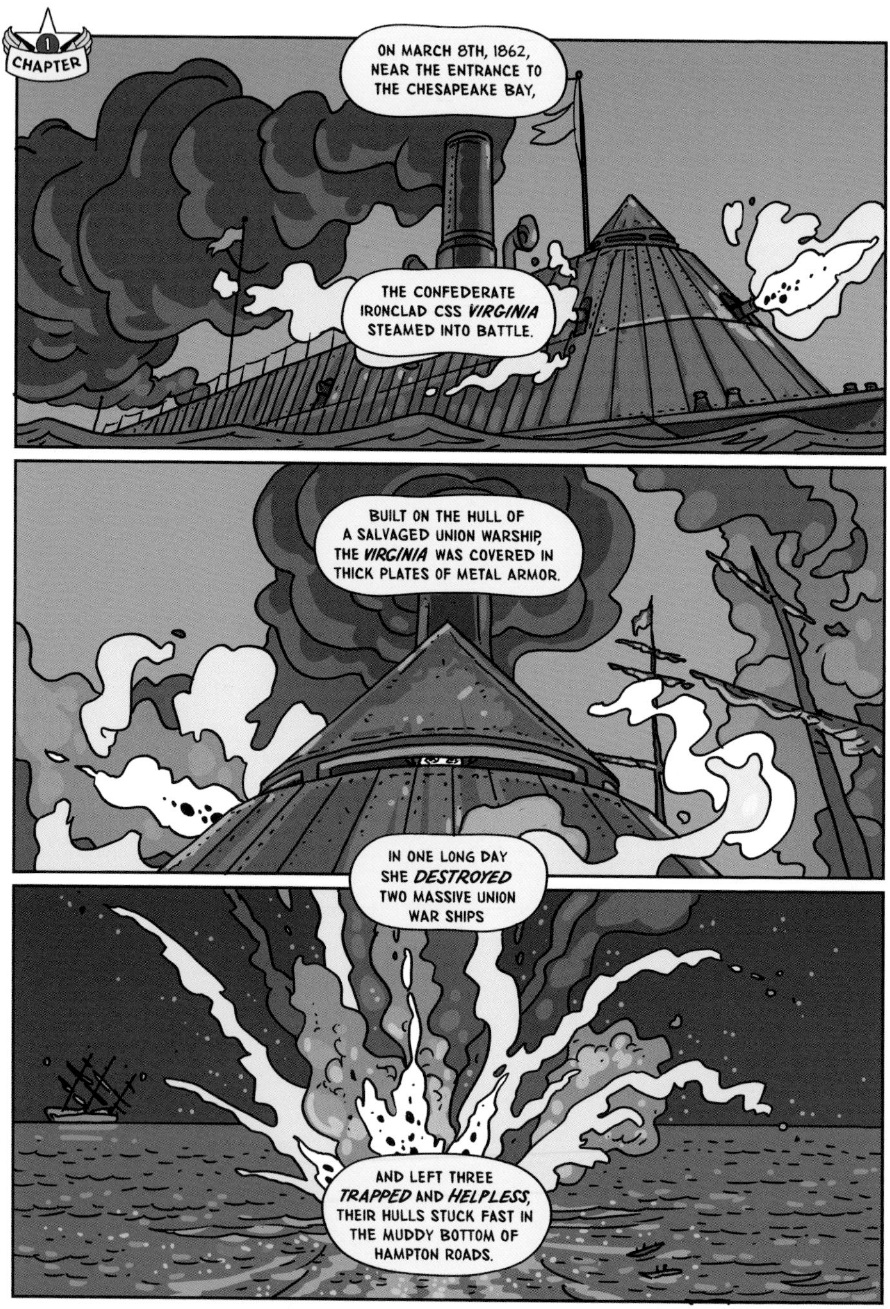
CHAPTER 1
ON MARCH 8TH, 1862, NEAR THE ENTRANCE TO THE CHESAPEAKE BAY,
THE CONFEDERATE IRONCLAD CSS *VIRGINIA* STEAMED INTO BATTLE.
BUILT ON THE HULL OF A SALVAGED UNION WARSHIP, THE *VIRGINIA* WAS COVERED IN THICK PLATES OF METAL ARMOR.
IN ONE LONG DAY SHE *DESTROYED* TWO MASSIVE UNION WAR SHIPS
AND LEFT THREE *TRAPPED* AND *HELPLESS*, THEIR HULLS STUCK FAST IN THE MUDDY BOTTOM OF HAMPTON ROADS.

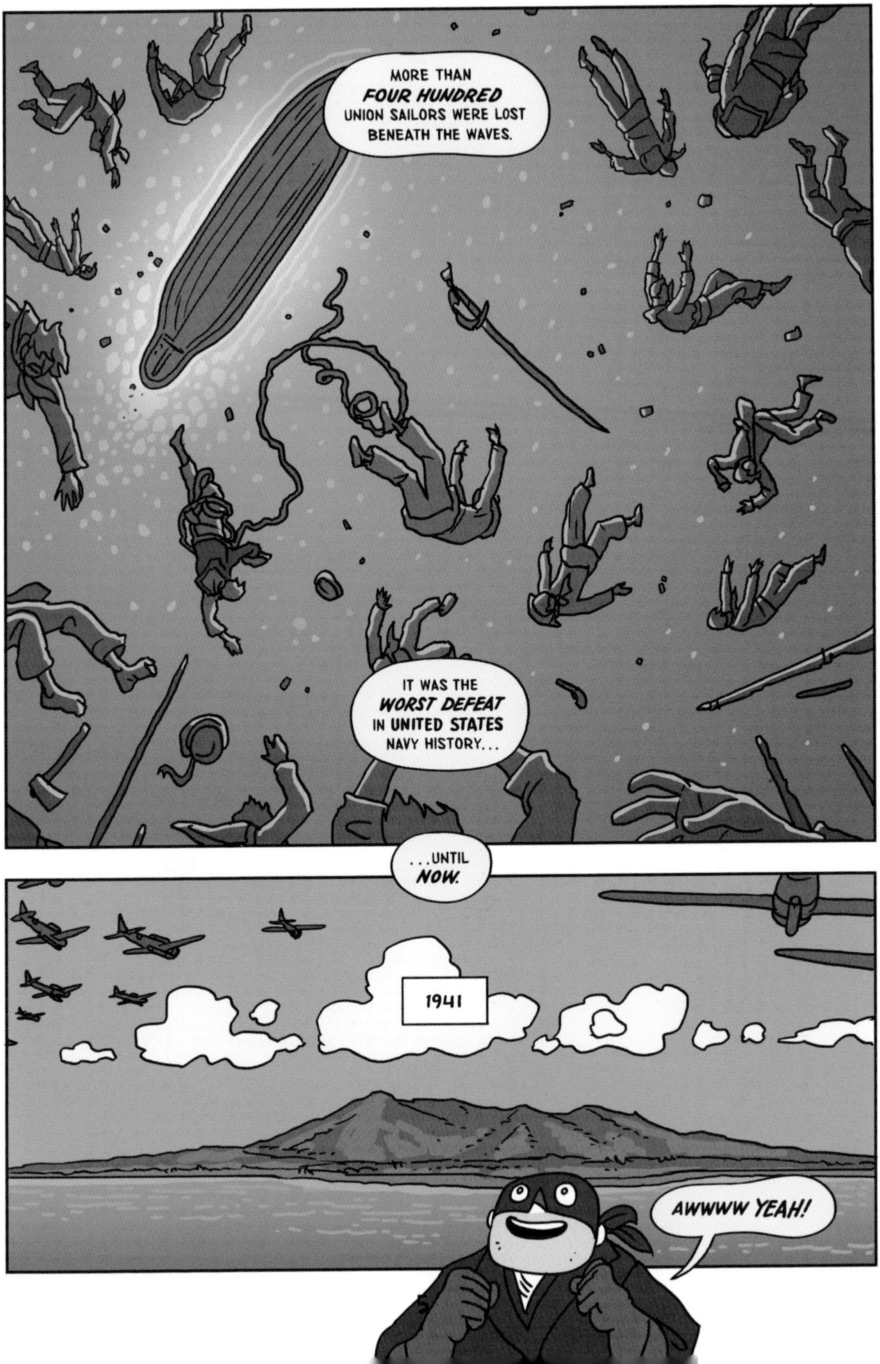
MORE THAN FOUR HUNDRED UNION SAILORS WERE LOST BENEATH THE WAVES.
IT WAS THE WORST DEFEAT IN UNITED STATES NAVY HISTORY...
...UNTIL NOW.
1941
AWWWW YEAH!

THE TARGET IS ON THE *EAST* SIDE OF THE ISLAND.
GET *CLOSER* TO THE WATER.
MMMRRRROOO
APPROACHING TARGET.
LOWER!
MMMRRROOOO
FIRE! FIRE TORPEDO!
TORPEDO AWAY!
CLICK
FWISSSSHH
IT'S LAUNCHED! IT'S *GOING TO MAKE IT!*

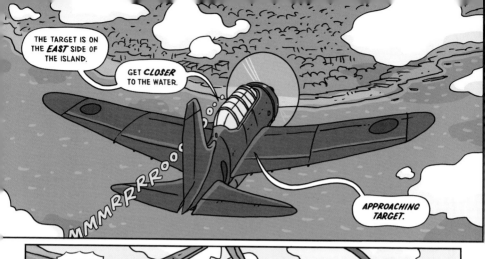

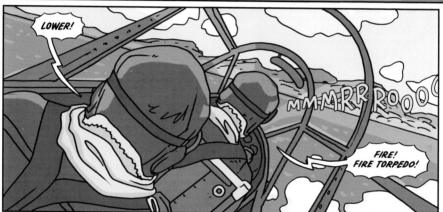

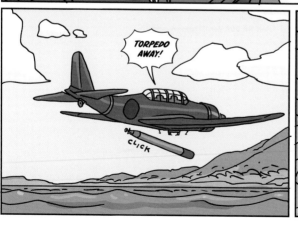

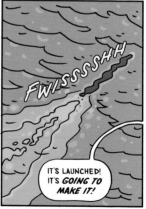

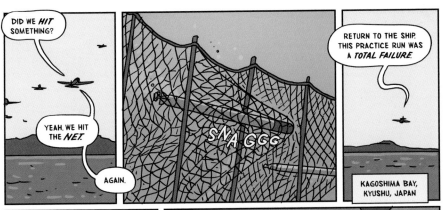

DID WE *HIT* SOMETHING?

YEAH. WE HIT THE *NET.*

AGAIN.

SNAGGG

RETURN TO THE SHIP. THIS PRACTICE RUN WAS A *TOTAL FAILURE.*

KAGOSHIMA BAY, KYUSHU, JAPAN

THE NETS ONLY GIVE US *FORTY FEET* OF WATER.

THERE'S *NO ROOM* FOR THE TORPEDOES TO LEVEL OUT!

OUR *ACTUAL* TARGET ZONE IS *FORTY* FEET DEEP ON AVERAGE.

YOU MUST FLY *EVEN LOWER,* LIKE A DRAGONFLY SKIMMING OVER A POND.

IT DOESN'T MATTER HOW *LOW* WE FLY-- THE TORPEDOES NEED *DEEPER WATER!*

SEVENTY FEET AT LEAST!

THIS PILOT IS CORRECT. OUR TORPEDOES WON'T SWIM IN THAT SHALLOW WATER.

COMMANDER GENDA! SIR!

SIR, WHAT CAN WE DO?

WE CAN EITHER WAIT FOR THE SEA TO RISE...

OR WE CAN TRY A *NEW* TYPE OF TORPEDO.

COME TAKE A LOOK.

7

SIR, THAT LOOKS LIKE OUR SAME *TYPE 91* TORPEDO.
YES. IT IS THE GOOD OLD *GYORAI*-- THE *THUNDERFISH.*
BUT LOOK CLOSER.
IT'S GOT A *WOODEN* BOX ON THE FINS.
THOSE PIECES OF WOOD WILL STABILIZE IT-- OUR *MODIFIED* THUNDERFISH WILL SWIM IN *SHALLOW* WATER.
HOW SHALLOW?
TIME TO FIND OUT.
REFUEL THESE BOMBERS AND ATTACH THE MODIFIED THUNDERFISH.
THIS WILL *NEVER* WORK.
I TRUST COMMANDER GENDA--HE'S A *PILOT,* JUST LIKE US.
FIRE! TORPEDO AWAY!
CLICK
HOW'S IT LOOKING?
I DON'T SEE IT. I DON'T THINK IT--
FWISSSSSHHHHHHHHHHHHHH
THEY WORK!
BONK
CONGRATULATIONS, COMMANDER GENDA, YOUR THUNDERFISH CAN *SWIM!*
REFUEL THE BOMBERS AND PUT MORE TARGETS OUT. WE WILL *PRACTICE* UNTIL WE ARE *PERFECT!*

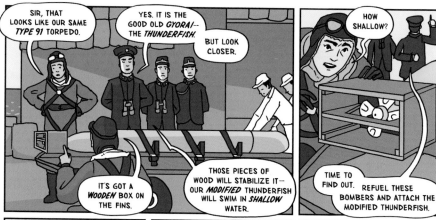

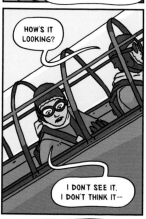

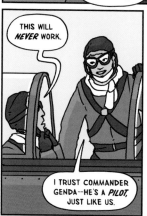

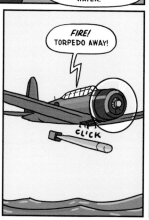

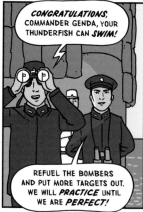

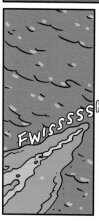

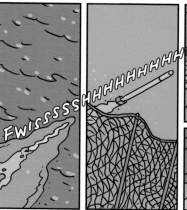

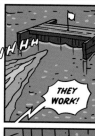

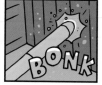

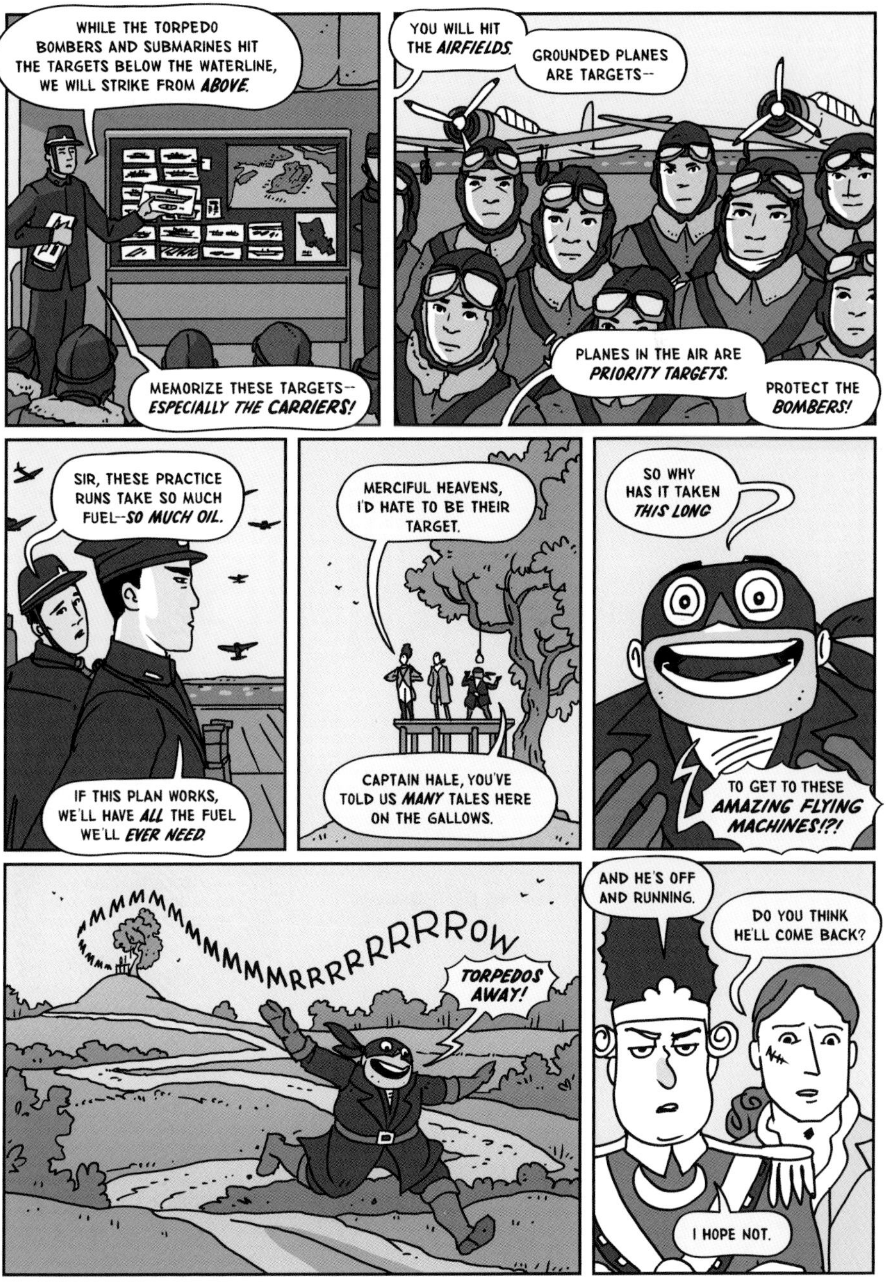
WHILE THE TORPEDO BOMBERS AND SUBMARINES HIT THE TARGETS BELOW THE WATERLINE, WE WILL STRIKE FROM ABOVE.
MEMORIZE THESE TARGETS-- ESPECIALLY THE CARRIERS!
YOU WILL HIT THE AIRFIELDS.
GROUNDED PLANES ARE TARGETS--
PLANES IN THE AIR ARE PRIORITY TARGETS.
PROTECT THE BOMBERS!
SIR, THESE PRACTICE RUNS TAKE SO MUCH FUEL--SO MUCH OIL.
IF THIS PLAN WORKS, WE'LL HAVE ALL THE FUEL WE'LL EVER NEED.
MERCIFUL HEAVENS, I'D HATE TO BE THEIR TARGET.
CAPTAIN HALE, YOU'VE TOLD US MANY TALES HERE ON THE GALLOWS.
SO WHY HAS IT TAKEN THIS LONG
TO GET TO THESE AMAZING FLYING MACHINES!?!
MMMMMMMMMMMMMMMMRRRRRRRRROW
TORPEDOS AWAY!
AND HE'S OFF AND RUNNING.
DO YOU THINK HE'LL COME BACK?
I HOPE NOT.

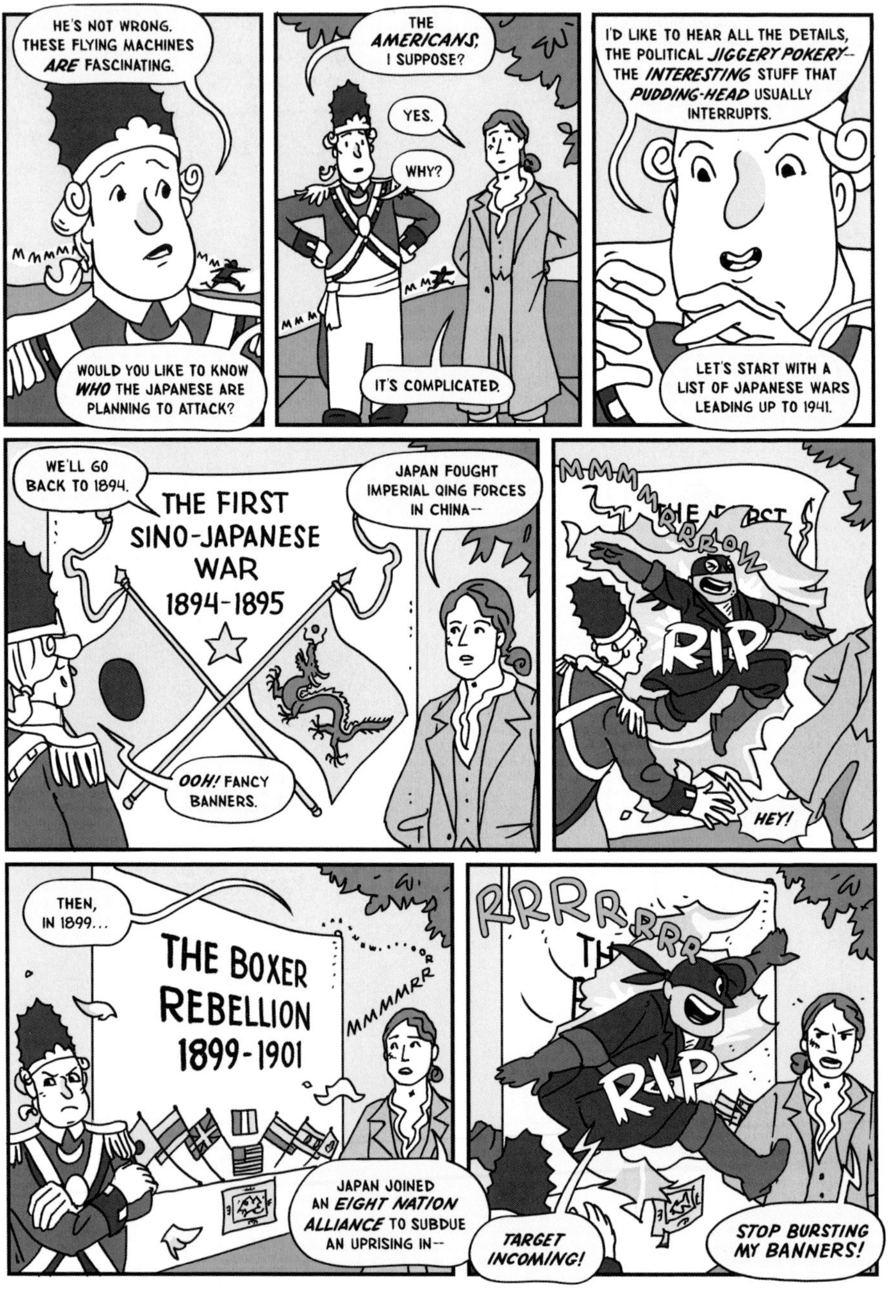

HE'S NOT WRONG. THESE FLYING MACHINES *ARE* FASCINATING.
MMMMM
MMM
WOULD YOU LIKE TO KNOW *WHO* THE JAPANESE ARE PLANNING TO ATTACK?
THE *AMERICANS,* I SUPPOSE?
YES.
WHY?
MMM
MMM
IT'S COMPLICATED.
I'D LIKE TO HEAR ALL THE DETAILS, THE POLITICAL *JIGGERY POKERY*— THE *INTERESTING* STUFF THAT *PUDDING-HEAD* USUALLY INTERRUPTS.
LET'S START WITH A LIST OF JAPANESE WARS LEADING UP TO 1941.
WE'LL GO BACK TO 1894.
THE FIRST SINO-JAPANESE WAR 1894-1895
JAPAN FOUGHT IMPERIAL QING FORCES IN CHINA—
OOH! FANCY BANNERS.
MMMMRRROW
RIP
HEY!
THEN, IN 1899...
THE BOXER REBELLION 1899-1901
MMMMRR
JAPAN JOINED AN *EIGHT NATION ALLIANCE* TO SUBDUE AN UPRISING IN—
RRRRRRRR
RIP
TARGET INCOMING!
STOP BURSTING MY BANNERS!

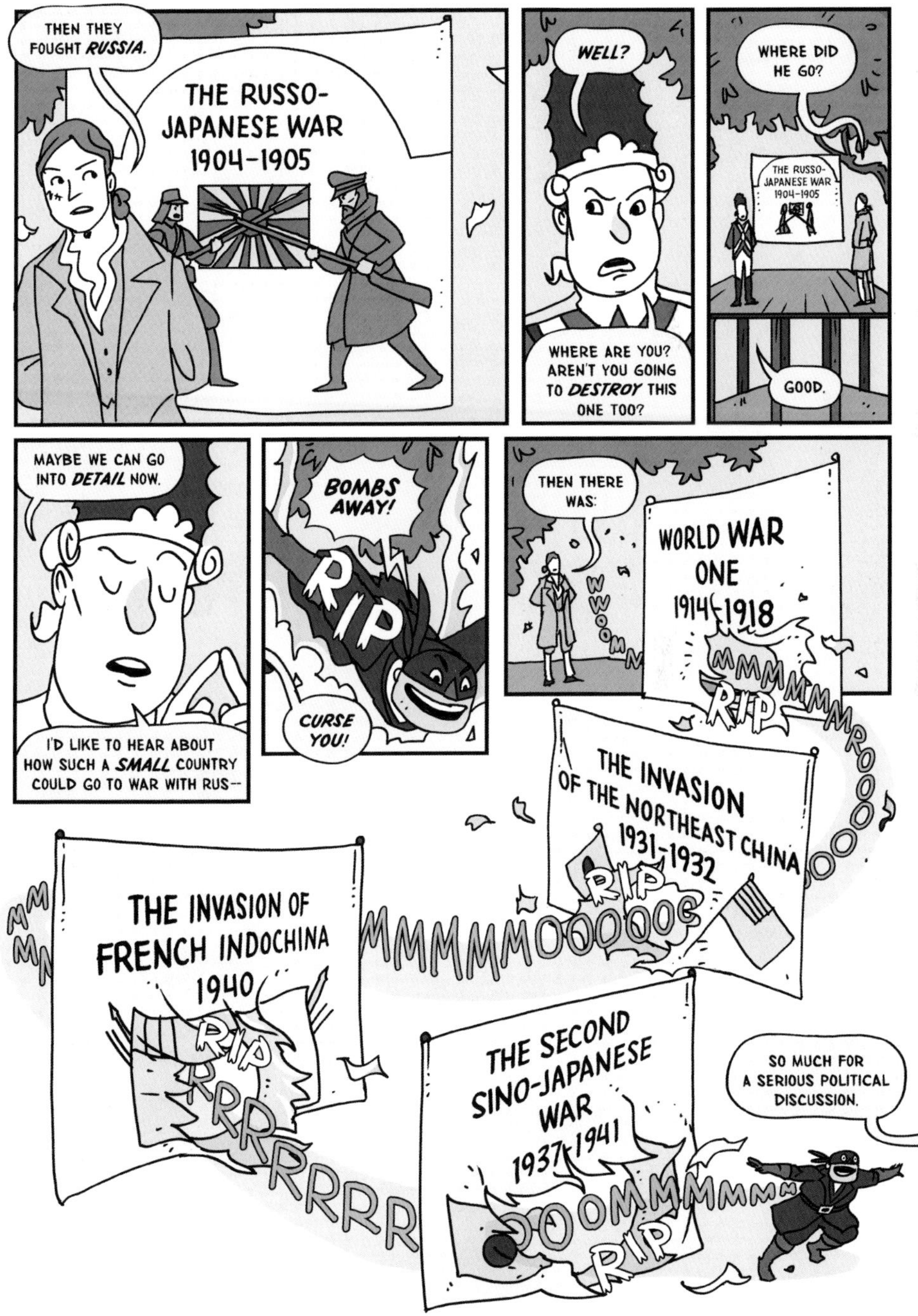
THEN THEY FOUGHT RUSSIA.
THE RUSSO-JAPANESE WAR 1904–1905
WELL?
WHERE ARE YOU? AREN'T YOU GOING TO DESTROY THIS ONE TOO?
WHERE DID HE GO?
THE RUSSO-JAPANESE WAR 1904–1905
GOOD.
MAYBE WE CAN GO INTO DETAIL NOW.
I'D LIKE TO HEAR ABOUT HOW SUCH A SMALL COUNTRY COULD GO TO WAR WITH RUS--
BOMBS AWAY!
RIP
CURSE YOU!
THEN THERE WAS:
WWOOMN
WORLD WAR ONE 1914-1918
MMMMMMROOOOOO
RIP
THE INVASION OF THE NORTHEAST CHINA 1931-1932
RIP
MMMMMMOOOOOO
THE INVASION OF FRENCH INDOCHINA 1940
RIP
RRRRRRRRR
THE SECOND SINO-JAPANESE WAR 1937-1941
OOOMMMMMM
RIP
SO MUCH FOR A SERIOUS POLITICAL DISCUSSION.

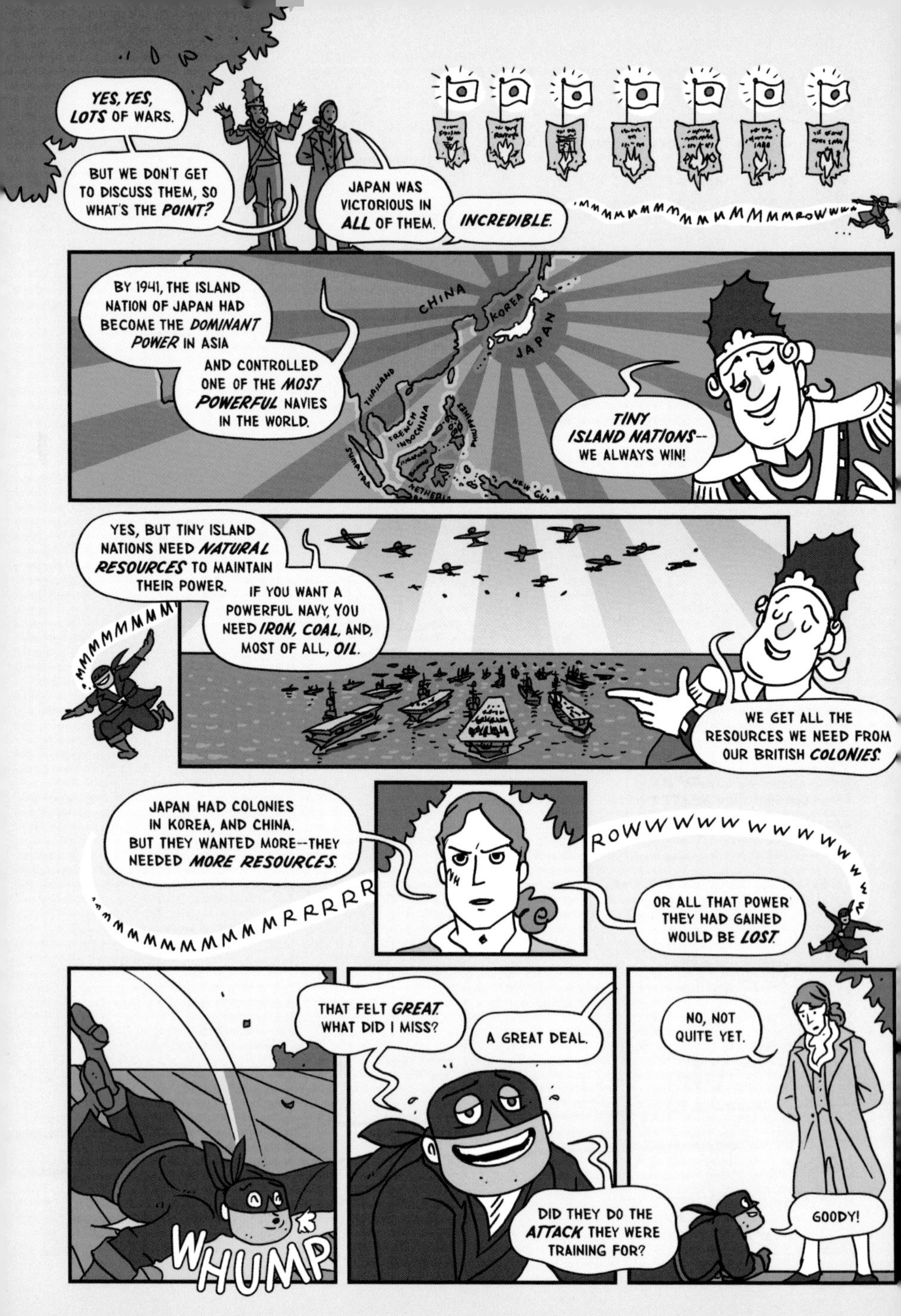
YES, YES, LOTS OF WARS.
BUT WE DON'T GET TO DISCUSS THEM, SO WHAT'S THE POINT?
JAPAN WAS VICTORIOUS IN ALL OF THEM.
INCREDIBLE.
MMMMMMMMMMMMMMMMMROWWW...
BY 1941, THE ISLAND NATION OF JAPAN HAD BECOME THE DOMINANT POWER IN ASIA
AND CONTROLLED ONE OF THE MOST POWERFUL NAVIES IN THE WORLD.
CHINA
KOREA
JAPAN
THAILAND
FRENCH INDOCHINA
SUMATRA
TINY ISLAND NATIONS-- WE ALWAYS WIN!
YES, BUT TINY ISLAND NATIONS NEED NATURAL RESOURCES TO MAINTAIN THEIR POWER.
IF YOU WANT A POWERFUL NAVY, YOU NEED IRON, COAL, AND, MOST OF ALL, OIL.
MMMMMMMMM
WE GET ALL THE RESOURCES WE NEED FROM OUR BRITISH COLONIES.
JAPAN HAD COLONIES IN KOREA, AND CHINA. BUT THEY WANTED MORE--THEY NEEDED MORE RESOURCES.
MMMMMMMMMMMMRRRRR
ROWWWWWWWWWWWWW
OR ALL THAT POWER THEY HAD GAINED WOULD BE LOST.
WHUMP
THAT FELT GREAT. WHAT DID I MISS?
A GREAT DEAL.
DID THEY DO THE ATTACK THEY WERE TRAINING FOR?
NO, NOT QUITE YET.
GOODY!

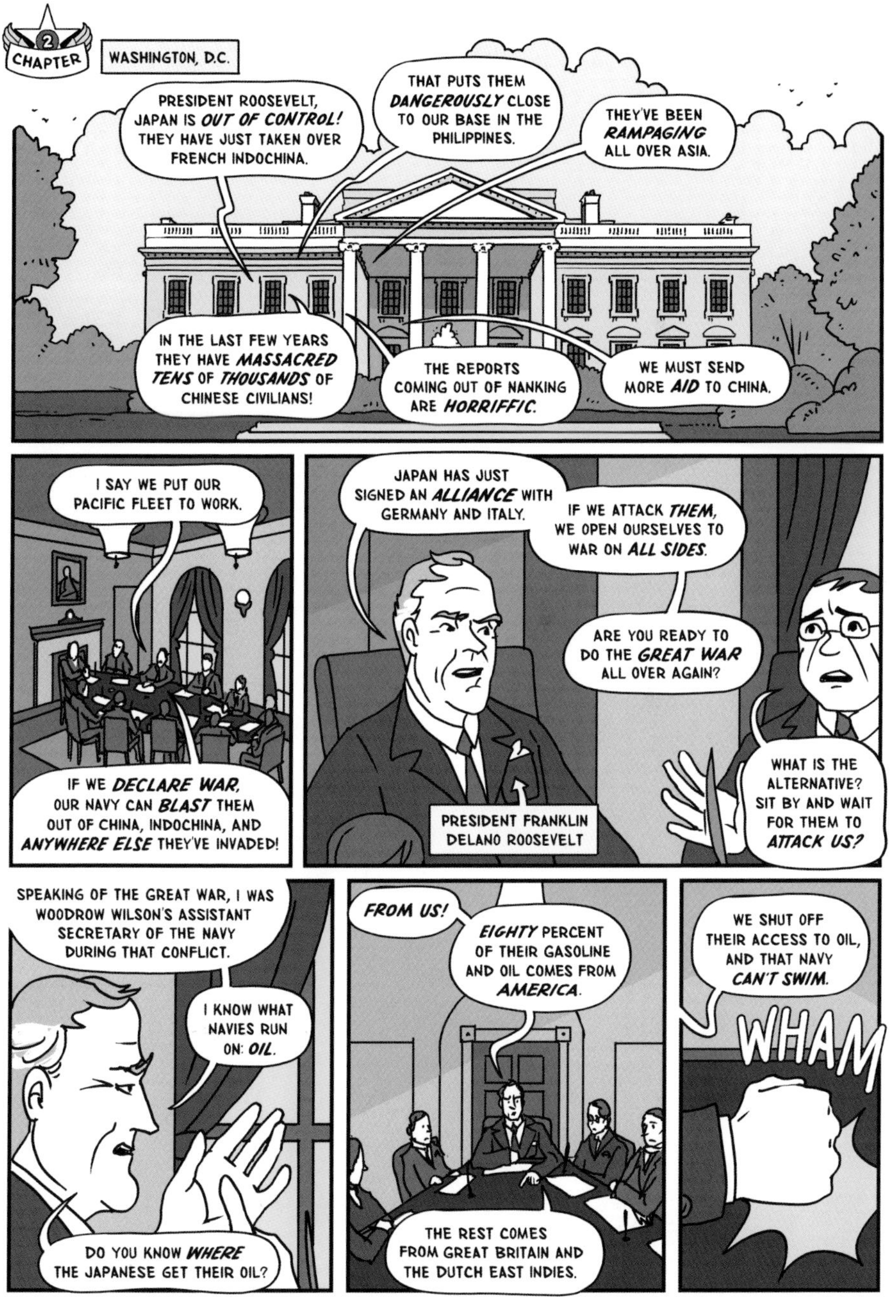
CHAPTER 2
WASHINGTON, D.C.
PRESIDENT ROOSEVELT, JAPAN IS OUT OF CONTROL! THEY HAVE JUST TAKEN OVER FRENCH INDOCHINA.
THAT PUTS THEM DANGEROUSLY CLOSE TO OUR BASE IN THE PHILIPPINES.
THEY'VE BEEN RAMPAGING ALL OVER ASIA.
IN THE LAST FEW YEARS THEY HAVE MASSACRED TENS OF THOUSANDS OF CHINESE CIVILIANS!
THE REPORTS COMING OUT OF NANKING ARE HORRIFFIC.
WE MUST SEND MORE AID TO CHINA.
I SAY WE PUT OUR PACIFIC FLEET TO WORK.
IF WE DECLARE WAR, OUR NAVY CAN BLAST THEM OUT OF CHINA, INDOCHINA, AND ANYWHERE ELSE THEY'VE INVADED!
JAPAN HAS JUST SIGNED AN ALLIANCE WITH GERMANY AND ITALY.
IF WE ATTACK THEM, WE OPEN OURSELVES TO WAR ON ALL SIDES.
ARE YOU READY TO DO THE GREAT WAR ALL OVER AGAIN?
PRESIDENT FRANKLIN DELANO ROOSEVELT
WHAT IS THE ALTERNATIVE? SIT BY AND WAIT FOR THEM TO ATTACK US?
SPEAKING OF THE GREAT WAR, I WAS WOODROW WILSON'S ASSISTANT SECRETARY OF THE NAVY DURING THAT CONFLICT.
I KNOW WHAT NAVIES RUN ON: OIL.
DO YOU KNOW WHERE THE JAPANESE GET THEIR OIL?
FROM US!
EIGHTY PERCENT OF THEIR GASOLINE AND OIL COMES FROM AMERICA.
THE REST COMES FROM GREAT BRITAIN AND THE DUTCH EAST INDIES.
WE SHUT OFF THEIR ACCESS TO OIL, AND THAT NAVY CAN'T SWIM.
WHAM

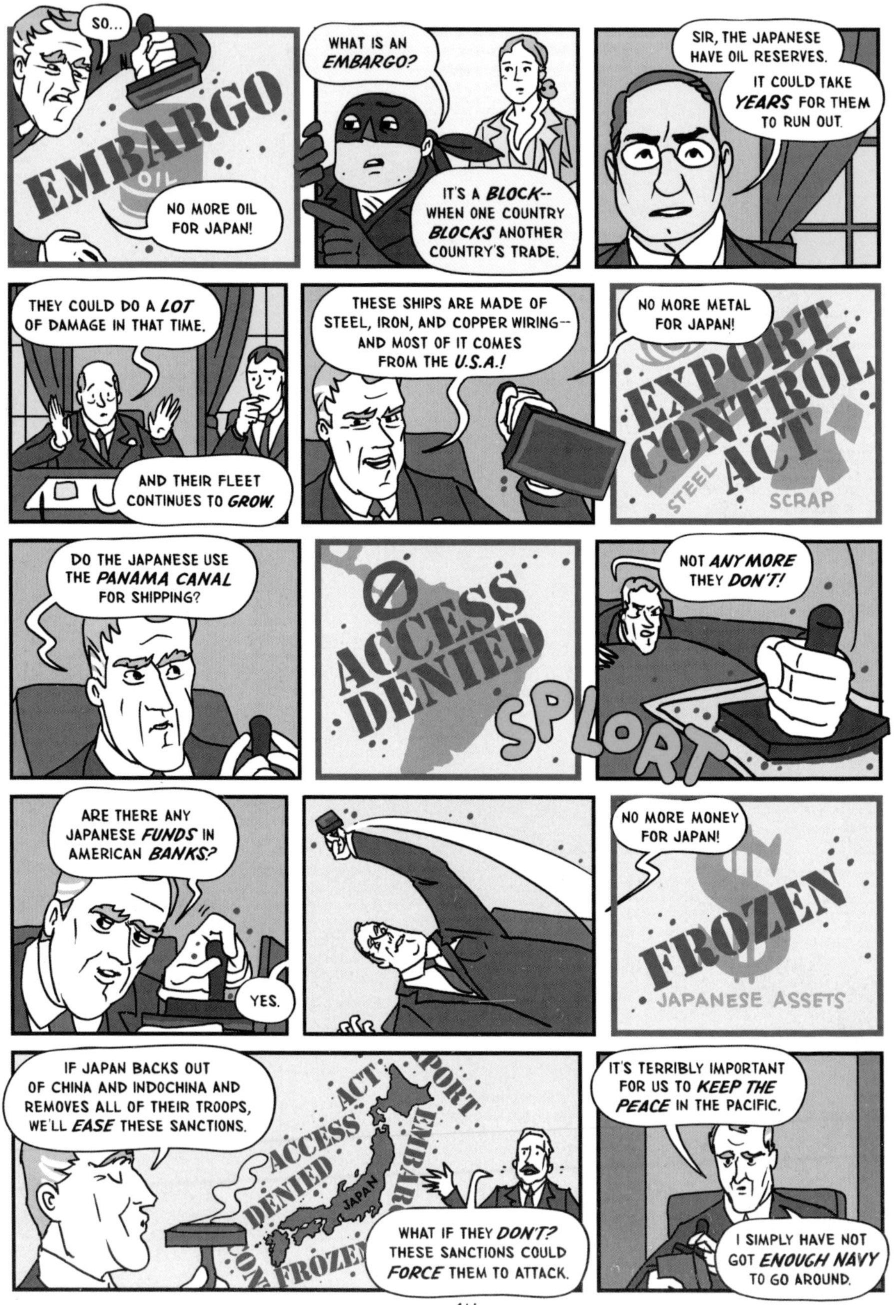
SO...
EMBARGO
OIL
NO MORE OIL FOR JAPAN!
WHAT IS AN *EMBARGO?*
IT'S A *BLOCK*-- WHEN ONE COUNTRY *BLOCKS* ANOTHER COUNTRY'S TRADE.
SIR, THE JAPANESE HAVE OIL RESERVES.
IT COULD TAKE *YEARS* FOR THEM TO RUN OUT.
THEY COULD DO A *LOT* OF DAMAGE IN THAT TIME.
AND THEIR FLEET CONTINUES TO *GROW.*
THESE SHIPS ARE MADE OF STEEL, IRON, AND COPPER WIRING-- AND MOST OF IT COMES FROM THE *U.S.A.!*
NO MORE METAL FOR JAPAN!
EXPORT CONTROL ACT
STEEL
SCRAP
DO THE JAPANESE USE THE *PANAMA CANAL* FOR SHIPPING?
ACCESS DENIED
SPLORT
NOT *ANY MORE* THEY *DON'T!*
ARE THERE ANY JAPANESE *FUNDS* IN AMERICAN *BANKS?*
YES.
NO MORE MONEY FOR JAPAN!
FROZEN
JAPANESE ASSETS
IF JAPAN BACKS OUT OF CHINA AND INDOCHINA AND REMOVES ALL OF THEIR TROOPS, WE'LL *EASE* THESE SANCTIONS.
ACCESS DENIED
ACT
EXPORT
EMBARGO
JAPAN
FROZEN
WHAT IF THEY *DON'T?* THESE SANCTIONS COULD *FORCE* THEM TO ATTACK.
IT'S TERRIBLY IMPORTANT FOR US TO *KEEP THE PEACE* IN THE PACIFIC.
I SIMPLY HAVE NOT GOT *ENOUGH NAVY* TO GO AROUND.

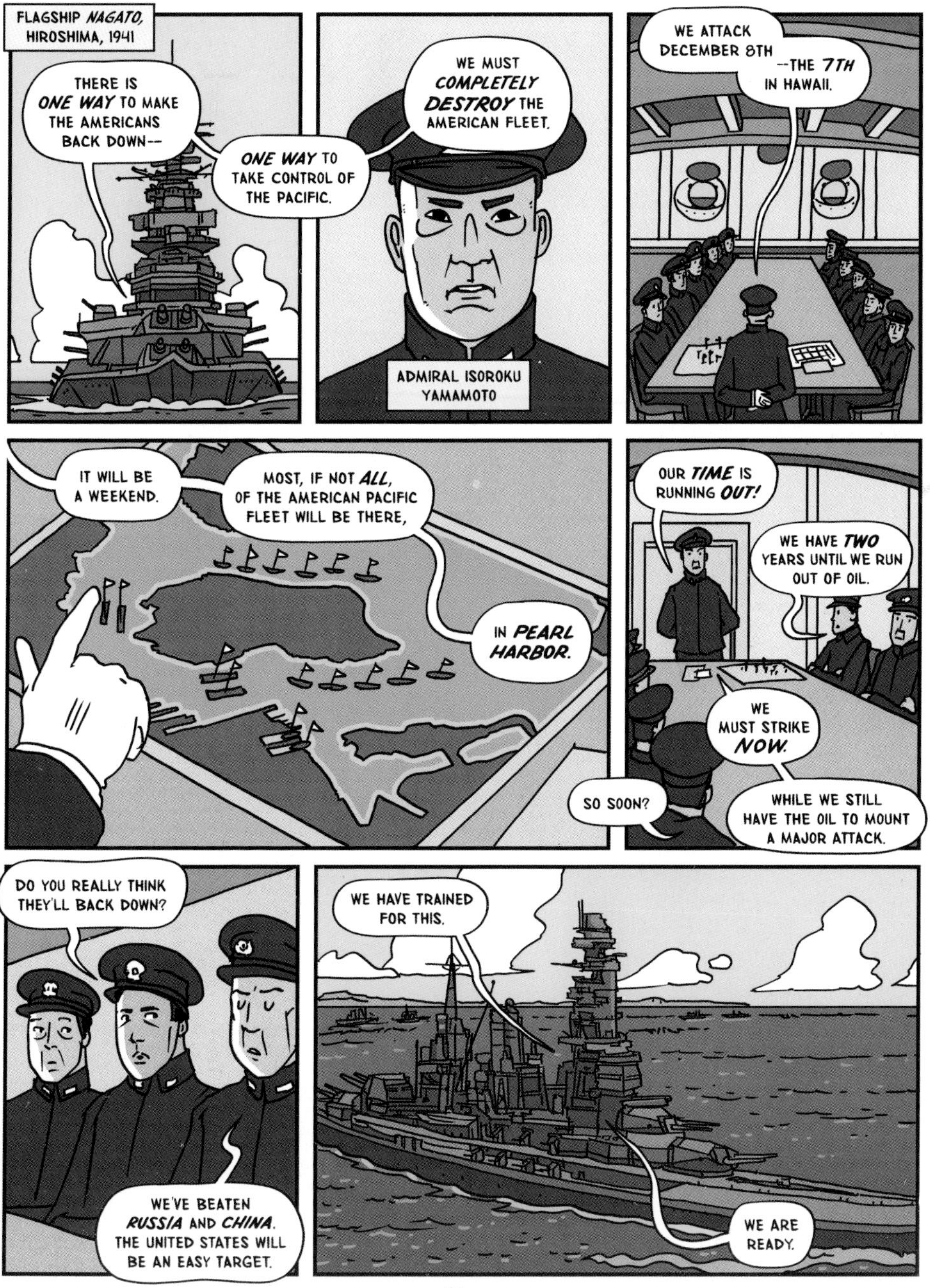
FLAGSHIP NAGATO, HIROSHIMA, 1941
THERE IS ONE WAY TO MAKE THE AMERICANS BACK DOWN--
ONE WAY TO TAKE CONTROL OF THE PACIFIC.
WE MUST COMPLETELY DESTROY THE AMERICAN FLEET.
ADMIRAL ISOROKU YAMAMOTO
WE ATTACK DECEMBER 8TH
--THE 7TH IN HAWAII.
IT WILL BE A WEEKEND.
MOST, IF NOT ALL, OF THE AMERICAN PACIFIC FLEET WILL BE THERE,
IN PEARL HARBOR.
OUR TIME IS RUNNING OUT!
WE HAVE TWO YEARS UNTIL WE RUN OUT OF OIL.
SO SOON?
WE MUST STRIKE NOW.
WHILE WE STILL HAVE THE OIL TO MOUNT A MAJOR ATTACK.
DO YOU REALLY THINK THEY'LL BACK DOWN?
WE'VE BEATEN RUSSIA AND CHINA. THE UNITED STATES WILL BE AN EASY TARGET.
WE HAVE TRAINED FOR THIS.
WE ARE READY.

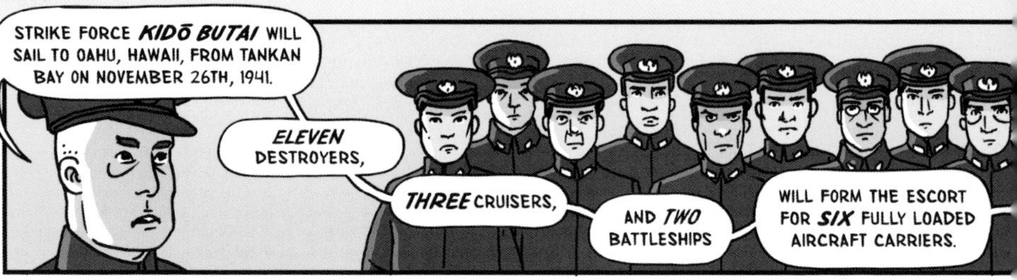

STRIKE FORCE *KIDŌ BUTAI* WILL SAIL TO OAHU, HAWAII, FROM TANKAN BAY ON NOVEMBER 26TH, 1941.
ELEVEN DESTROYERS,
THREE CRUISERS,
AND *TWO* BATTLESHIPS
WILL FORM THE ESCORT FOR ***SIX*** FULLY LOADED AIRCRAFT CARRIERS.

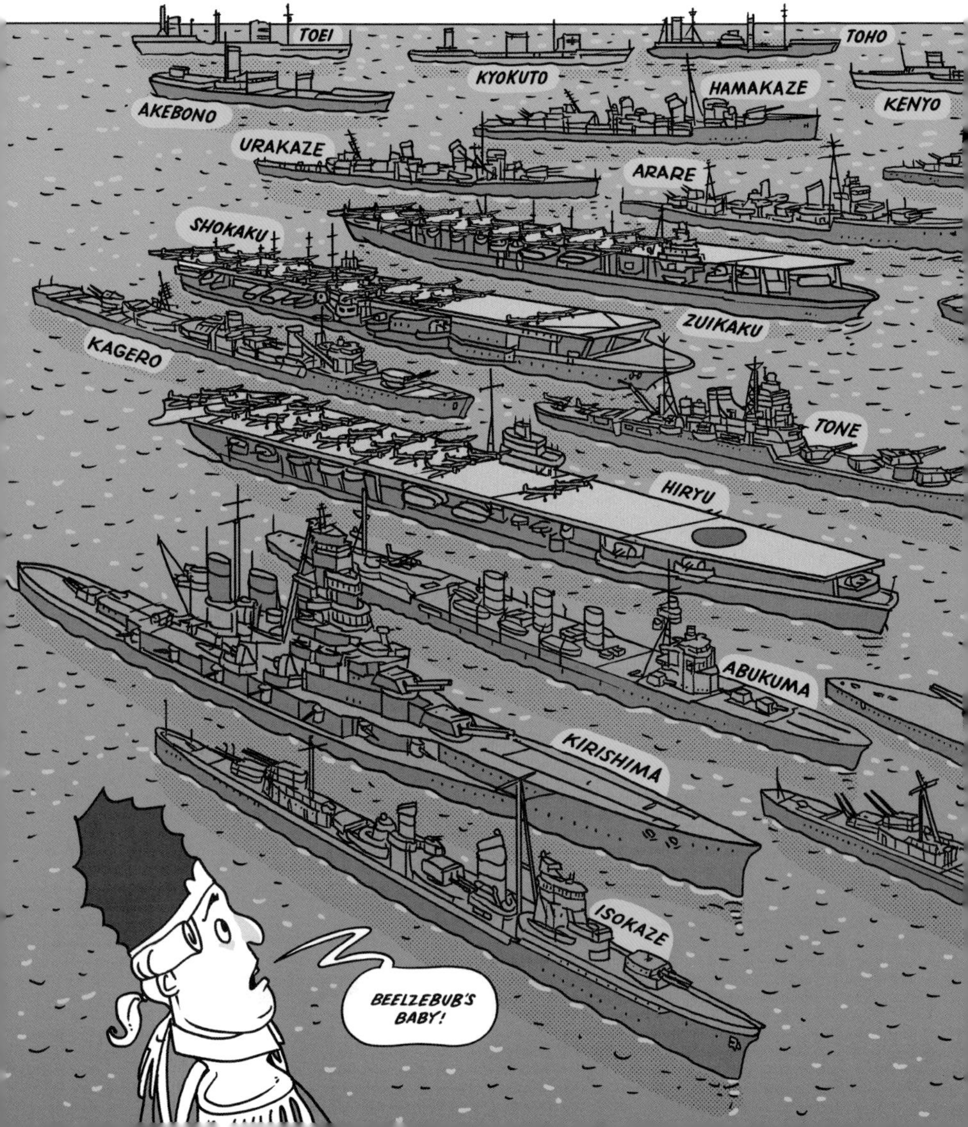

TOEI
KYOKUTO
TOHO
AKEBONO
HAMAKAZE
KENYO
URAKAZE
ARARE
SHOKAKU
ZUIKAKU
KAGERO
TONE
HIRYU
ABUKUMA
KIRISHIMA
ISOKAZE
BEELZEBUB'S BABY!

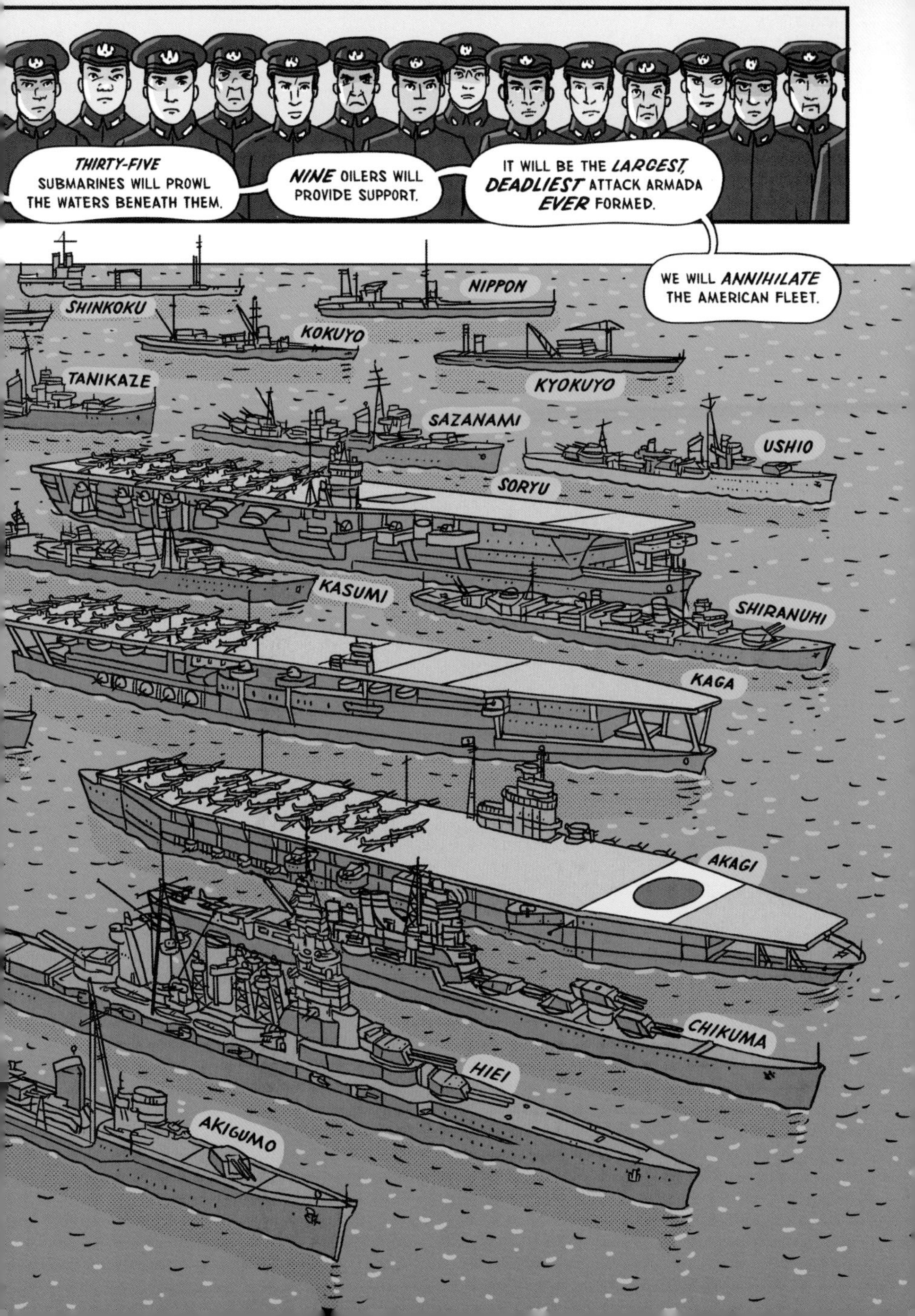
THIRTY-FIVE SUBMARINES WILL PROWL THE WATERS BENEATH THEM.
NINE OILERS WILL PROVIDE SUPPORT.
IT WILL BE THE LARGEST, DEADLIEST ATTACK ARMADA EVER FORMED.
WE WILL ANNIHILATE THE AMERICAN FLEET.
NIPPON
SHINKOKU
KOKUYO
KYOKUYO
TANIKAZE
SAZANAMI
USHIO
SORYU
KASUMI
SHIRANUHI
KAGA
AKAGI
CHIKUMA
HIEI
AKIGUMO

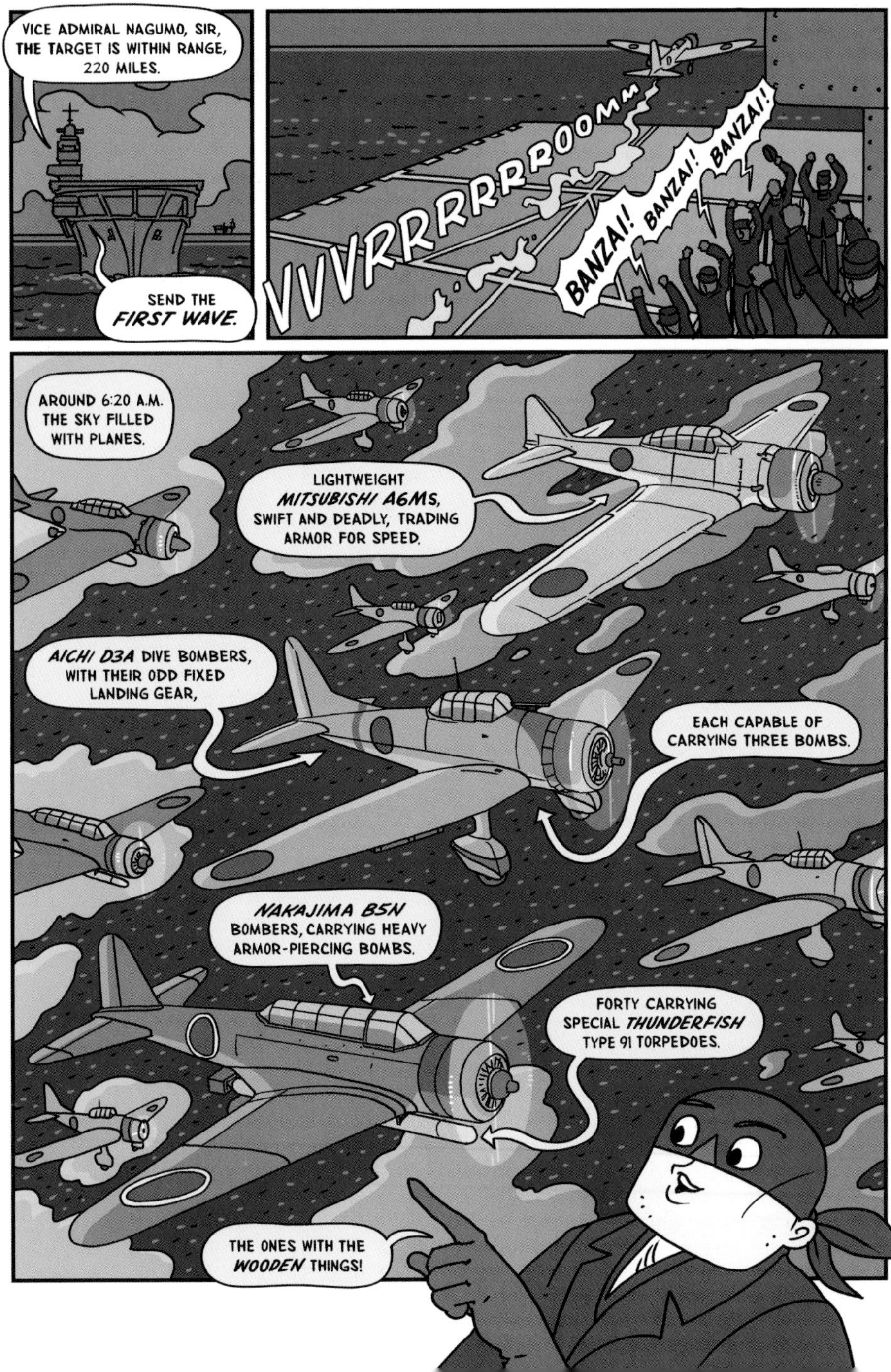
VICE ADMIRAL NAGUMO, SIR, THE TARGET IS WITHIN RANGE, 220 MILES.
SEND THE *FIRST WAVE.*
VVVRRRRRROOMᴹᴹ
BANZAI! BANZAI! BANZAI!
AROUND 6:20 A.M. THE SKY FILLED WITH PLANES.
LIGHTWEIGHT *MITSUBISHI A6MS*, SWIFT AND DEADLY, TRADING ARMOR FOR SPEED.
AICHI D3A DIVE BOMBERS, WITH THEIR ODD FIXED LANDING GEAR,
EACH CAPABLE OF CARRYING THREE BOMBS.
NAKAJIMA B5N BOMBERS, CARRYING HEAVY ARMOR-PIERCING BOMBS.
FORTY CARRYING SPECIAL *THUNDERFISH* TYPE 91 TORPEDOES.
THE ONES WITH THE *WOODEN* THINGS!

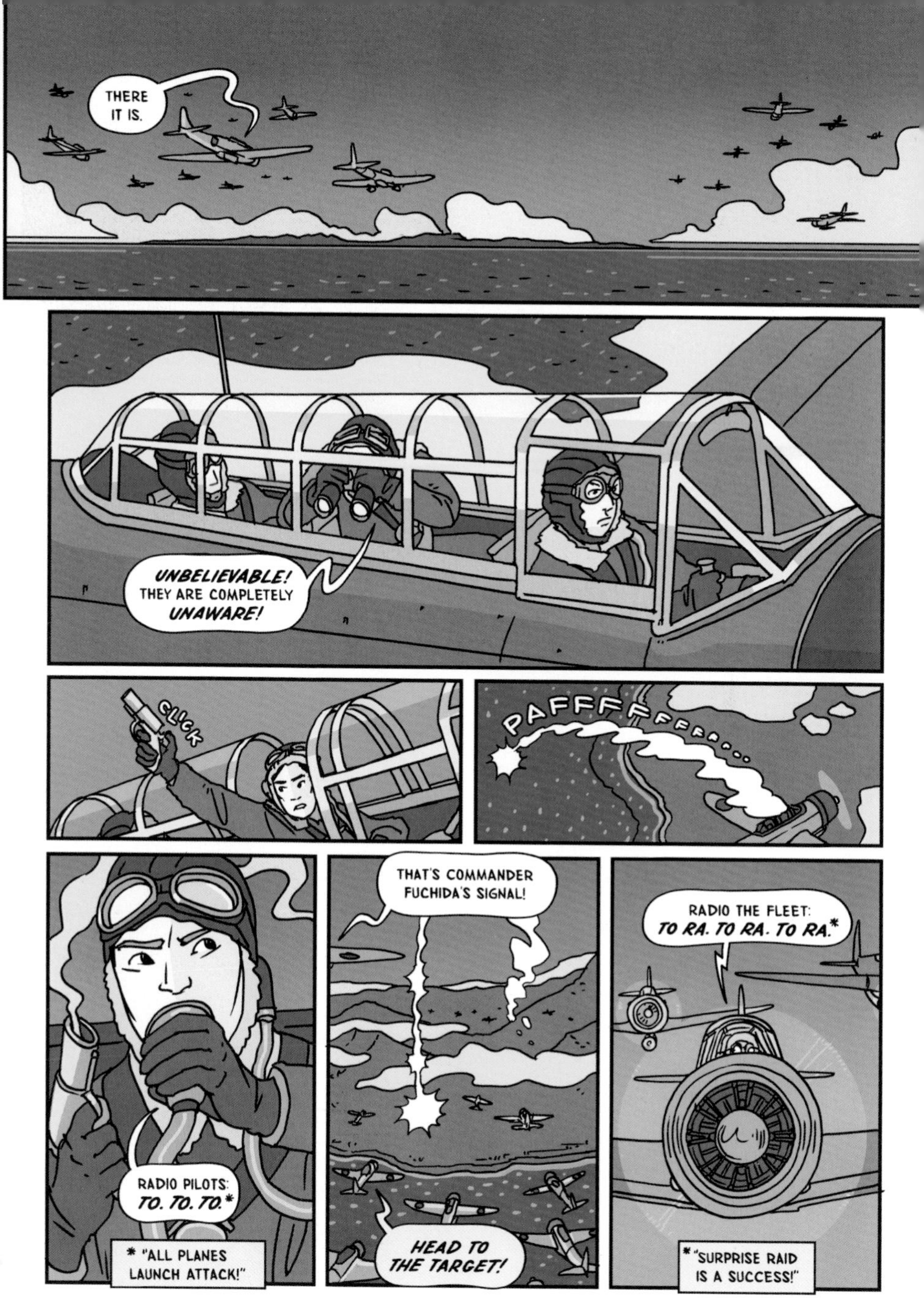
THERE IT IS.
UNBELIEVABLE! THEY ARE COMPLETELY UNAWARE!
CLICK
PAFFFFFFFFF.....
RADIO PILOTS: TO. TO. TO.*
* "ALL PLANES LAUNCH ATTACK!"
THAT'S COMMANDER FUCHIDA'S SIGNAL!
HEAD TO THE TARGET!
RADIO THE FLEET: TO RA. TO RA. TO RA.*
*"SURPRISE RAID IS A SUCCESS!"

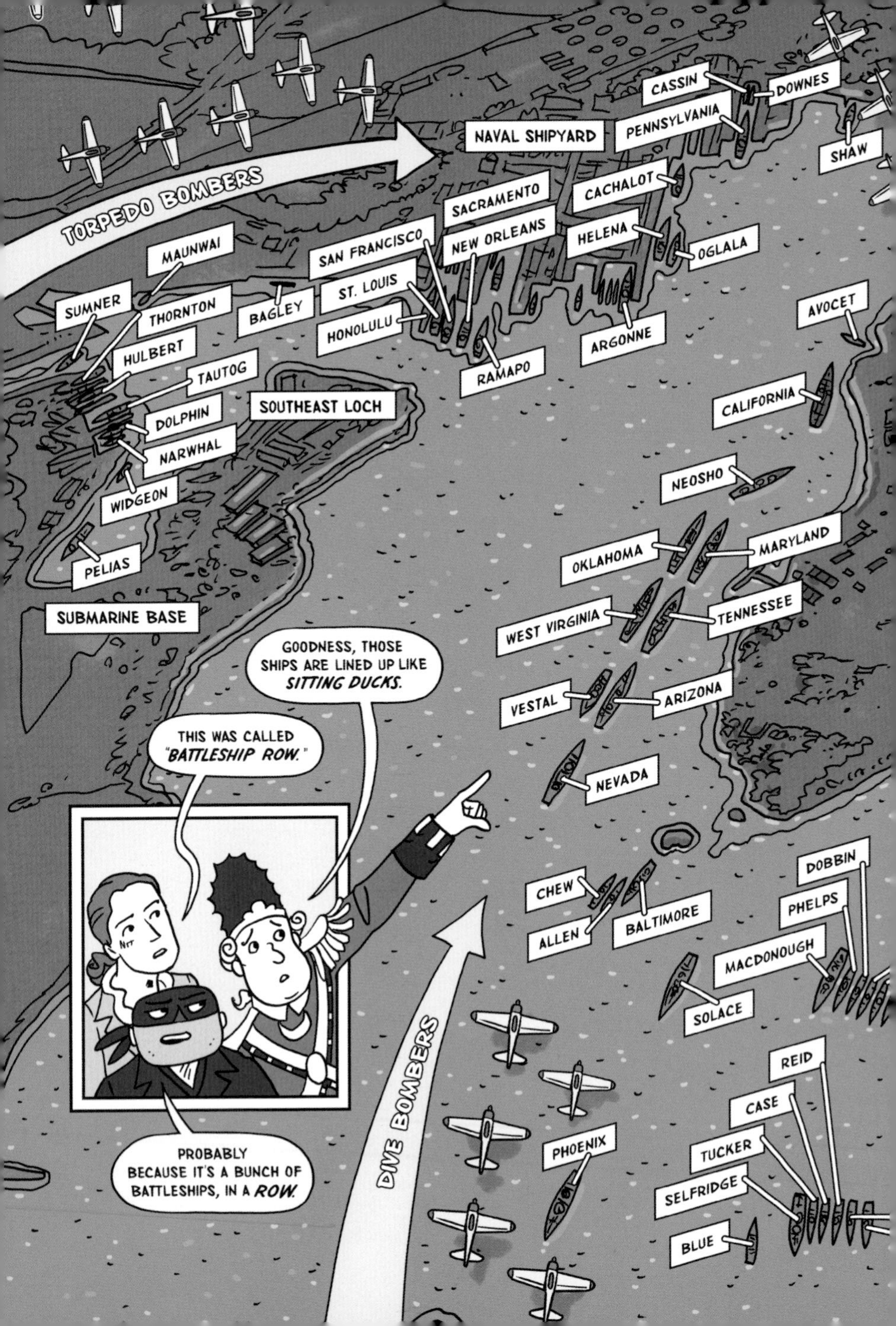
TORPEDO BOMBERS
NAVAL SHIPYARD
CASSIN
DOWNES
PENNSYLVANIA
SHAW
CACHALOT
SACRAMENTO
NEW ORLEANS
HELENA
OGLALA
SAN FRANCISCO
MAUNWAI
ST. LOUIS
BAGLEY
SUMNER
THORNTON
HONOLULU
ARGONNE
AVOCET
HULBERT
RAMAPO
TAUTOG
SOUTHEAST LOCH
CALIFORNIA
DOLPHIN
NARWHAL
NEOSHO
WIDGEON
OKLAHOMA
MARYLAND
PELIAS
SUBMARINE BASE
WEST VIRGINIA
TENNESSEE
GOODNESS, THOSE SHIPS ARE LINED UP LIKE SITTING DUCKS.
VESTAL
ARIZONA
THIS WAS CALLED "BATTLESHIP ROW."
NEVADA
DOBBIN
CHEW
PHELPS
ALLEN
BALTIMORE
MACDONOUGH
SOLACE
DIVE BOMBERS
REID
CASE
PHOENIX
TUCKER
PROBABLY BECAUSE IT'S A BUNCH OF BATTLESHIPS, IN A ROW.
SELFRIDGE
BLUE

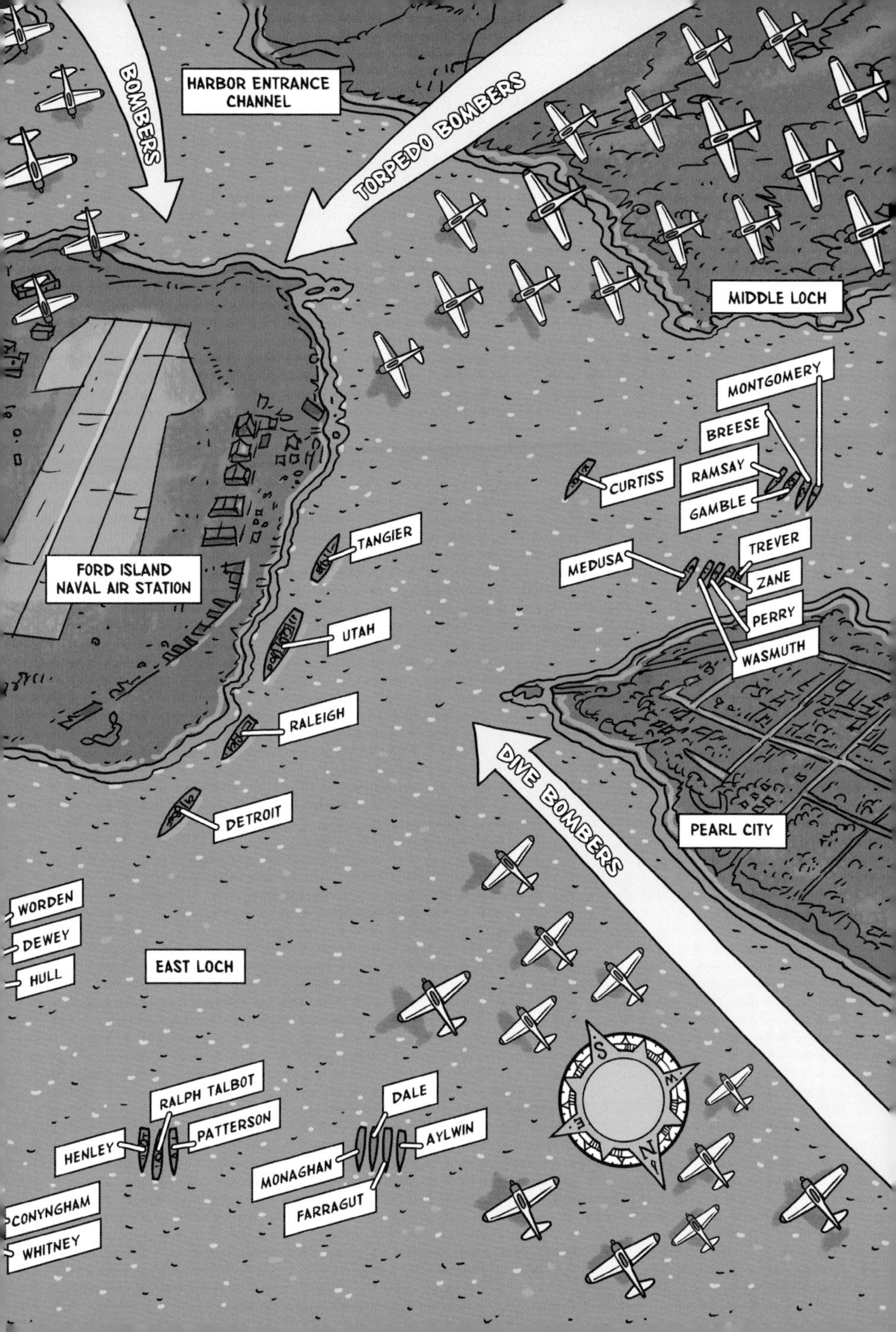
BOMBERS
HARBOR ENTRANCE CHANNEL
TORPEDO BOMBERS
MIDDLE LOCH
MONTGOMERY
BREESE
CURTISS
RAMSAY
GAMBLE
TANGIER
TREVER
MEDUSA
ZANE
FORD ISLAND NAVAL AIR STATION
PERRY
UTAH
WASMUTH
RALEIGH
DIVE BOMBERS
DETROIT
PEARL CITY
WORDEN
DEWEY
EAST LOCH
HULL
RALPH TALBOT
DALE
PATTERSON
AYLWIN
HENLEY
MONAGHAN
FARRAGUT
CONYNGHAM
WHITNEY

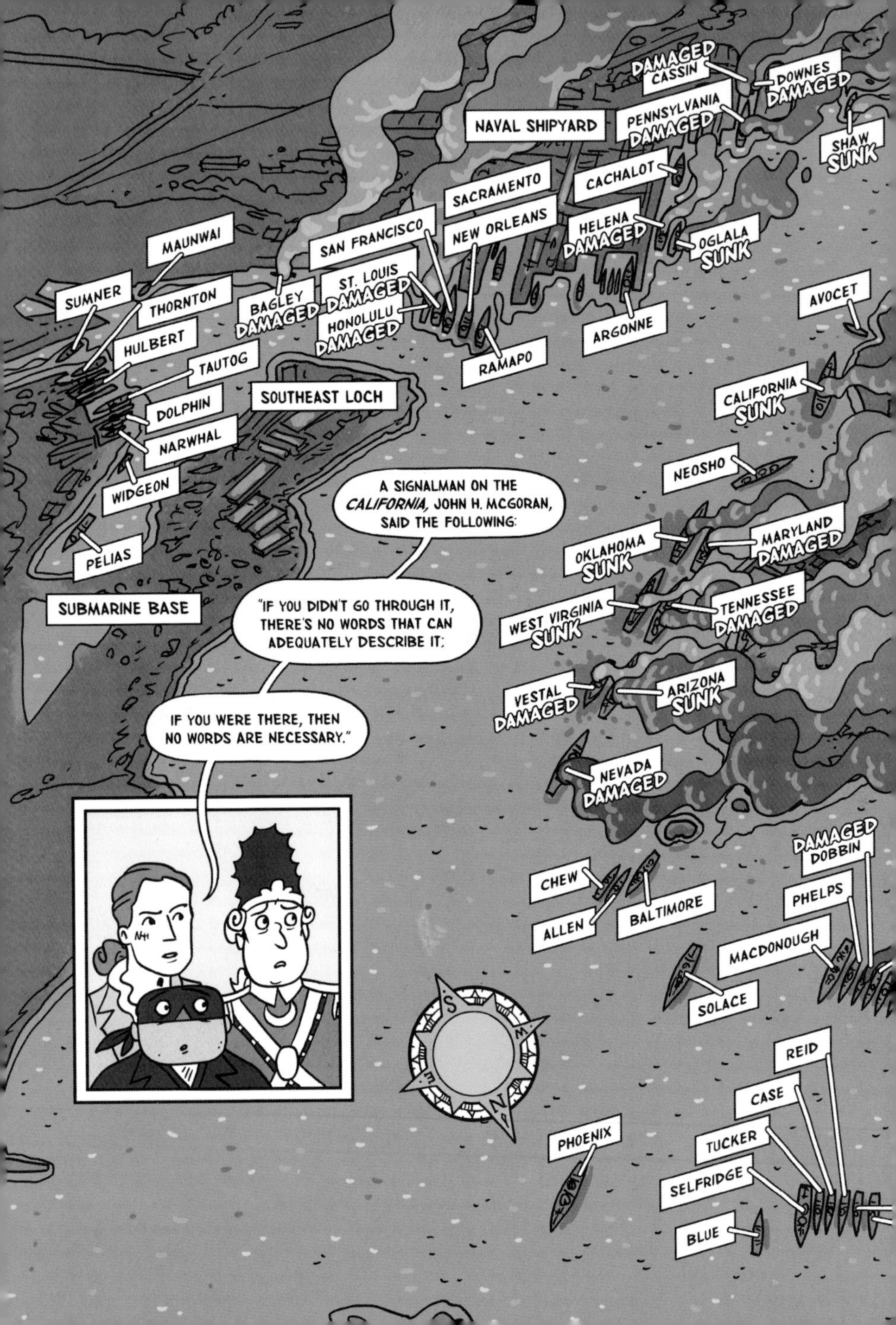

DAMAGED CASSIN
DOWNES DAMAGED
NAVAL SHIPYARD
PENNSYLVANIA DAMAGED
SHAW SUNK
CACHALOT
SACRAMENTO
NEW ORLEANS
SAN FRANCISCO
HELENA DAMAGED
OGLALA SUNK
MAUNWAI
SUMNER
THORNTON
BAGLEY DAMAGED
ST. LOUIS DAMAGED
HONOLULU DAMAGED
ARGONNE
AVOCET
HULBERT
RAMAPO
TAUTOG
SOUTHEAST LOCH
DOLPHIN
CALIFORNIA SUNK
NARWHAL
NEOSHO
WIDGEON
A SIGNALMAN ON THE *CALIFORNIA,* JOHN H. MCGORAN, SAID THE FOLLOWING:
PELIAS
OKLAHOMA SUNK
MARYLAND DAMAGED
SUBMARINE BASE
"IF YOU DIDN'T GO THROUGH IT, THERE'S NO WORDS THAT CAN ADEQUATELY DESCRIBE IT;
WEST VIRGINIA SUNK
TENNESSEE DAMAGED
VESTAL DAMAGED
ARIZONA SUNK
IF YOU WERE THERE, THEN NO WORDS ARE NECESSARY."
NEVADA DAMAGED
DAMAGED DOBBIN
CHEW
PHELPS
ALLEN
BALTIMORE
MACDONOUGH
SOLACE
REID
CASE
PHOENIX
TUCKER
SELFRIDGE
BLUE

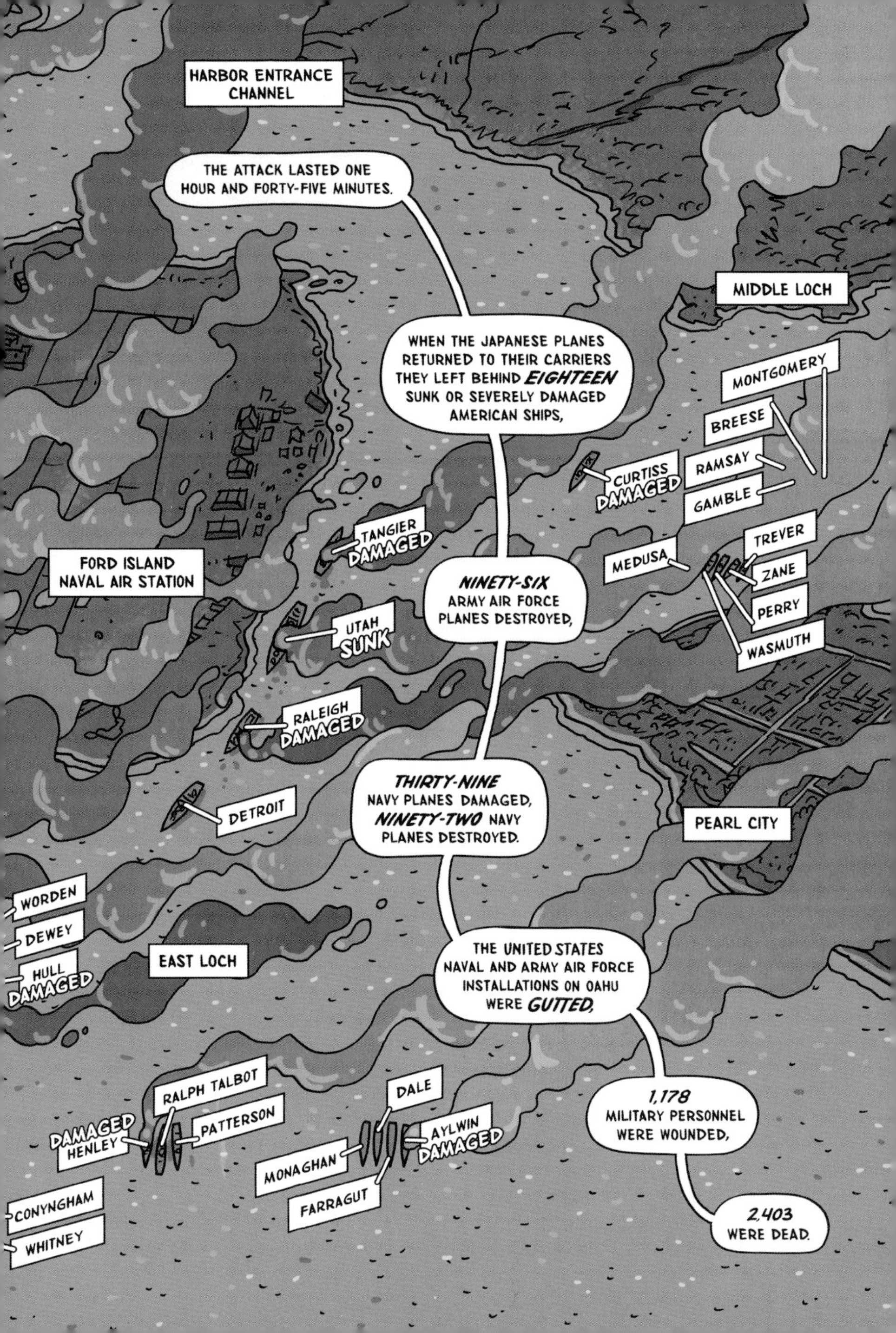

HARBOR ENTRANCE CHANNEL
THE ATTACK LASTED ONE HOUR AND FORTY-FIVE MINUTES.
MIDDLE LOCH
WHEN THE JAPANESE PLANES RETURNED TO THEIR CARRIERS THEY LEFT BEHIND *EIGHTEEN* SUNK OR SEVERELY DAMAGED AMERICAN SHIPS,
MONTGOMERY
BREESE
RAMSAY
GAMBLE
CURTISS DAMAGED
TANGIER DAMAGED
FORD ISLAND NAVAL AIR STATION
NINETY-SIX ARMY AIR FORCE PLANES DESTROYED,
MEDUSA
TREVER
ZANE
PERRY
WASMUTH
UTAH SUNK
RALEIGH DAMAGED
THIRTY-NINE NAVY PLANES DAMAGED, *NINETY-TWO* NAVY PLANES DESTROYED.
DETROIT
PEARL CITY
WORDEN
DEWEY
HULL DAMAGED
EAST LOCH
THE UNITED STATES NAVAL AND ARMY AIR FORCE INSTALLATIONS ON OAHU WERE *GUTTED*,
RALPH TALBOT
DALE
DAMAGED HENLEY
PATTERSON
AYLWIN DAMAGED
MONAGHAN
FARRAGUT
1,178 MILITARY PERSONNEL WERE WOUNDED,
CONYNGHAM
WHITNEY
2,403 WERE DEAD.

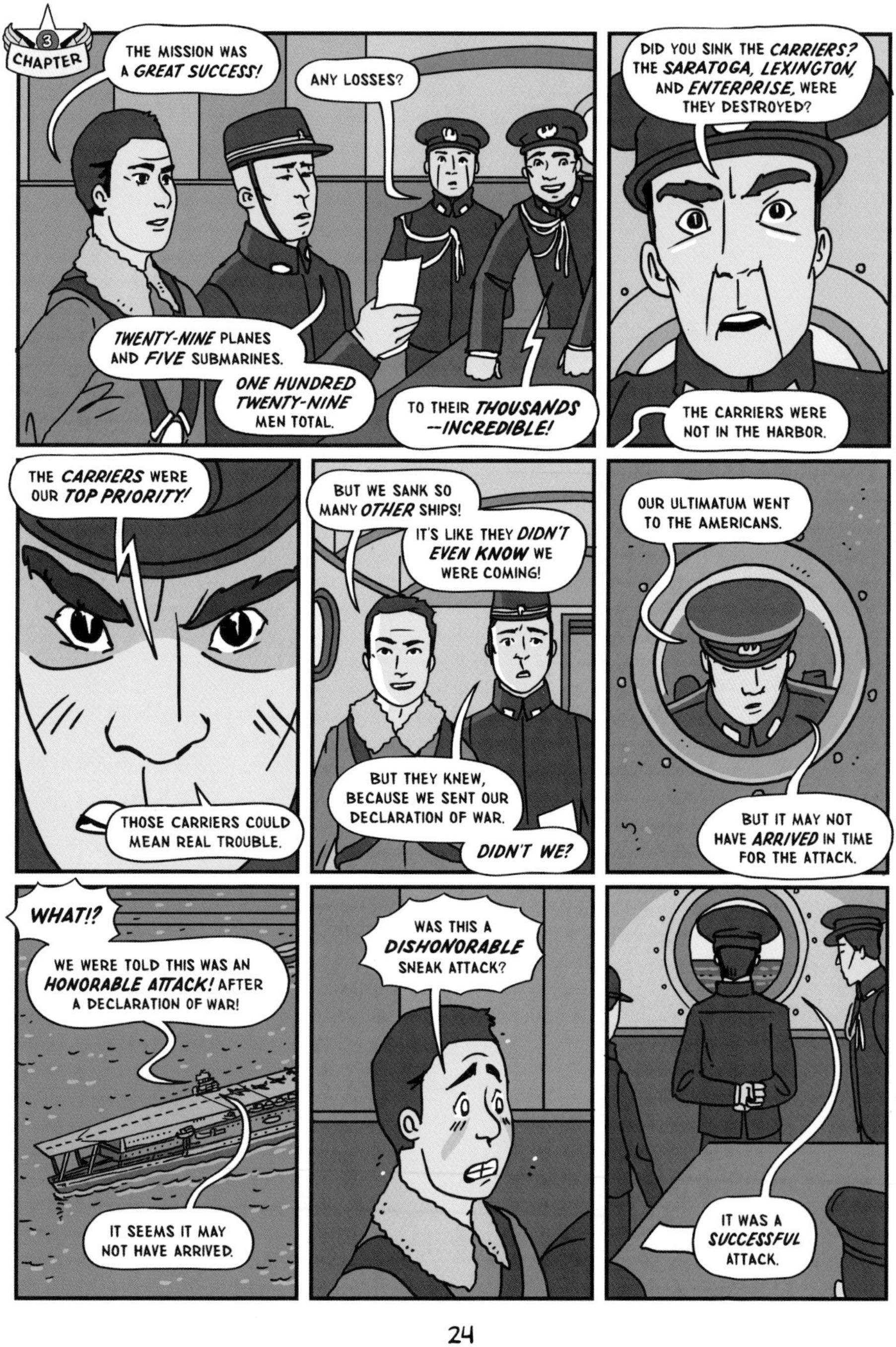
3 CHAPTER
THE MISSION WAS A GREAT SUCCESS!
ANY LOSSES?
TWENTY-NINE PLANES AND FIVE SUBMARINES.
ONE HUNDRED TWENTY-NINE MEN TOTAL.
TO THEIR THOUSANDS --INCREDIBLE!
DID YOU SINK THE CARRIERS? THE SARATOGA, LEXINGTON, AND ENTERPRISE, WERE THEY DESTROYED?
THE CARRIERS WERE NOT IN THE HARBOR.
THE CARRIERS WERE OUR TOP PRIORITY!
THOSE CARRIERS COULD MEAN REAL TROUBLE.
BUT WE SANK SO MANY OTHER SHIPS!
IT'S LIKE THEY DIDN'T EVEN KNOW WE WERE COMING!
BUT THEY KNEW, BECAUSE WE SENT OUR DECLARATION OF WAR.
DIDN'T WE?
OUR ULTIMATUM WENT TO THE AMERICANS.
BUT IT MAY NOT HAVE ARRIVED IN TIME FOR THE ATTACK.
WHAT!?
WE WERE TOLD THIS WAS AN HONORABLE ATTACK! AFTER A DECLARATION OF WAR!
IT SEEMS IT MAY NOT HAVE ARRIVED.
WAS THIS A DISHONORABLE SNEAK ATTACK?
IT WAS A SUCCESSFUL ATTACK.

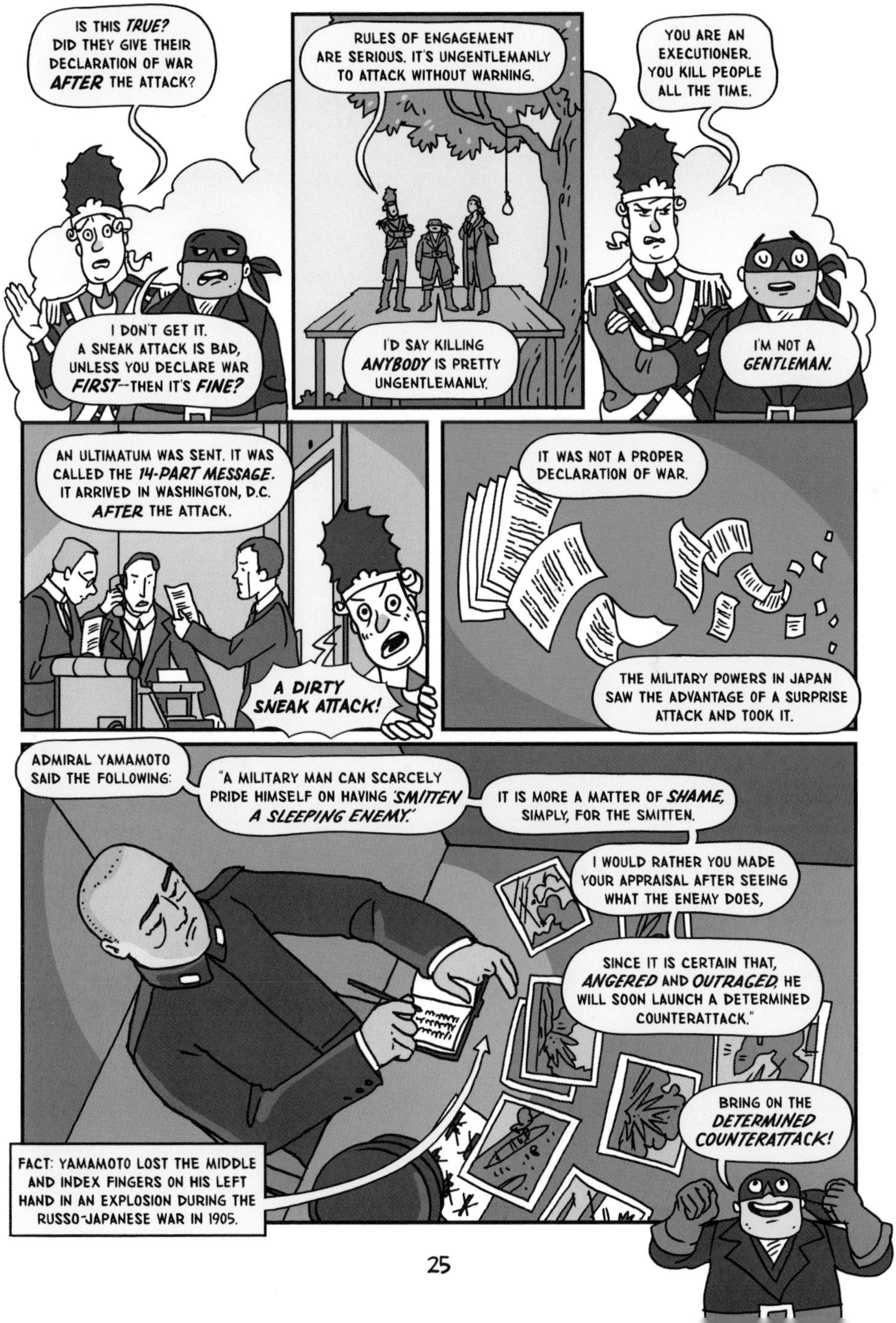
IS THIS *TRUE?* DID THEY GIVE THEIR DECLARATION OF WAR *AFTER* THE ATTACK?
I DON'T GET IT. A SNEAK ATTACK IS BAD, UNLESS YOU DECLARE WAR *FIRST*--THEN IT'S *FINE?*
RULES OF ENGAGEMENT ARE SERIOUS. IT'S UNGENTLEMANLY TO ATTACK WITHOUT WARNING.
I'D SAY KILLING *ANYBODY* IS PRETTY UNGENTLEMANLY.
YOU ARE AN EXECUTIONER. YOU KILL PEOPLE ALL THE TIME.
I'M NOT A *GENTLEMAN.*
AN ULTIMATUM WAS SENT. IT WAS CALLED THE *14-PART MESSAGE.* IT ARRIVED IN WASHINGTON, D.C. *AFTER* THE ATTACK.
A DIRTY SNEAK ATTACK!
IT WAS NOT A PROPER DECLARATION OF WAR.
THE MILITARY POWERS IN JAPAN SAW THE ADVANTAGE OF A SURPRISE ATTACK AND TOOK IT.
ADMIRAL YAMAMOTO SAID THE FOLLOWING:
"A MILITARY MAN CAN SCARCELY PRIDE HIMSELF ON HAVING *'SMITTEN A SLEEPING ENEMY.'*
IT IS MORE A MATTER OF *SHAME,* SIMPLY, FOR THE SMITTEN.
I WOULD RATHER YOU MADE YOUR APPRAISAL AFTER SEEING WHAT THE ENEMY DOES,
SINCE IT IS CERTAIN THAT, *ANGERED* AND *OUTRAGED,* HE WILL SOON LAUNCH A DETERMINED COUNTERATTACK."
BRING ON THE *DETERMINED COUNTERATTACK!*
FACT: YAMAMOTO LOST THE MIDDLE AND INDEX FINGERS ON HIS LEFT HAND IN AN EXPLOSION DURING THE RUSSO-JAPANESE WAR IN 1905.

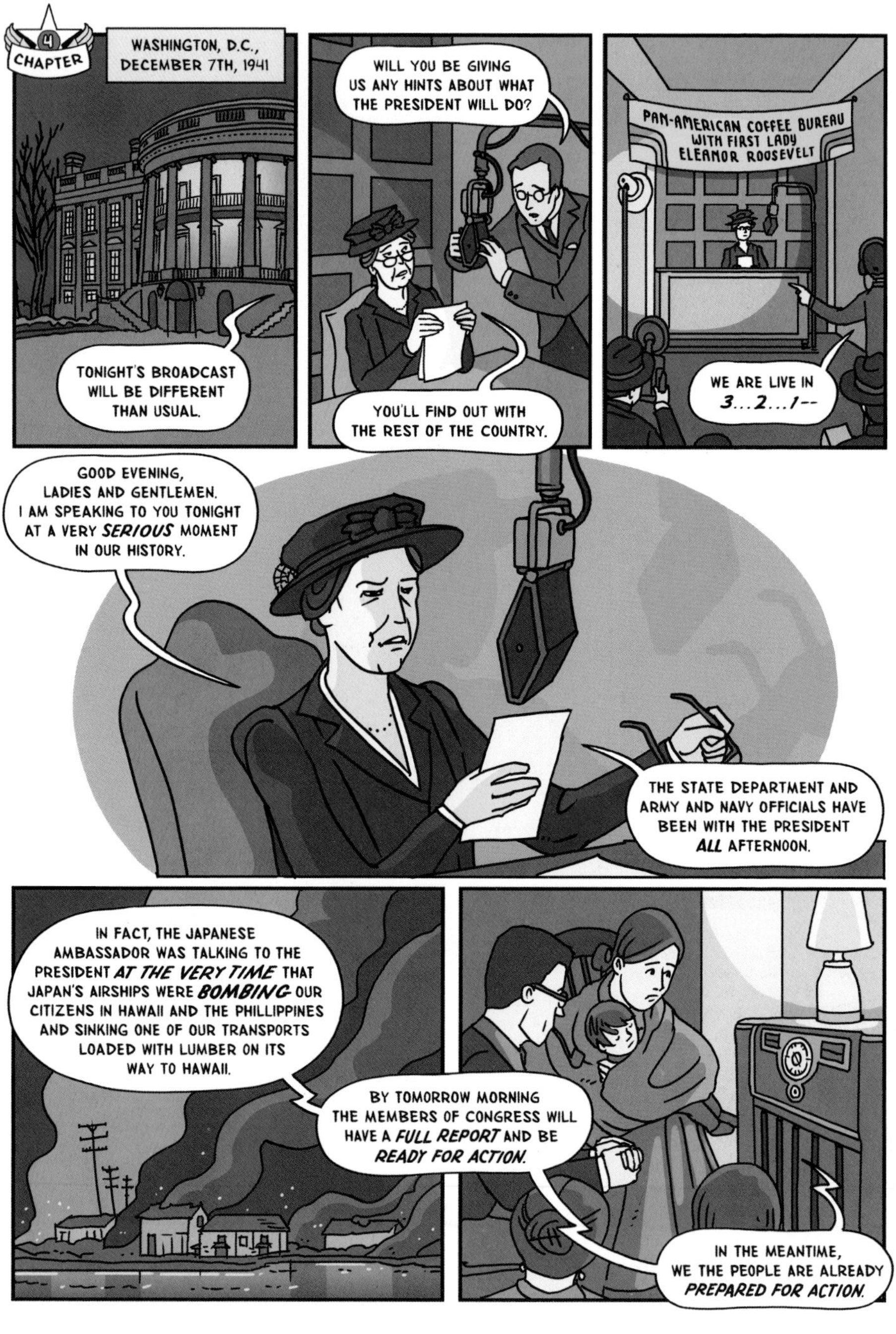

4 CHAPTER
WASHINGTON, D.C., DECEMBER 7TH, 1941
TONIGHT'S BROADCAST WILL BE DIFFERENT THAN USUAL.
WILL YOU BE GIVING US ANY HINTS ABOUT WHAT THE PRESIDENT WILL DO?
YOU'LL FIND OUT WITH THE REST OF THE COUNTRY.
PAN-AMERICAN COFFEE BUREAU WITH FIRST LADY ELEANOR ROOSEVELT
WE ARE LIVE IN 3...2...1--
GOOD EVENING, LADIES AND GENTLEMEN. I AM SPEAKING TO YOU TONIGHT AT A VERY SERIOUS MOMENT IN OUR HISTORY.
THE STATE DEPARTMENT AND ARMY AND NAVY OFFICIALS HAVE BEEN WITH THE PRESIDENT ALL AFTERNOON.
IN FACT, THE JAPANESE AMBASSADOR WAS TALKING TO THE PRESIDENT AT THE VERY TIME THAT JAPAN'S AIRSHIPS WERE BOMBING OUR CITIZENS IN HAWAII AND THE PHILLIPPINES AND SINKING ONE OF OUR TRANSPORTS LOADED WITH LUMBER ON ITS WAY TO HAWAII.
BY TOMORROW MORNING THE MEMBERS OF CONGRESS WILL HAVE A FULL REPORT AND BE READY FOR ACTION.
IN THE MEANTIME, WE THE PEOPLE ARE ALREADY PREPARED FOR ACTION.

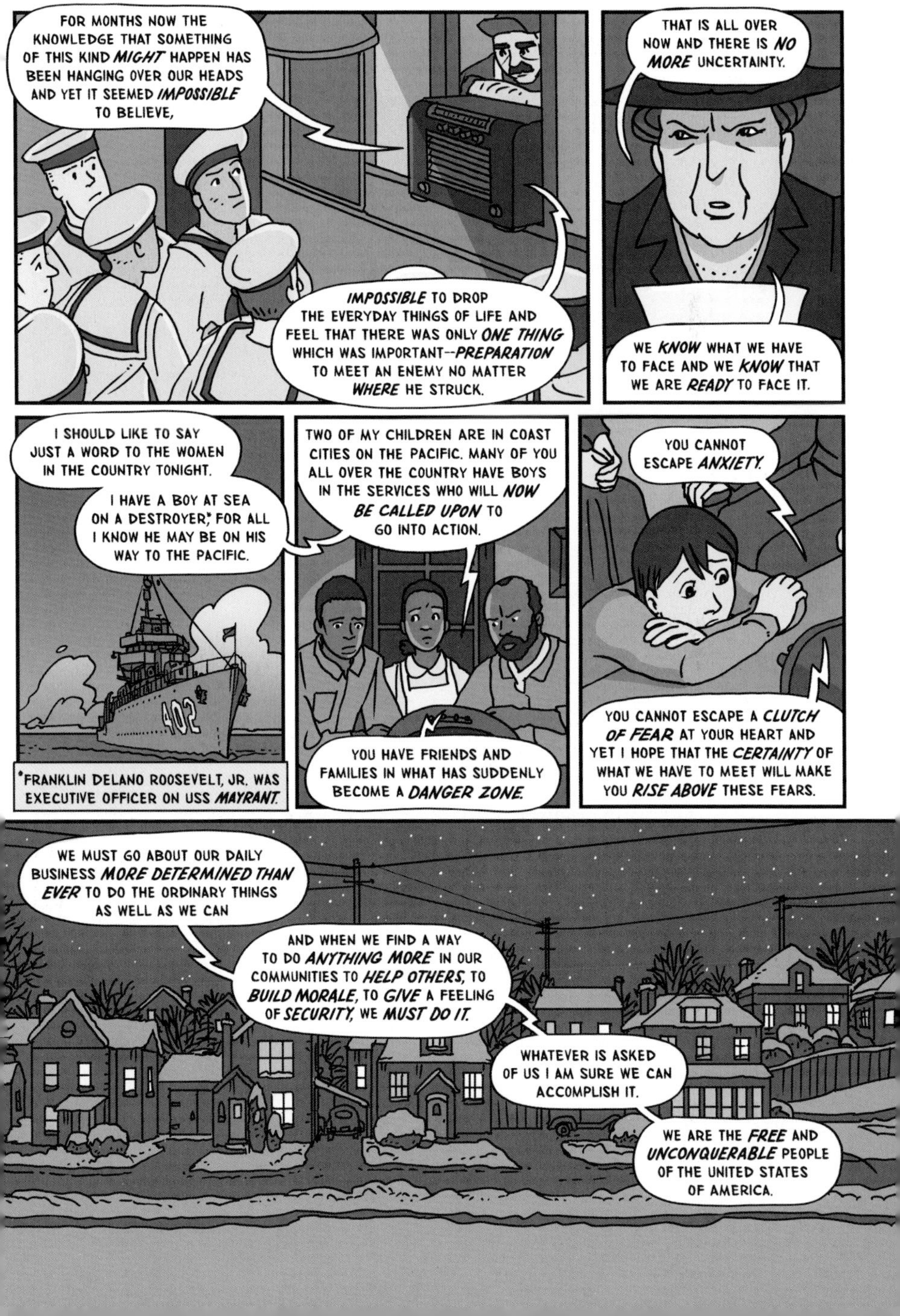
FOR MONTHS NOW THE KNOWLEDGE THAT SOMETHING OF THIS KIND *MIGHT* HAPPEN HAS BEEN HANGING OVER OUR HEADS AND YET IT SEEMED *IMPOSSIBLE* TO BELIEVE,
IMPOSSIBLE TO DROP THE EVERYDAY THINGS OF LIFE AND FEEL THAT THERE WAS ONLY *ONE THING* WHICH WAS IMPORTANT--*PREPARATION* TO MEET AN ENEMY NO MATTER *WHERE* HE STRUCK.
THAT IS ALL OVER NOW AND THERE IS *NO MORE* UNCERTAINTY.
WE *KNOW* WHAT WE HAVE TO FACE AND WE *KNOW* THAT WE ARE *READY* TO FACE IT.
I SHOULD LIKE TO SAY JUST A WORD TO THE WOMEN IN THE COUNTRY TONIGHT.
I HAVE A BOY AT SEA ON A DESTROYER;* FOR ALL I KNOW HE MAY BE ON HIS WAY TO THE PACIFIC.
402
*FRANKLIN DELANO ROOSEVELT, JR. WAS EXECUTIVE OFFICER ON USS *MAYRANT.*
TWO OF MY CHILDREN ARE IN COAST CITIES ON THE PACIFIC. MANY OF YOU ALL OVER THE COUNTRY HAVE BOYS IN THE SERVICES WHO WILL *NOW BE CALLED UPON* TO GO INTO ACTION.
YOU HAVE FRIENDS AND FAMILIES IN WHAT HAS SUDDENLY BECOME A *DANGER ZONE.*
YOU CANNOT ESCAPE *ANXIETY.*
YOU CANNOT ESCAPE A *CLUTCH OF FEAR* AT YOUR HEART AND YET I HOPE THAT THE *CERTAINTY* OF WHAT WE HAVE TO MEET WILL MAKE YOU *RISE ABOVE* THESE FEARS.
WE MUST GO ABOUT OUR DAILY BUSINESS *MORE DETERMINED THAN EVER* TO DO THE ORDINARY THINGS AS WELL AS WE CAN
AND WHEN WE FIND A WAY TO DO *ANYTHING MORE* IN OUR COMMUNITIES TO *HELP OTHERS,* TO *BUILD MORALE,* TO *GIVE* A FEELING OF *SECURITY,* WE *MUST DO IT.*
WHATEVER IS ASKED OF US I AM SURE WE CAN ACCOMPLISH IT.
WE ARE THE *FREE* AND *UNCONQUERABLE* PEOPLE OF THE UNITED STATES OF AMERICA.

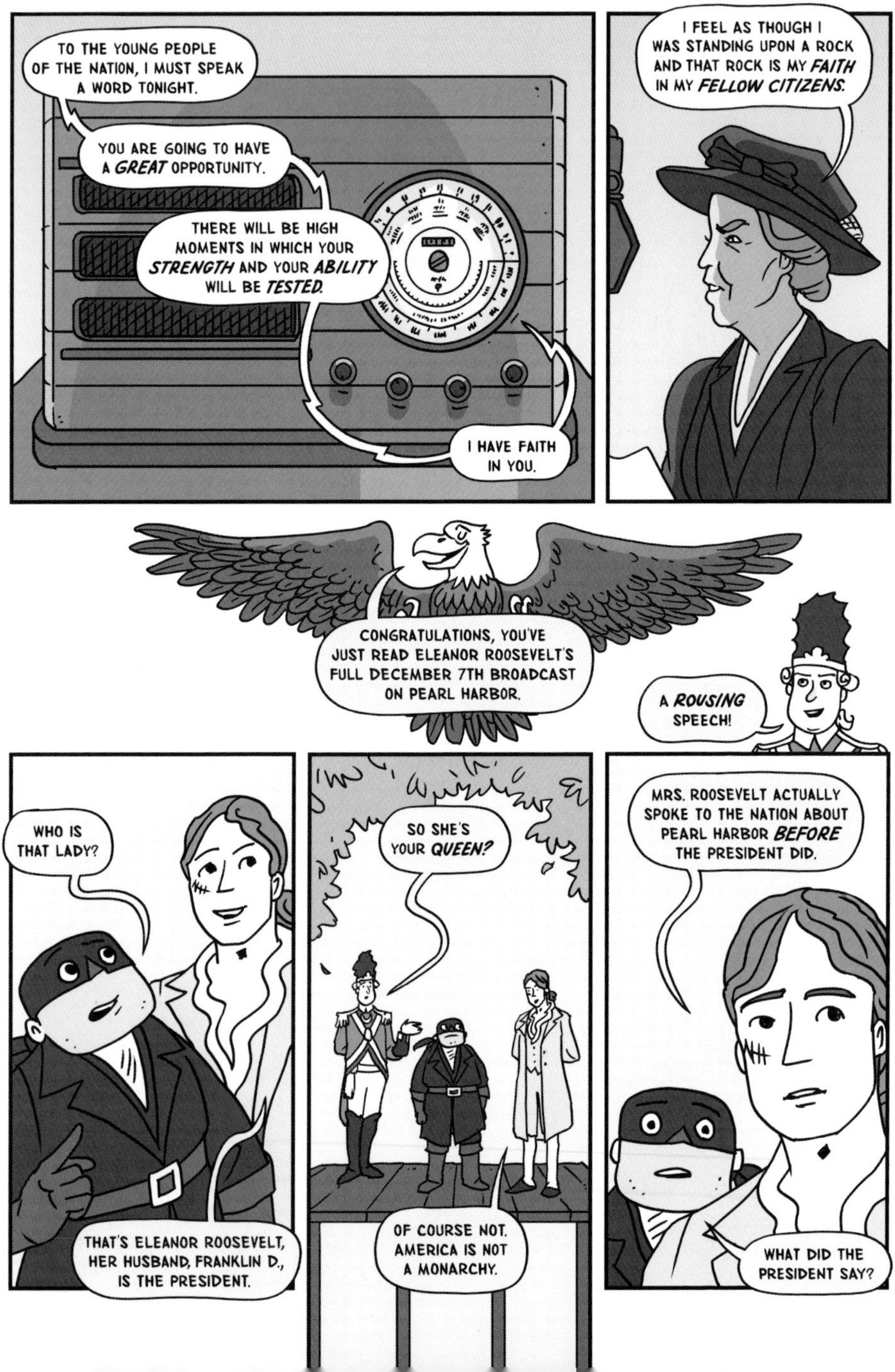
TO THE YOUNG PEOPLE OF THE NATION, I MUST SPEAK A WORD TONIGHT.
YOU ARE GOING TO HAVE A *GREAT* OPPORTUNITY.
THERE WILL BE HIGH MOMENTS IN WHICH YOUR *STRENGTH* AND YOUR *ABILITY* WILL BE *TESTED.*
I HAVE FAITH IN YOU.
I FEEL AS THOUGH I WAS STANDING UPON A ROCK AND THAT ROCK IS MY *FAITH* IN MY *FELLOW CITIZENS.*
CONGRATULATIONS, YOU'VE JUST READ ELEANOR ROOSEVELT'S FULL DECEMBER 7TH BROADCAST ON PEARL HARBOR.
A *ROUSING* SPEECH!
WHO IS THAT LADY?
THAT'S ELEANOR ROOSEVELT, HER HUSBAND, FRANKLIN D., IS THE PRESIDENT.
SO SHE'S YOUR *QUEEN?*
OF COURSE NOT. AMERICA IS NOT A MONARCHY.
MRS. ROOSEVELT ACTUALLY SPOKE TO THE NATION ABOUT PEARL HARBOR *BEFORE* THE PRESIDENT DID.
WHAT DID THE PRESIDENT SAY?

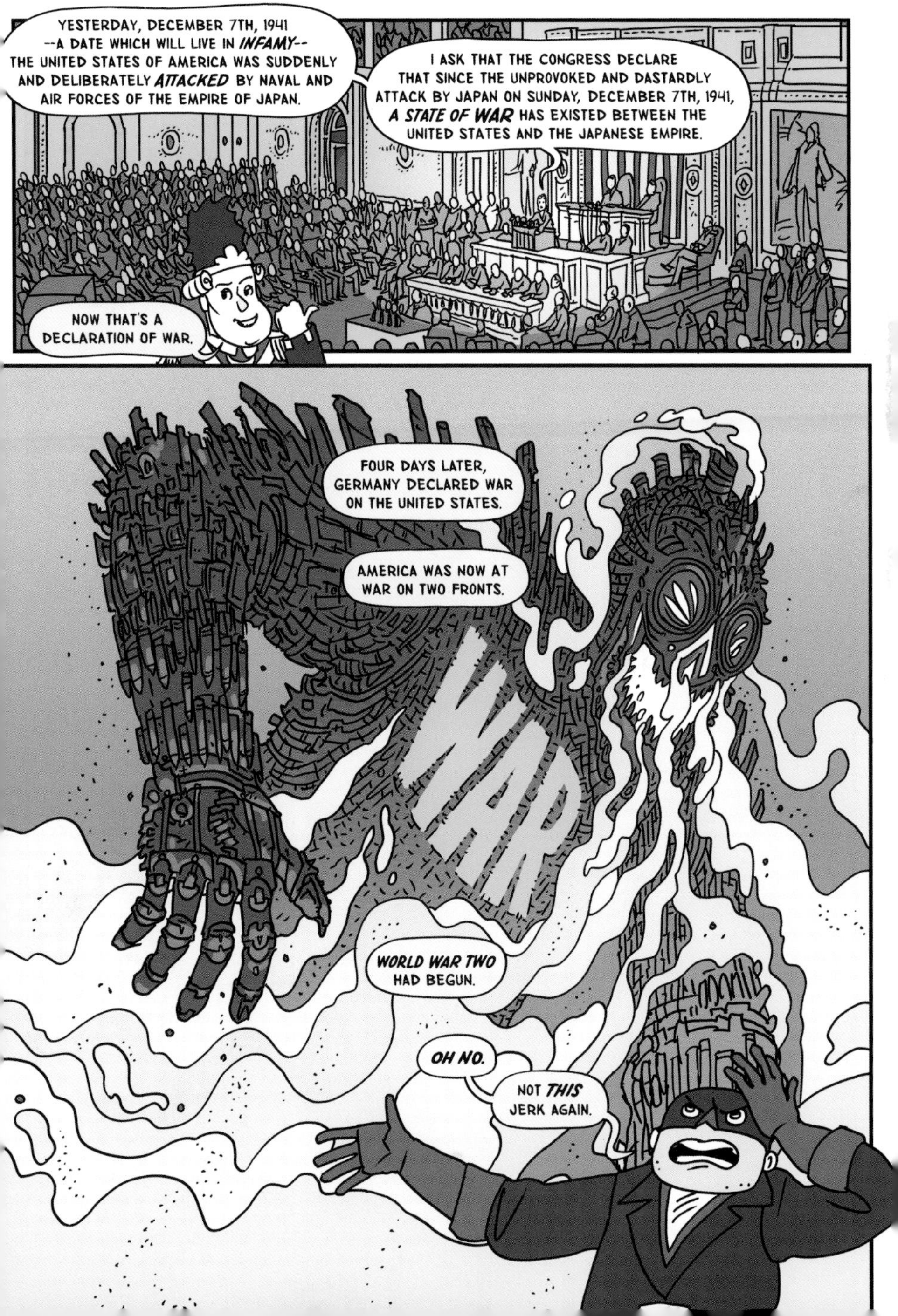
YESTERDAY, DECEMBER 7TH, 1941 --A DATE WHICH WILL LIVE IN *INFAMY*-- THE UNITED STATES OF AMERICA WAS SUDDENLY AND DELIBERATELY *ATTACKED* BY NAVAL AND AIR FORCES OF THE EMPIRE OF JAPAN.
I ASK THAT THE CONGRESS DECLARE THAT SINCE THE UNPROVOKED AND DASTARDLY ATTACK BY JAPAN ON SUNDAY, DECEMBER 7TH, 1941, *A STATE OF WAR* HAS EXISTED BETWEEN THE UNITED STATES AND THE JAPANESE EMPIRE.
NOW THAT'S A DECLARATION OF WAR.
FOUR DAYS LATER, GERMANY DECLARED WAR ON THE UNITED STATES.
AMERICA WAS NOW AT WAR ON TWO FRONTS.
WAR
WORLD WAR TWO HAD BEGUN.
OH NO.
NOT *THIS* JERK AGAIN.

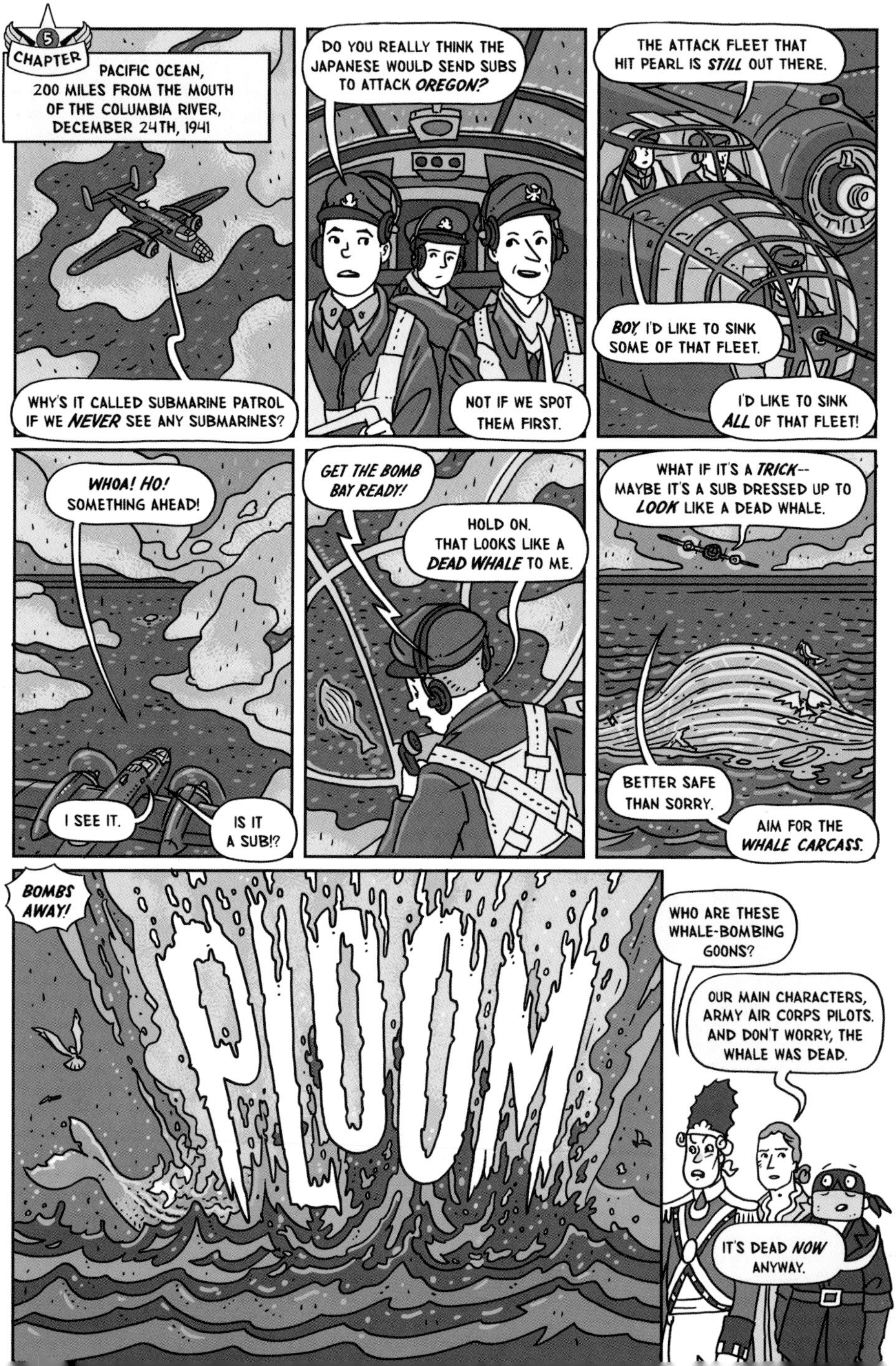
CHAPTER 5
PACIFIC OCEAN, 200 MILES FROM THE MOUTH OF THE COLUMBIA RIVER, DECEMBER 24TH, 1941
WHY'S IT CALLED SUBMARINE PATROL IF WE *NEVER* SEE ANY SUBMARINES?
DO YOU REALLY THINK THE JAPANESE WOULD SEND SUBS TO ATTACK *OREGON?*
NOT IF WE SPOT THEM FIRST.
THE ATTACK FLEET THAT HIT PEARL IS *STILL* OUT THERE.
BOY, I'D LIKE TO SINK SOME OF THAT FLEET.
I'D LIKE TO SINK *ALL* OF THAT FLEET!
WHOA! HO! SOMETHING AHEAD!
I SEE IT.
IS IT A SUB!?
GET THE BOMB BAY READY!
HOLD ON. THAT LOOKS LIKE A *DEAD WHALE* TO ME.
WHAT IF IT'S A *TRICK*-- MAYBE IT'S A SUB DRESSED UP TO *LOOK* LIKE A DEAD WHALE.
BETTER SAFE THAN SORRY.
AIM FOR THE *WHALE CARCASS.*
BOMBS AWAY!
PLOOM
WHO ARE THESE WHALE-BOMBING GOONS?
OUR MAIN CHARACTERS, ARMY AIR CORPS PILOTS. AND DON'T WORRY, THE WHALE WAS DEAD.
IT'S DEAD *NOW* ANYWAY.

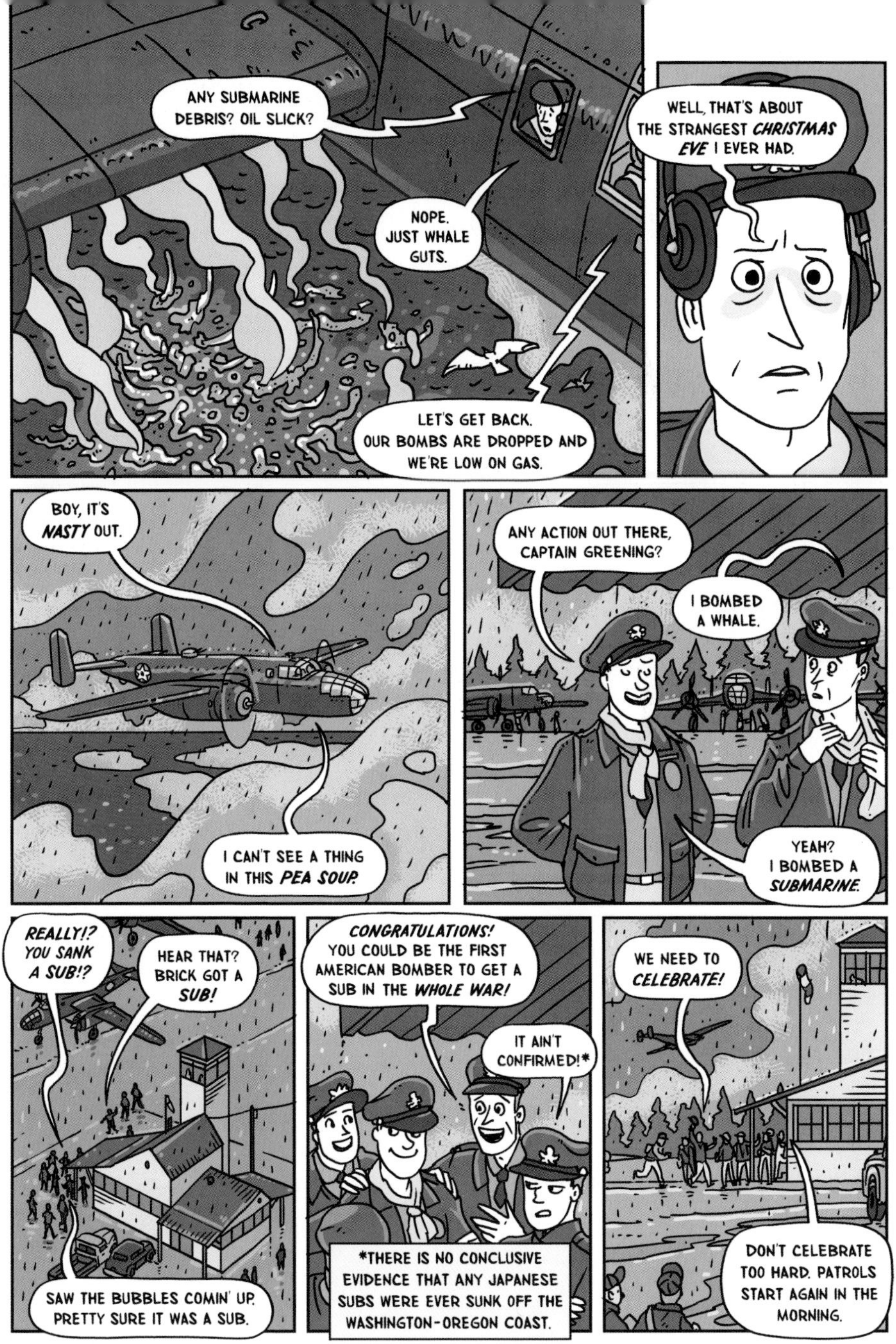

ANY SUBMARINE DEBRIS? OIL SLICK?
NOPE. JUST WHALE GUTS.
LET'S GET BACK. OUR BOMBS ARE DROPPED AND WE'RE LOW ON GAS.
WELL, THAT'S ABOUT THE STRANGEST CHRISTMAS EVE I EVER HAD.
BOY, IT'S NASTY OUT.
I CAN'T SEE A THING IN THIS PEA SOUP.
ANY ACTION OUT THERE, CAPTAIN GREENING?
I BOMBED A WHALE.
YEAH? I BOMBED A SUBMARINE.
REALLY!? YOU SANK A SUB!?
HEAR THAT? BRICK GOT A SUB!
SAW THE BUBBLES COMIN' UP. PRETTY SURE IT WAS A SUB.
CONGRATULATIONS! YOU COULD BE THE FIRST AMERICAN BOMBER TO GET A SUB IN THE WHOLE WAR!
IT AIN'T CONFIRMED!*
*THERE IS NO CONCLUSIVE EVIDENCE THAT ANY JAPANESE SUBS WERE EVER SUNK OFF THE WASHINGTON-OREGON COAST.
WE NEED TO CELEBRATE!
DON'T CELEBRATE TOO HARD. PATROLS START AGAIN IN THE MORNING.

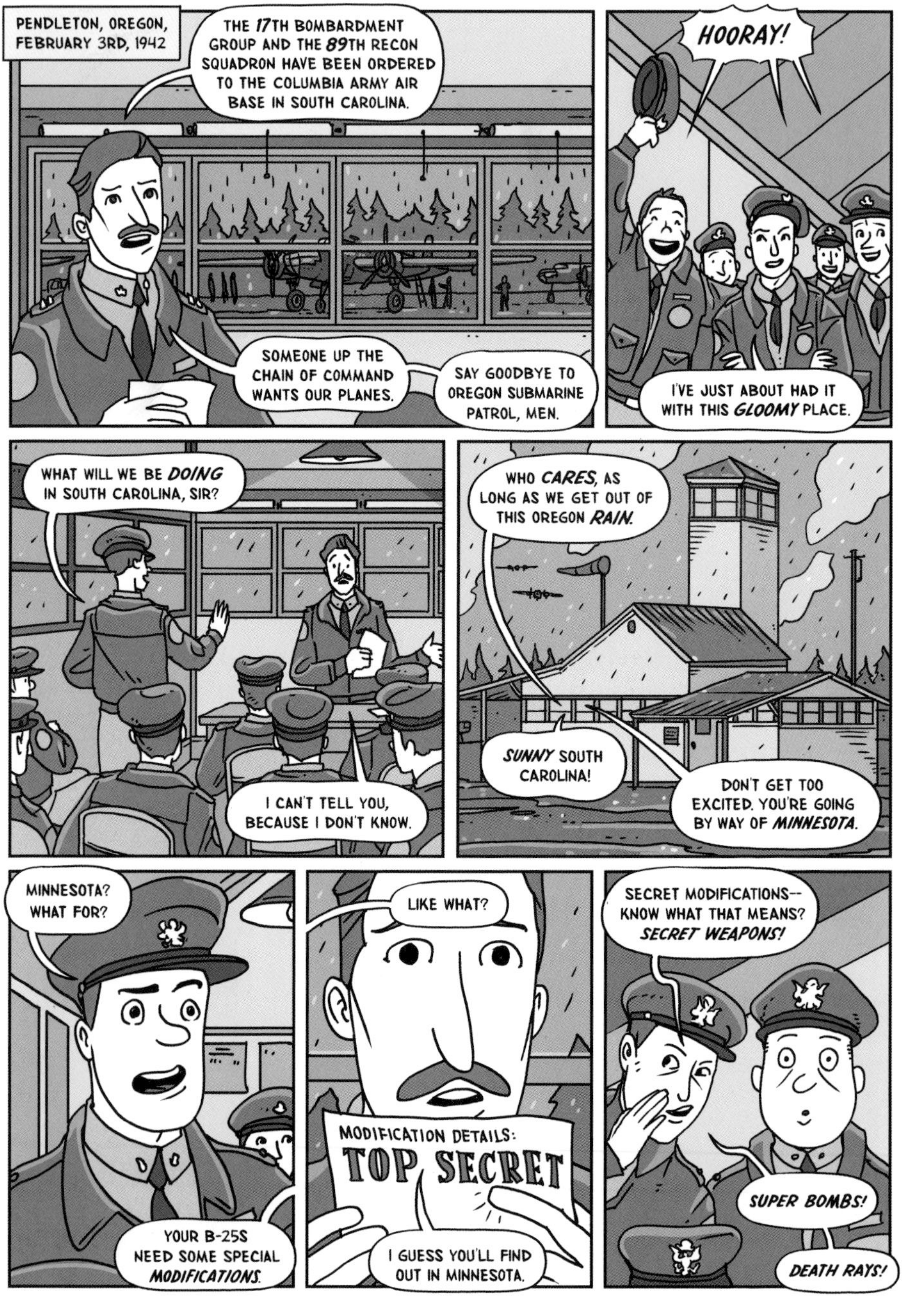
PENDLETON, OREGON, FEBRUARY 3RD, 1942
THE 17TH BOMBARDMENT GROUP AND THE 89TH RECON SQUADRON HAVE BEEN ORDERED TO THE COLUMBIA ARMY AIR BASE IN SOUTH CAROLINA.
SOMEONE UP THE CHAIN OF COMMAND WANTS OUR PLANES.
SAY GOODBYE TO OREGON SUBMARINE PATROL, MEN.
HOORAY!
I'VE JUST ABOUT HAD IT WITH THIS GLOOMY PLACE.
WHAT WILL WE BE DOING IN SOUTH CAROLINA, SIR?
I CAN'T TELL YOU, BECAUSE I DON'T KNOW.
WHO CARES, AS LONG AS WE GET OUT OF THIS OREGON RAIN.
SUNNY SOUTH CAROLINA!
DON'T GET TOO EXCITED. YOU'RE GOING BY WAY OF MINNESOTA.
MINNESOTA? WHAT FOR?
YOUR B-25S NEED SOME SPECIAL MODIFICATIONS.
LIKE WHAT?
MODIFICATION DETAILS:
TOP SECRET
I GUESS YOU'LL FIND OUT IN MINNESOTA.
SECRET MODIFICATIONS-- KNOW WHAT THAT MEANS? SECRET WEAPONS!
SUPER BOMBS!
DEATH RAYS!

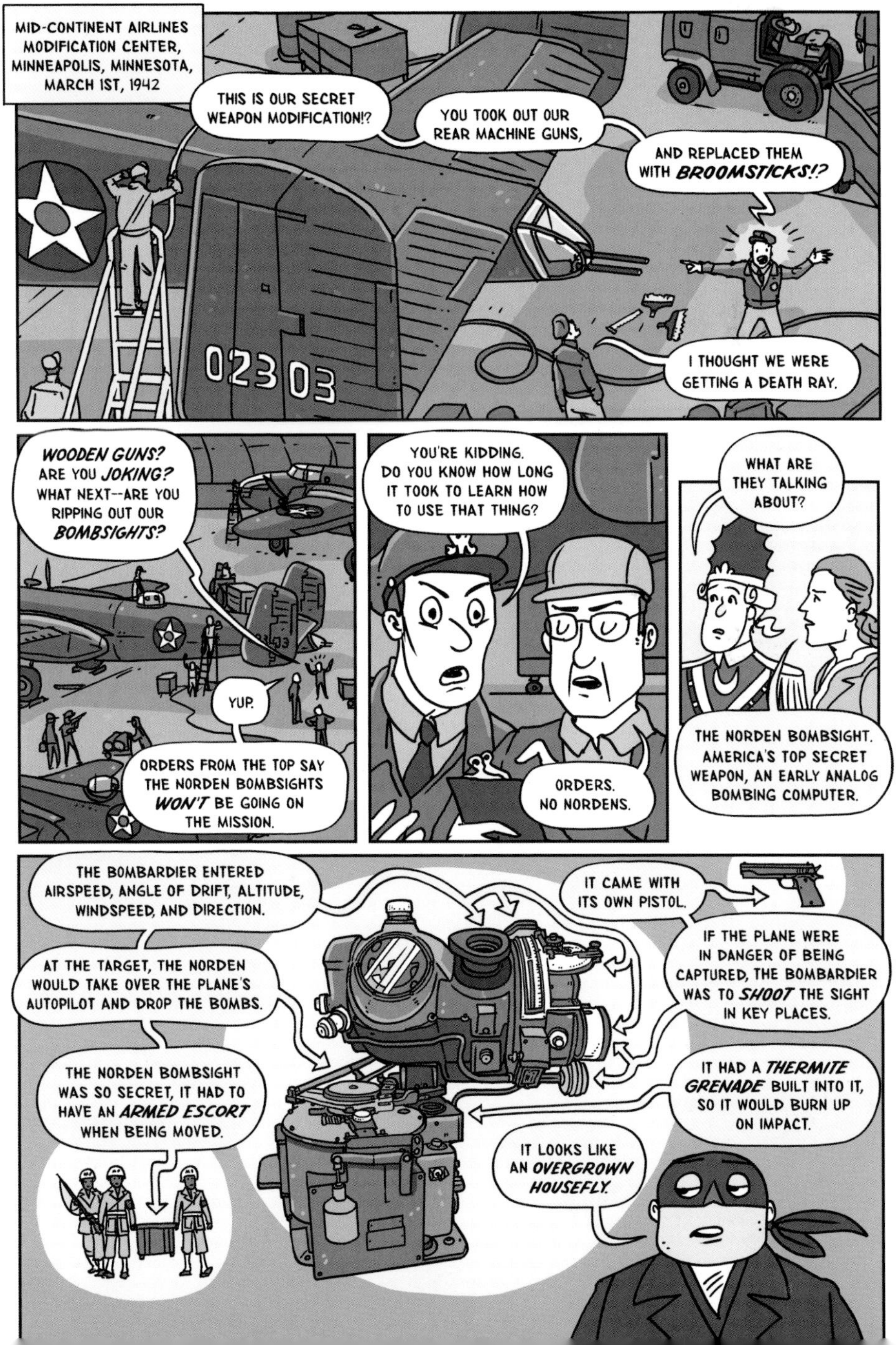
MID-CONTINENT AIRLINES MODIFICATION CENTER, MINNEAPOLIS, MINNESOTA, MARCH 1ST, 1942
THIS IS OUR SECRET WEAPON MODIFICATION!?
YOU TOOK OUT OUR REAR MACHINE GUNS,
AND REPLACED THEM WITH BROOMSTICKS!?
02303
I THOUGHT WE WERE GETTING A DEATH RAY.
WOODEN GUNS? ARE YOU JOKING? WHAT NEXT--ARE YOU RIPPING OUT OUR BOMBSIGHTS?
YUP.
ORDERS FROM THE TOP SAY THE NORDEN BOMBSIGHTS WON'T BE GOING ON THE MISSION.
YOU'RE KIDDING. DO YOU KNOW HOW LONG IT TOOK TO LEARN HOW TO USE THAT THING?
ORDERS. NO NORDENS.
WHAT ARE THEY TALKING ABOUT?
THE NORDEN BOMBSIGHT. AMERICA'S TOP SECRET WEAPON, AN EARLY ANALOG BOMBING COMPUTER.
THE BOMBARDIER ENTERED AIRSPEED, ANGLE OF DRIFT, ALTITUDE, WINDSPEED, AND DIRECTION.
IT CAME WITH ITS OWN PISTOL.
AT THE TARGET, THE NORDEN WOULD TAKE OVER THE PLANE'S AUTOPILOT AND DROP THE BOMBS.
IF THE PLANE WERE IN DANGER OF BEING CAPTURED, THE BOMBARDIER WAS TO SHOOT THE SIGHT IN KEY PLACES.
THE NORDEN BOMBSIGHT WAS SO SECRET, IT HAD TO HAVE AN ARMED ESCORT WHEN BEING MOVED.
IT HAD A THERMITE GRENADE BUILT INTO IT, SO IT WOULD BURN UP ON IMPACT.
IT LOOKS LIKE AN OVERGROWN HOUSEFLY.

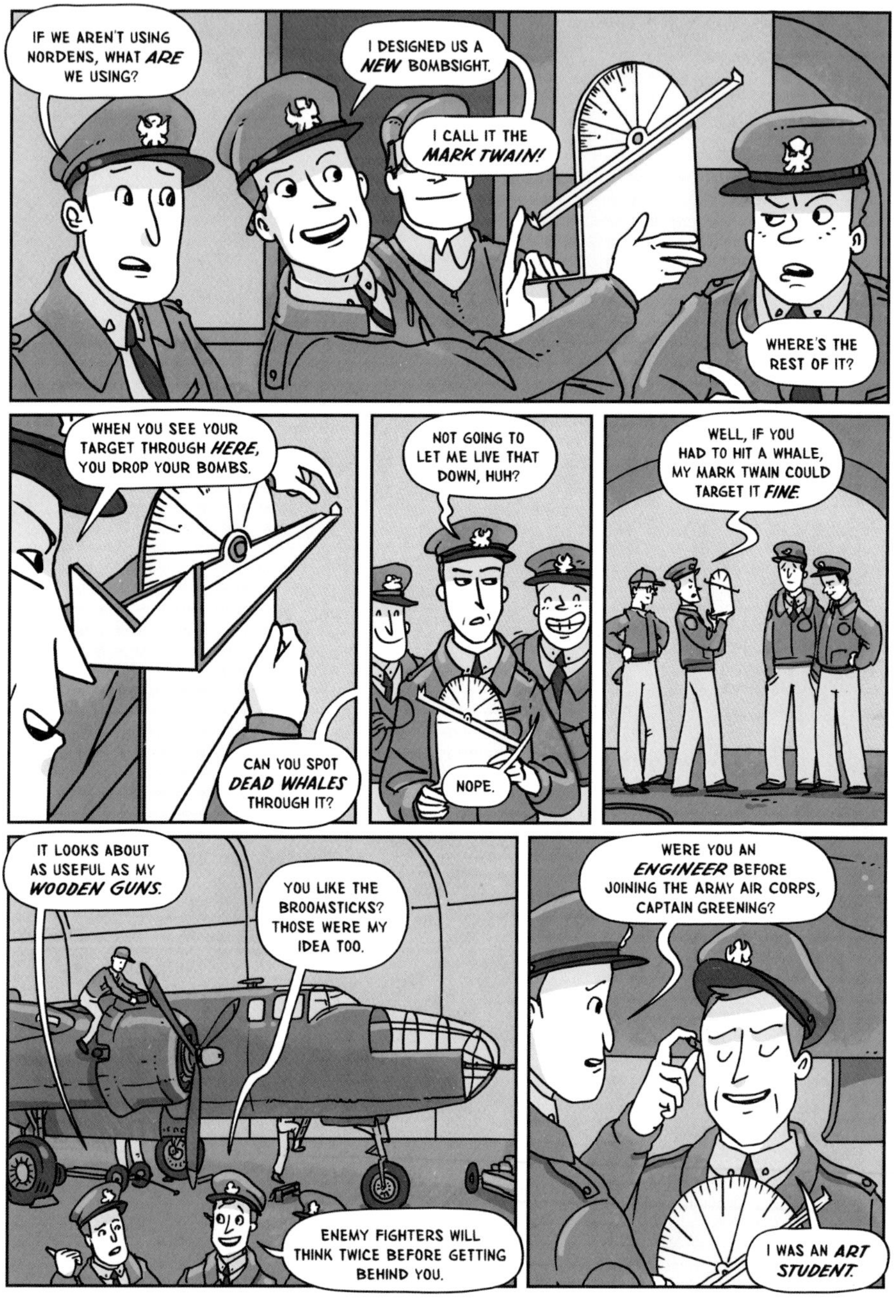

IF WE AREN'T USING NORDENS, WHAT ARE WE USING?
I DESIGNED US A NEW BOMBSIGHT.
I CALL IT THE MARK TWAIN!
WHERE'S THE REST OF IT?
WHEN YOU SEE YOUR TARGET THROUGH HERE, YOU DROP YOUR BOMBS.
CAN YOU SPOT DEAD WHALES THROUGH IT?
NOT GOING TO LET ME LIVE THAT DOWN, HUH?
NOPE.
WELL, IF YOU HAD TO HIT A WHALE, MY MARK TWAIN COULD TARGET IT FINE.
IT LOOKS ABOUT AS USEFUL AS MY WOODEN GUNS.
YOU LIKE THE BROOMSTICKS? THOSE WERE MY IDEA TOO.
ENEMY FIGHTERS WILL THINK TWICE BEFORE GETTING BEHIND YOU.
WERE YOU AN ENGINEER BEFORE JOINING THE ARMY AIR CORPS, CAPTAIN GREENING?
I WAS AN ART STUDENT.

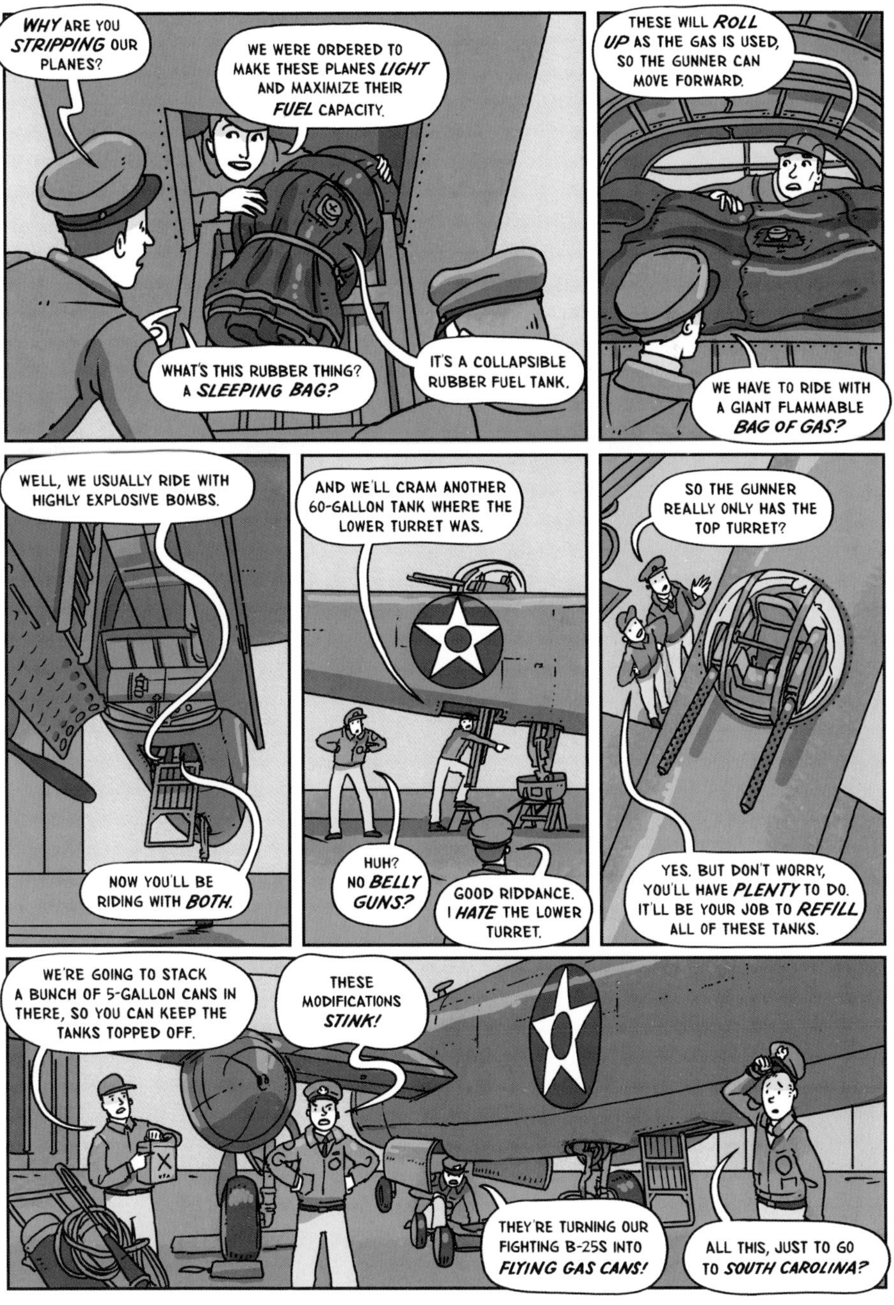
WHY ARE YOU STRIPPING OUR PLANES?
WE WERE ORDERED TO MAKE THESE PLANES LIGHT AND MAXIMIZE THEIR FUEL CAPACITY.
WHAT'S THIS RUBBER THING? A SLEEPING BAG?
IT'S A COLLAPSIBLE RUBBER FUEL TANK.
THESE WILL ROLL UP AS THE GAS IS USED, SO THE GUNNER CAN MOVE FORWARD.
WE HAVE TO RIDE WITH A GIANT FLAMMABLE BAG OF GAS?
WELL, WE USUALLY RIDE WITH HIGHLY EXPLOSIVE BOMBS.
NOW YOU'LL BE RIDING WITH BOTH.
AND WE'LL CRAM ANOTHER 60-GALLON TANK WHERE THE LOWER TURRET WAS.
HUH? NO BELLY GUNS?
GOOD RIDDANCE. I HATE THE LOWER TURRET.
SO THE GUNNER REALLY ONLY HAS THE TOP TURRET?
YES. BUT DON'T WORRY, YOU'LL HAVE PLENTY TO DO. IT'LL BE YOUR JOB TO REFILL ALL OF THESE TANKS.
WE'RE GOING TO STACK A BUNCH OF 5-GALLON CANS IN THERE, SO YOU CAN KEEP THE TANKS TOPPED OFF.
THESE MODIFICATIONS STINK!
THEY'RE TURNING OUR FIGHTING B-25S INTO FLYING GAS CANS!
ALL THIS, JUST TO GO TO SOUTH CAROLINA?

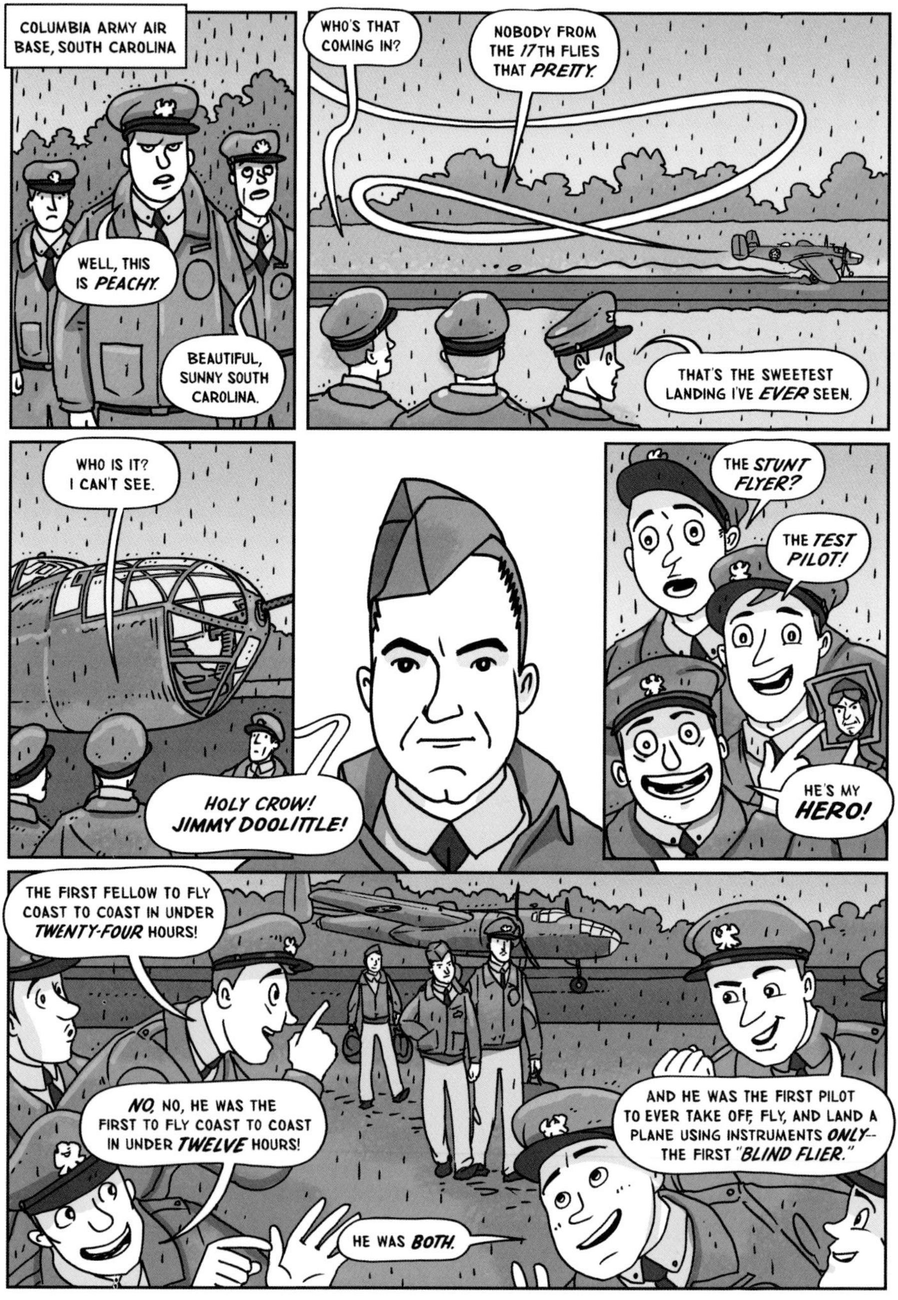

COLUMBIA ARMY AIR BASE, SOUTH CAROLINA
WELL, THIS IS *PEACHY.*
BEAUTIFUL, SUNNY SOUTH CAROLINA.
WHO'S THAT COMING IN?
NOBODY FROM THE *17*TH FLIES THAT *PRETTY.*
THAT'S THE SWEETEST LANDING I'VE *EVER* SEEN.
WHO IS IT? I CAN'T SEE.
HOLY CROW! JIMMY DOOLITTLE!
THE *STUNT FLYER?*
THE *TEST PILOT!*
HE'S MY **HERO!**
THE FIRST FELLOW TO FLY COAST TO COAST IN UNDER *TWENTY-FOUR* HOURS!
NO, NO, HE WAS THE FIRST TO FLY COAST TO COAST IN UNDER *TWELVE* HOURS!
AND HE WAS THE FIRST PILOT TO EVER TAKE OFF, FLY, AND LAND A PLANE USING INSTRUMENTS *ONLY*-- THE FIRST "*BLIND FLIER.*"
HE WAS *BOTH.*

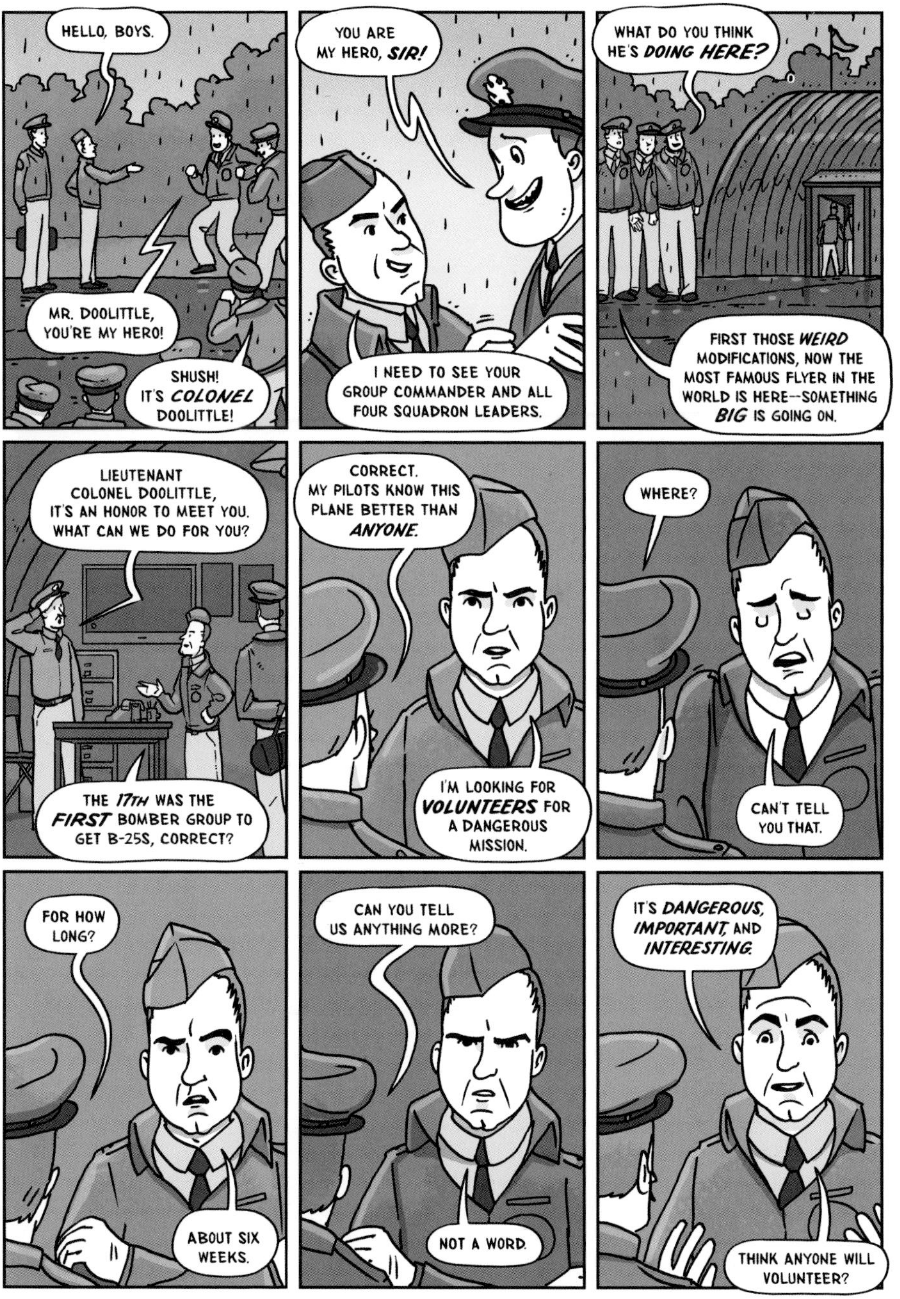
HELLO, BOYS.
MR. DOOLITTLE, YOU'RE MY HERO!
SHUSH! IT'S COLONEL DOOLITTLE!
YOU ARE MY HERO, SIR!
I NEED TO SEE YOUR GROUP COMMANDER AND ALL FOUR SQUADRON LEADERS.
WHAT DO YOU THINK HE'S DOING HERE?
FIRST THOSE WEIRD MODIFICATIONS, NOW THE MOST FAMOUS FLYER IN THE WORLD IS HERE--SOMETHING BIG IS GOING ON.
LIEUTENANT COLONEL DOOLITTLE, IT'S AN HONOR TO MEET YOU. WHAT CAN WE DO FOR YOU?
THE 17TH WAS THE FIRST BOMBER GROUP TO GET B-25S, CORRECT?
CORRECT. MY PILOTS KNOW THIS PLANE BETTER THAN ANYONE.
I'M LOOKING FOR VOLUNTEERS FOR A DANGEROUS MISSION.
WHERE?
CAN'T TELL YOU THAT.
FOR HOW LONG?
ABOUT SIX WEEKS.
CAN YOU TELL US ANYTHING MORE?
NOT A WORD.
IT'S DANGEROUS, IMPORTANT, AND INTERESTING.
THINK ANYONE WILL VOLUNTEER?

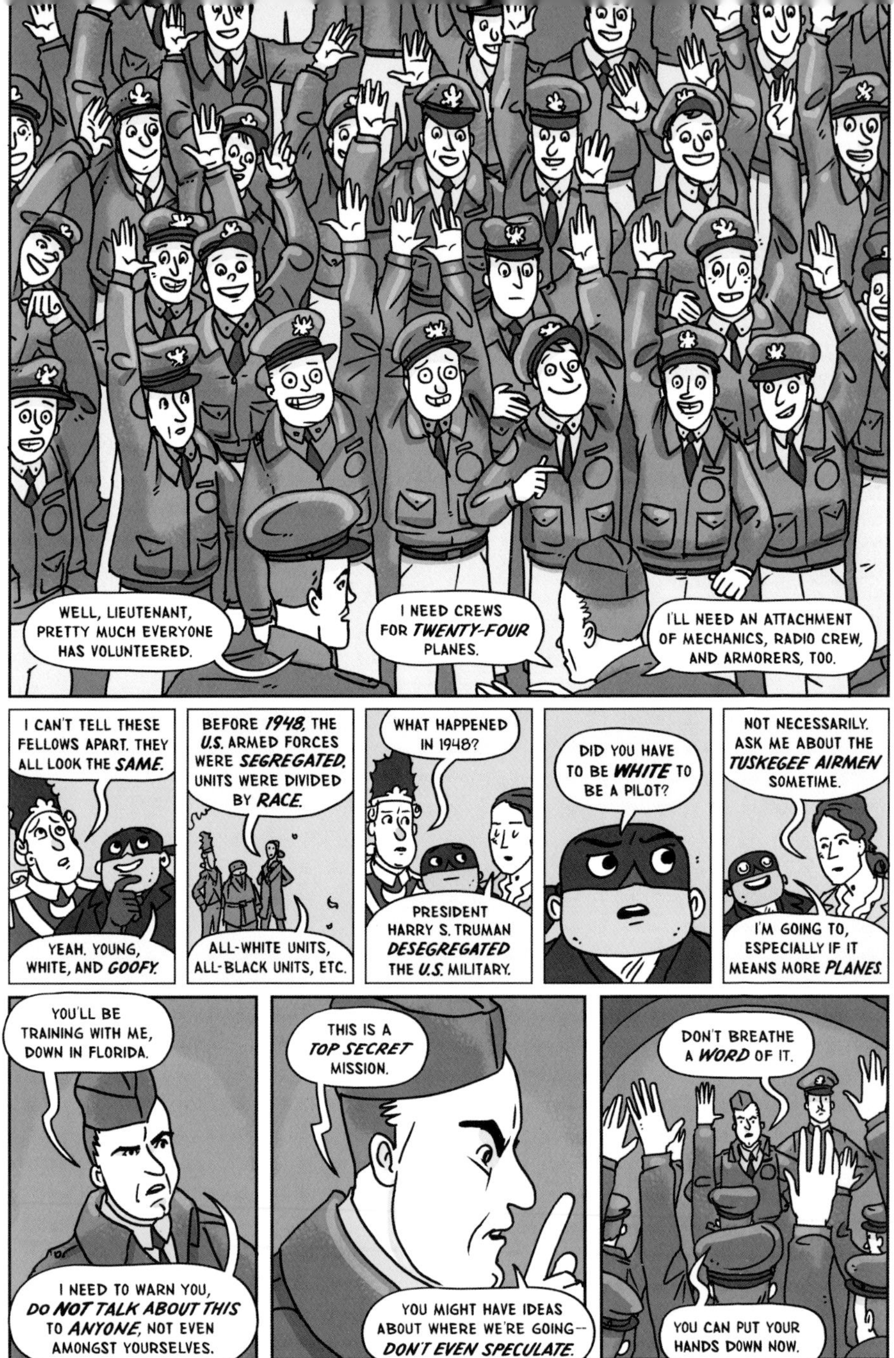
WELL, LIEUTENANT, PRETTY MUCH EVERYONE HAS VOLUNTEERED.
I NEED CREWS FOR TWENTY-FOUR PLANES.
I'LL NEED AN ATTACHMENT OF MECHANICS, RADIO CREW, AND ARMORERS, TOO.
I CAN'T TELL THESE FELLOWS APART. THEY ALL LOOK THE SAME.
YEAH. YOUNG, WHITE, AND GOOFY.
BEFORE 1948, THE U.S. ARMED FORCES WERE SEGREGATED. UNITS WERE DIVIDED BY RACE.
ALL-WHITE UNITS, ALL-BLACK UNITS, ETC.
WHAT HAPPENED IN 1948?
PRESIDENT HARRY S. TRUMAN DESEGREGATED THE U.S. MILITARY.
DID YOU HAVE TO BE WHITE TO BE A PILOT?
NOT NECESSARILY. ASK ME ABOUT THE TUSKEGEE AIRMEN SOMETIME.
I'M GOING TO, ESPECIALLY IF IT MEANS MORE PLANES.
YOU'LL BE TRAINING WITH ME, DOWN IN FLORIDA.
I NEED TO WARN YOU, DO NOT TALK ABOUT THIS TO ANYONE, NOT EVEN AMONGST YOURSELVES.
THIS IS A TOP SECRET MISSION.
YOU MIGHT HAVE IDEAS ABOUT WHERE WE'RE GOING-- DON'T EVEN SPECULATE.
DON'T BREATHE A WORD OF IT.
YOU CAN PUT YOUR HANDS DOWN NOW.

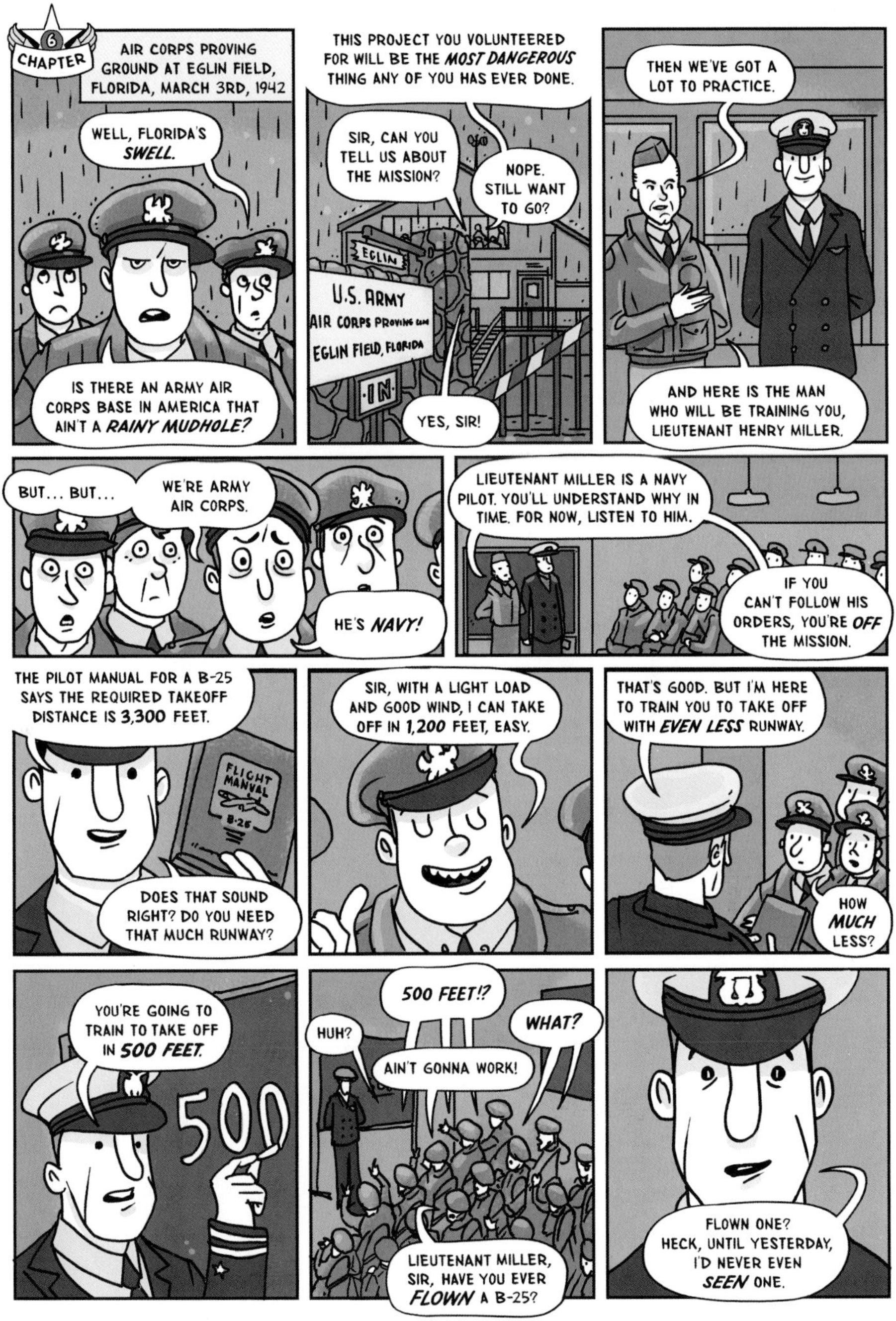
CHAPTER 6
AIR CORPS PROVING GROUND AT EGLIN FIELD, FLORIDA, MARCH 3RD, 1942
WELL, FLORIDA'S *SWELL.*
IS THERE AN ARMY AIR CORPS BASE IN AMERICA THAT AIN'T A *RAINY MUDHOLE?*
THIS PROJECT YOU VOLUNTEERED FOR WILL BE THE *MOST DANGEROUS* THING ANY OF YOU HAS EVER DONE.
SIR, CAN YOU TELL US ABOUT THE MISSION?
NOPE. STILL WANT TO GO?
EGLIN
U.S. ARMY
AIR CORPS PROVING GROUND
EGLIN FIELD, FLORIDA
IN
YES, SIR!
THEN WE'VE GOT A LOT TO PRACTICE.
AND HERE IS THE MAN WHO WILL BE TRAINING YOU, LIEUTENANT HENRY MILLER.
BUT... BUT...
WE'RE ARMY AIR CORPS.
HE'S *NAVY!*
LIEUTENANT MILLER IS A NAVY PILOT. YOU'LL UNDERSTAND WHY IN TIME. FOR NOW, LISTEN TO HIM.
IF YOU CAN'T FOLLOW HIS ORDERS, YOU'RE *OFF* THE MISSION.
THE PILOT MANUAL FOR A B-25 SAYS THE REQUIRED TAKEOFF DISTANCE IS 3,300 FEET.
FLIGHT MANUAL
B-25
DOES THAT SOUND RIGHT? DO YOU NEED THAT MUCH RUNWAY?
SIR, WITH A LIGHT LOAD AND GOOD WIND, I CAN TAKE OFF IN 1,200 FEET, EASY.
THAT'S GOOD. BUT I'M HERE TO TRAIN YOU TO TAKE OFF WITH *EVEN LESS* RUNWAY.
HOW *MUCH* LESS?
YOU'RE GOING TO TRAIN TO TAKE OFF IN *500 FEET.*
500
HUH?
500 FEET!?
WHAT?
AIN'T GONNA WORK!
LIEUTENANT MILLER, SIR, HAVE YOU EVER *FLOWN* A B-25?
FLOWN ONE? HECK, UNTIL YESTERDAY, I'D NEVER EVEN *SEEN* ONE.

MYSELF, CAPTAIN YORK, CAPTAIN JONES, AND CAPTAIN GREENING SUCCESSFULLY EXECUTED A 500-FOOT B-25 LAUNCH YESTERDAY.

HOW *FAST* WERE YOU GOING?

WE TOOK OFF AT *50* MILES PER HOUR.

NOT A CHANCE!

IMPOSSIBLE!

YOU NEED TO BE GOING *AT LEAST* 100 MILES AN HOUR TO TAKEOFF!

PREFERABLY *110!*

TRAINING BEGINS TOMORROW AT 0600. WE'LL BEGIN WITH A DEMONSTRATION.

BBB RRRRR

FIRST, GET YOUR ENGINES UP TO *FULL* CAPACITY.

BBB RRRRR

PUT YOUR FLAPS ALL THE WAY DOWN.

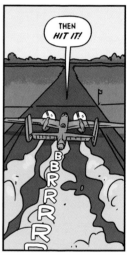

THEN *HIT IT!*

BBRRRR

BBRRRRRUMMM

SKONK

MMMMMM

IMPOSSIBLE.

500

40

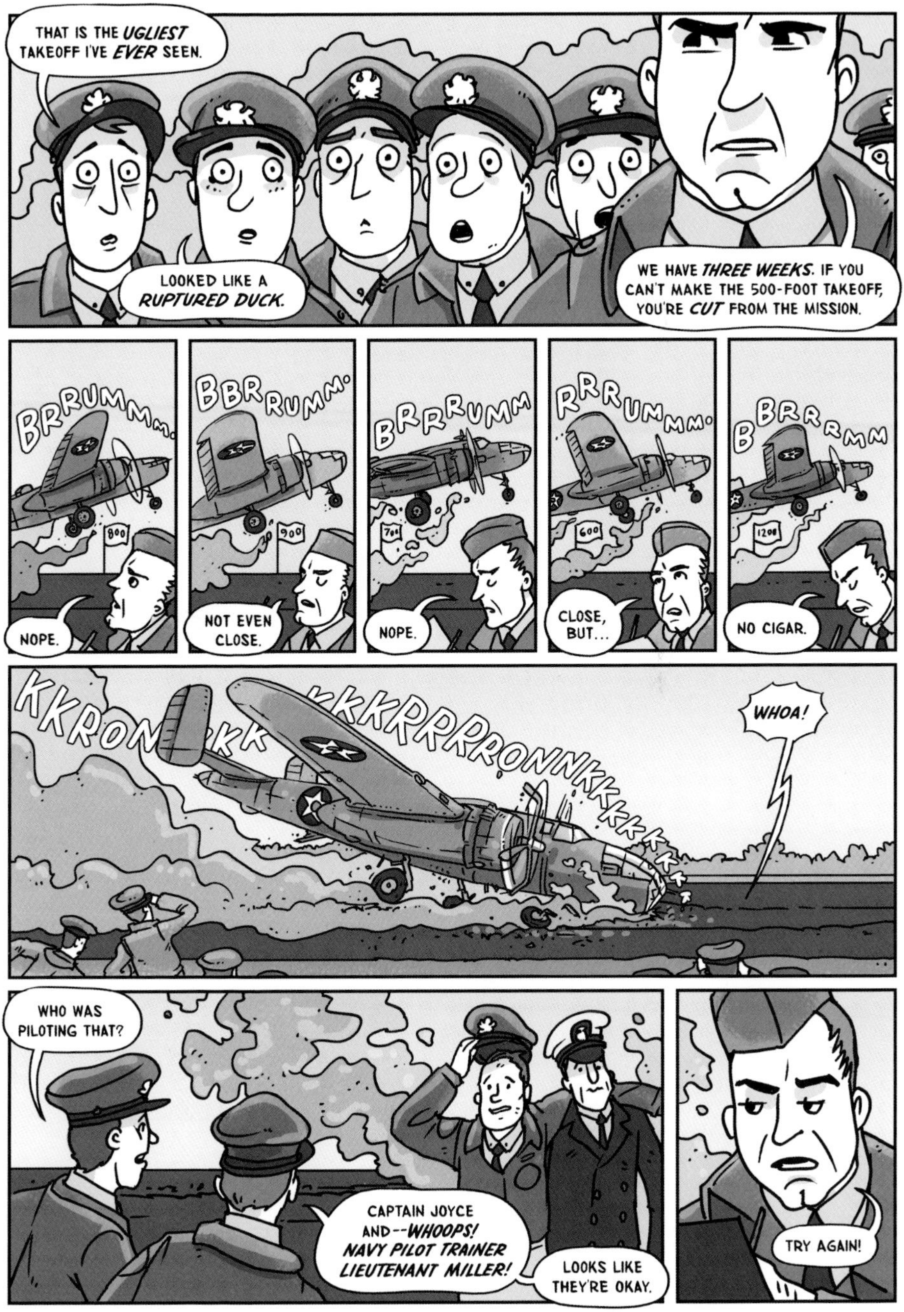

THAT IS THE UGLIEST TAKEOFF I'VE EVER SEEN.
LOOKED LIKE A RUPTURED DUCK.
WE HAVE THREE WEEKS. IF YOU CAN'T MAKE THE 500-FOOT TAKEOFF, YOU'RE CUT FROM THE MISSION.
BRRUMMM.
800
NOPE.
BBRRUMM.
900
NOT EVEN CLOSE.
BRRRUMM
700
NOPE.
RRRUMMM.
600
CLOSE, BUT...
BBRRRRMM
1200
NO CIGAR.
KKRONKK KKKRRRRONNKKKKKKKT
WHOA!
WHO WAS PILOTING THAT?
CAPTAIN JOYCE AND--WHOOPS! NAVY PILOT TRAINER LIEUTENANT MILLER!
LOOKS LIKE THEY'RE OKAY.
TRY AGAIN!

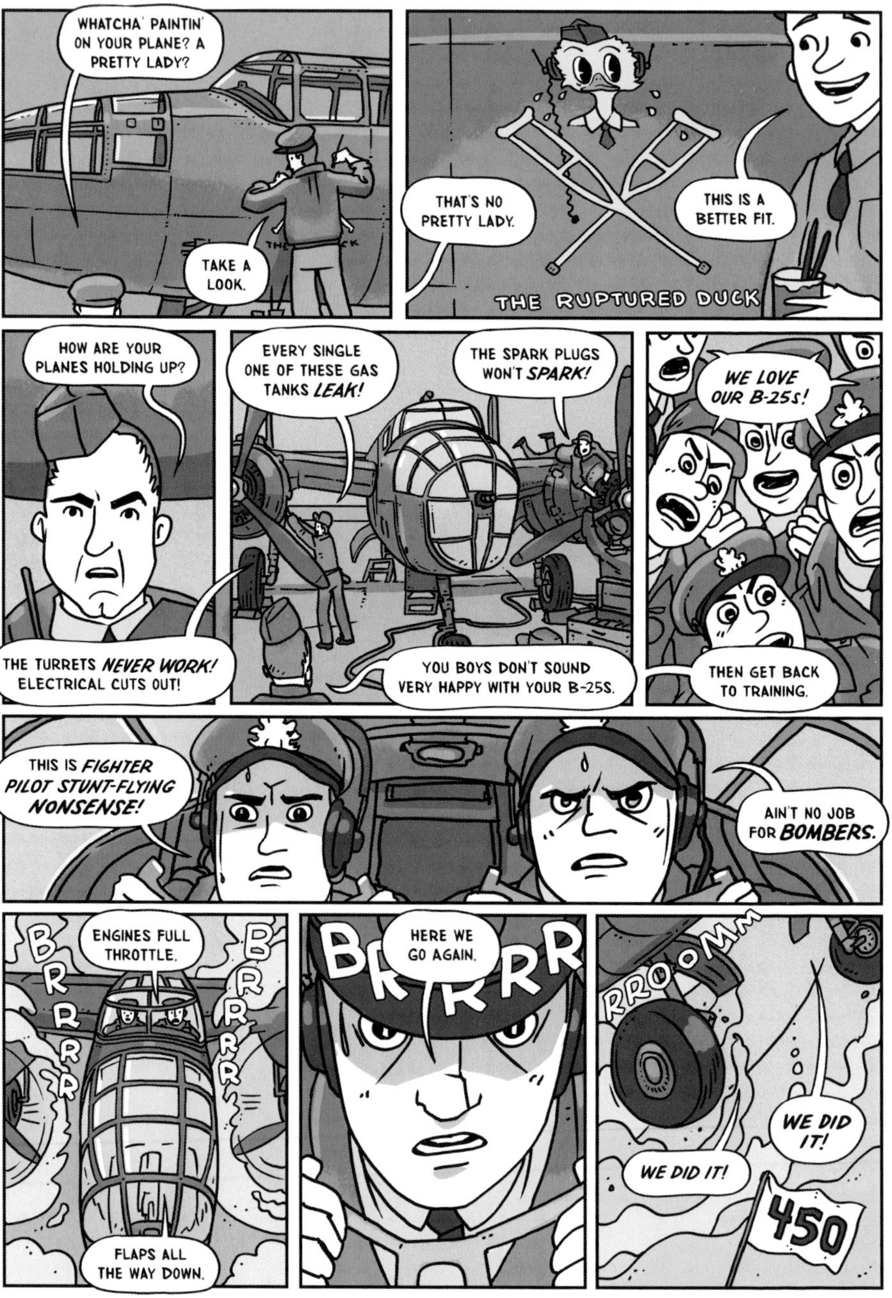
WHATCHA' PAINTIN' ON YOUR PLANE? A PRETTY LADY?
TAKE A LOOK.
THAT'S NO PRETTY LADY.
THIS IS A BETTER FIT.
THE RUPTURED DUCK
HOW ARE YOUR PLANES HOLDING UP?
THE TURRETS *NEVER WORK!* ELECTRICAL CUTS OUT!
EVERY SINGLE ONE OF THESE GAS TANKS *LEAK!*
THE SPARK PLUGS WON'T *SPARK!*
YOU BOYS DON'T SOUND VERY HAPPY WITH YOUR B-25S.
WE LOVE OUR B-25s!
THEN GET BACK TO TRAINING.
THIS IS *FIGHTER PILOT STUNT-FLYING NONSENSE!*
AIN'T NO JOB FOR **BOMBERS.**
BRRRR
ENGINES FULL THROTTLE.
BRRRR
FLAPS ALL THE WAY DOWN.
BRRRR
HERE WE GO AGAIN.
RROOMM
WE DID IT!
WE DID IT!
450

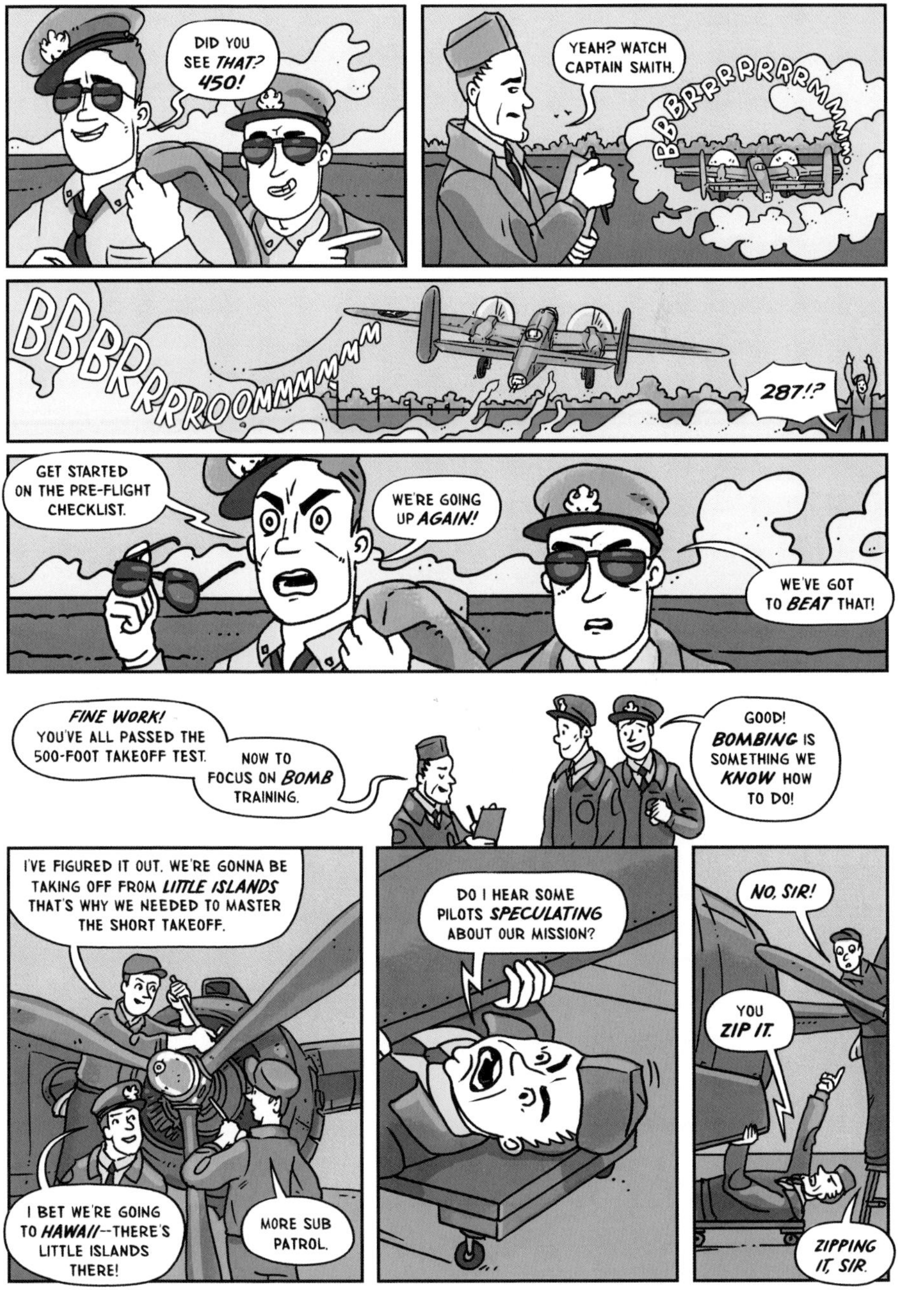
DID YOU SEE THAT? 450!
YEAH? WATCH CAPTAIN SMITH.
BBBRRRRRRRMMMM.
BBBRRRRROOMMMMMMM
287!?
GET STARTED ON THE PRE-FLIGHT CHECKLIST.
WE'RE GOING UP AGAIN!
WE'VE GOT TO BEAT THAT!
FINE WORK! YOU'VE ALL PASSED THE 500-FOOT TAKEOFF TEST.
NOW TO FOCUS ON BOMB TRAINING.
GOOD! BOMBING IS SOMETHING WE KNOW HOW TO DO!
I'VE FIGURED IT OUT. WE'RE GONNA BE TAKING OFF FROM LITTLE ISLANDS THAT'S WHY WE NEEDED TO MASTER THE SHORT TAKEOFF.
I BET WE'RE GOING TO HAWAII--THERE'S LITTLE ISLANDS THERE!
MORE SUB PATROL.
DO I HEAR SOME PILOTS SPECULATING ABOUT OUR MISSION?
NO, SIR!
YOU ZIP IT.
ZIPPING IT, SIR.

WE NEED TO GET IN AS *LOW* AS POSSIBLE. WHEN WE'RE ABOVE THE OCEAN, I WANT YOUR PROPELLERS TO BE ALMOST TOUCHING WATER.

THAT'S LOW.

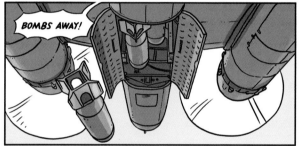

ACCURACY IS IMPROVED THE LOWER WE FLY.

WE'RE *500 FEET* FROM GROUND LEVEL.

BOMBS AWAY!

BOOOM

WHUMP

WHONK

THAT WAS TOO LOW.

44

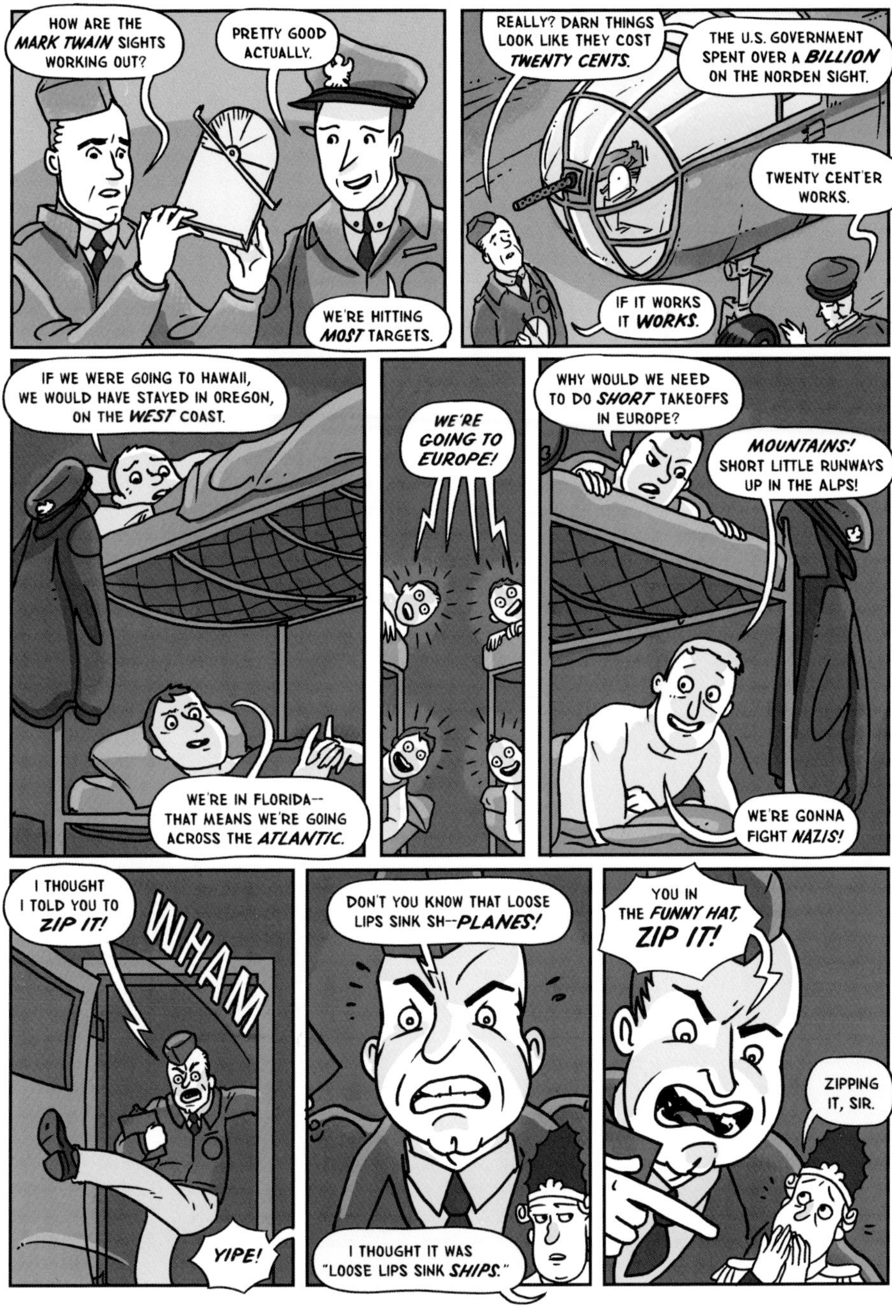
HOW ARE THE MARK TWAIN SIGHTS WORKING OUT?
PRETTY GOOD ACTUALLY.
WE'RE HITTING MOST TARGETS.
REALLY? DARN THINGS LOOK LIKE THEY COST TWENTY CENTS.
THE U.S. GOVERNMENT SPENT OVER A BILLION ON THE NORDEN SIGHT.
THE TWENTY CENT'ER WORKS.
IF IT WORKS IT WORKS.
IF WE WERE GOING TO HAWAII, WE WOULD HAVE STAYED IN OREGON, ON THE WEST COAST.
WE'RE IN FLORIDA-- THAT MEANS WE'RE GOING ACROSS THE ATLANTIC.
WE'RE GOING TO EUROPE!
WHY WOULD WE NEED TO DO SHORT TAKEOFFS IN EUROPE?
MOUNTAINS! SHORT LITTLE RUNWAYS UP IN THE ALPS!
WE'RE GONNA FIGHT NAZIS!
I THOUGHT I TOLD YOU TO ZIP IT!
WHAM
YIPE!
DON'T YOU KNOW THAT LOOSE LIPS SINK SH--PLANES!
I THOUGHT IT WAS "LOOSE LIPS SINK SHIPS."
YOU IN THE FUNNY HAT, ZIP IT!
ZIPPING IT, SIR.

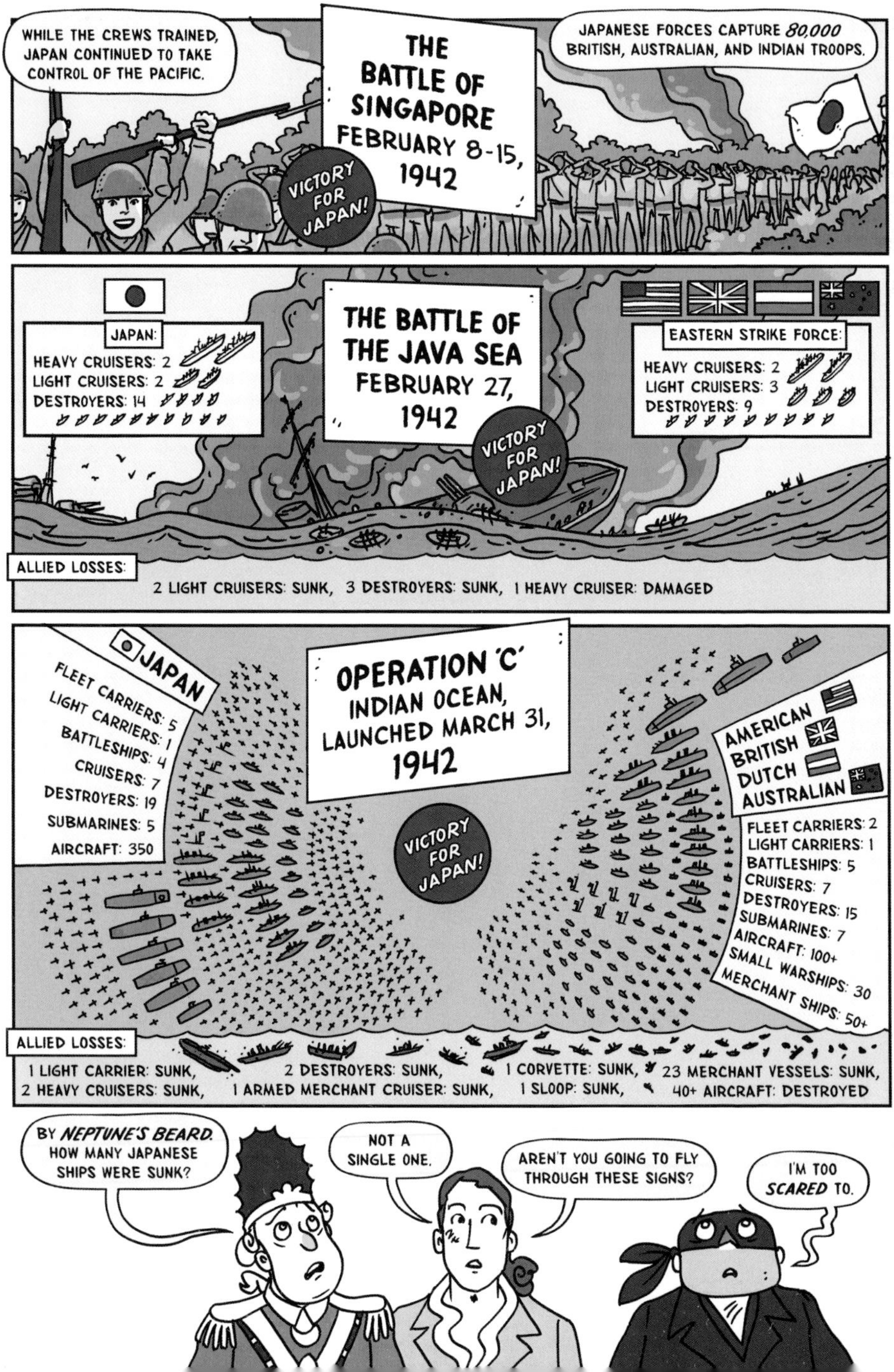
WHILE THE CREWS TRAINED, JAPAN CONTINUED TO TAKE CONTROL OF THE PACIFIC.
THE BATTLE OF SINGAPORE FEBRUARY 8-15, 1942
VICTORY FOR JAPAN!
JAPANESE FORCES CAPTURE *80,000* BRITISH, AUSTRALIAN, AND INDIAN TROOPS.
JAPAN:
HEAVY CRUISERS: 2
LIGHT CRUISERS: 2
DESTROYERS: 14
THE BATTLE OF THE JAVA SEA FEBRUARY 27, 1942
VICTORY FOR JAPAN!
EASTERN STRIKE FORCE:
HEAVY CRUISERS: 2
LIGHT CRUISERS: 3
DESTROYERS: 9
ALLIED LOSSES:
2 LIGHT CRUISERS: SUNK, 3 DESTROYERS: SUNK, 1 HEAVY CRUISER: DAMAGED
JAPAN
FLEET CARRIERS: 5
LIGHT CARRIERS: 1
BATTLESHIPS: 4
CRUISERS: 7
DESTROYERS: 19
SUBMARINES: 5
AIRCRAFT: 350
OPERATION 'C' INDIAN OCEAN, LAUNCHED MARCH 31, 1942
VICTORY FOR JAPAN!
AMERICAN
BRITISH
DUTCH
AUSTRALIAN
FLEET CARRIERS: 2
LIGHT CARRIERS: 1
BATTLESHIPS: 5
CRUISERS: 7
DESTROYERS: 15
SUBMARINES: 7
AIRCRAFT: 100+
SMALL WARSHIPS: 30
MERCHANT SHIPS: 50+
ALLIED LOSSES:
1 LIGHT CARRIER: SUNK,
2 HEAVY CRUISERS: SUNK,
2 DESTROYERS: SUNK,
1 ARMED MERCHANT CRUISER: SUNK,
1 CORVETTE: SUNK,
1 SLOOP: SUNK,
23 MERCHANT VESSELS: SUNK,
40+ AIRCRAFT: DESTROYED
BY *NEPTUNE'S BEARD*. HOW MANY JAPANESE SHIPS WERE SUNK?
NOT A SINGLE ONE.
AREN'T YOU GOING TO FLY THROUGH THESE SIGNS?
I'M TOO *SCARED* TO.

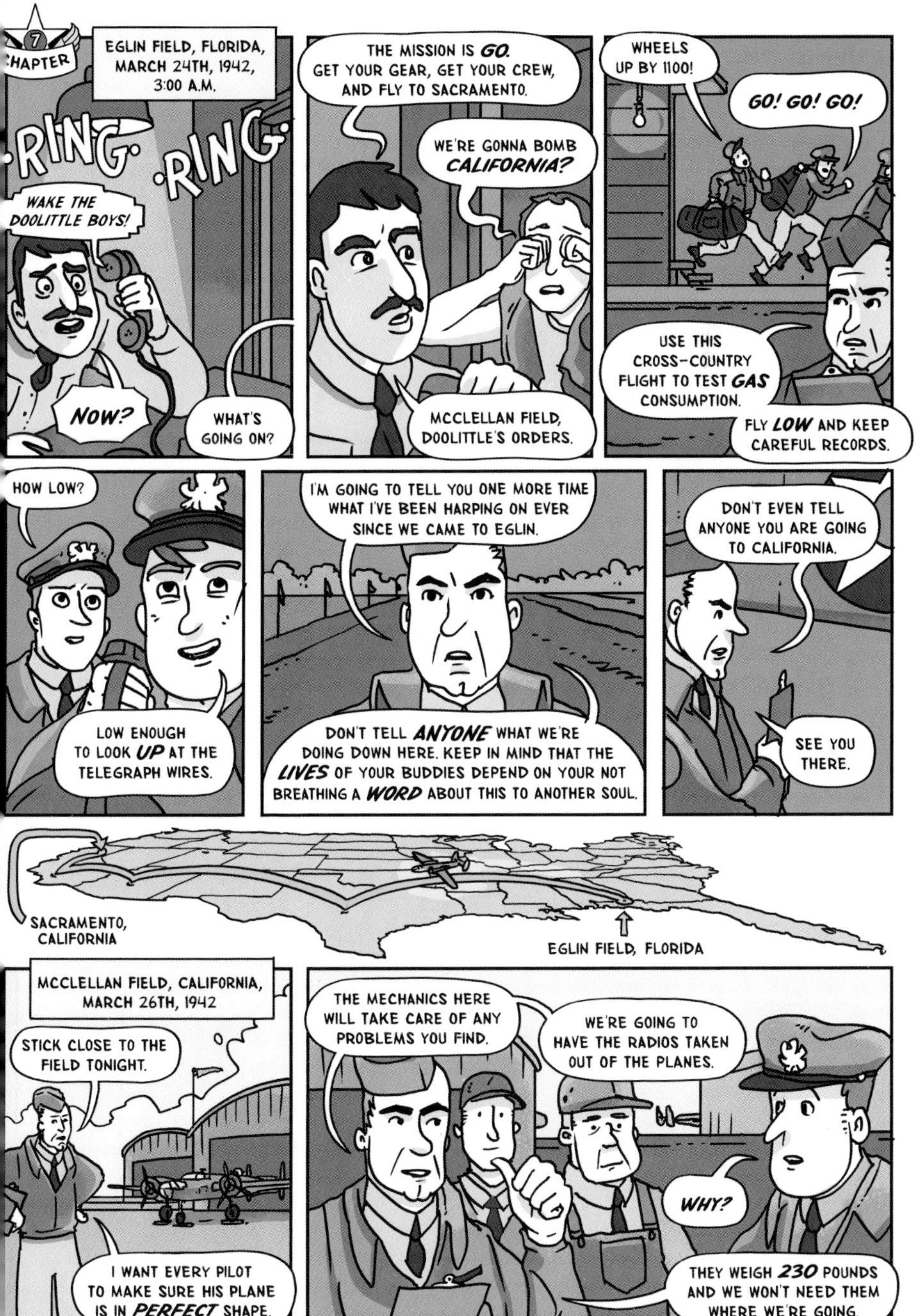
CHAPTER 7
EGLIN FIELD, FLORIDA, MARCH 24TH, 1942, 3:00 A.M.
RING RING
WAKE THE DOOLITTLE BOYS!
NOW?
WHAT'S GOING ON?
THE MISSION IS GO. GET YOUR GEAR, GET YOUR CREW, AND FLY TO SACRAMENTO.
WE'RE GONNA BOMB CALIFORNIA?
MCCLELLAN FIELD, DOOLITTLE'S ORDERS.
WHEELS UP BY 1100!
GO! GO! GO!
USE THIS CROSS-COUNTRY FLIGHT TO TEST GAS CONSUMPTION.
FLY LOW AND KEEP CAREFUL RECORDS.
HOW LOW?
LOW ENOUGH TO LOOK UP AT THE TELEGRAPH WIRES.
I'M GOING TO TELL YOU ONE MORE TIME WHAT I'VE BEEN HARPING ON EVER SINCE WE CAME TO EGLIN.
DON'T TELL ANYONE WHAT WE'RE DOING DOWN HERE. KEEP IN MIND THAT THE LIVES OF YOUR BUDDIES DEPEND ON YOUR NOT BREATHING A WORD ABOUT THIS TO ANOTHER SOUL.
DON'T EVEN TELL ANYONE YOU ARE GOING TO CALIFORNIA.
SEE YOU THERE.
SACRAMENTO, CALIFORNIA
EGLIN FIELD, FLORIDA
MCCLELLAN FIELD, CALIFORNIA, MARCH 26TH, 1942
STICK CLOSE TO THE FIELD TONIGHT.
I WANT EVERY PILOT TO MAKE SURE HIS PLANE IS IN PERFECT SHAPE.
THE MECHANICS HERE WILL TAKE CARE OF ANY PROBLEMS YOU FIND.
WE'RE GOING TO HAVE THE RADIOS TAKEN OUT OF THE PLANES.
WHY?
THEY WEIGH 230 POUNDS AND WE WON'T NEED THEM WHERE WE'RE GOING.

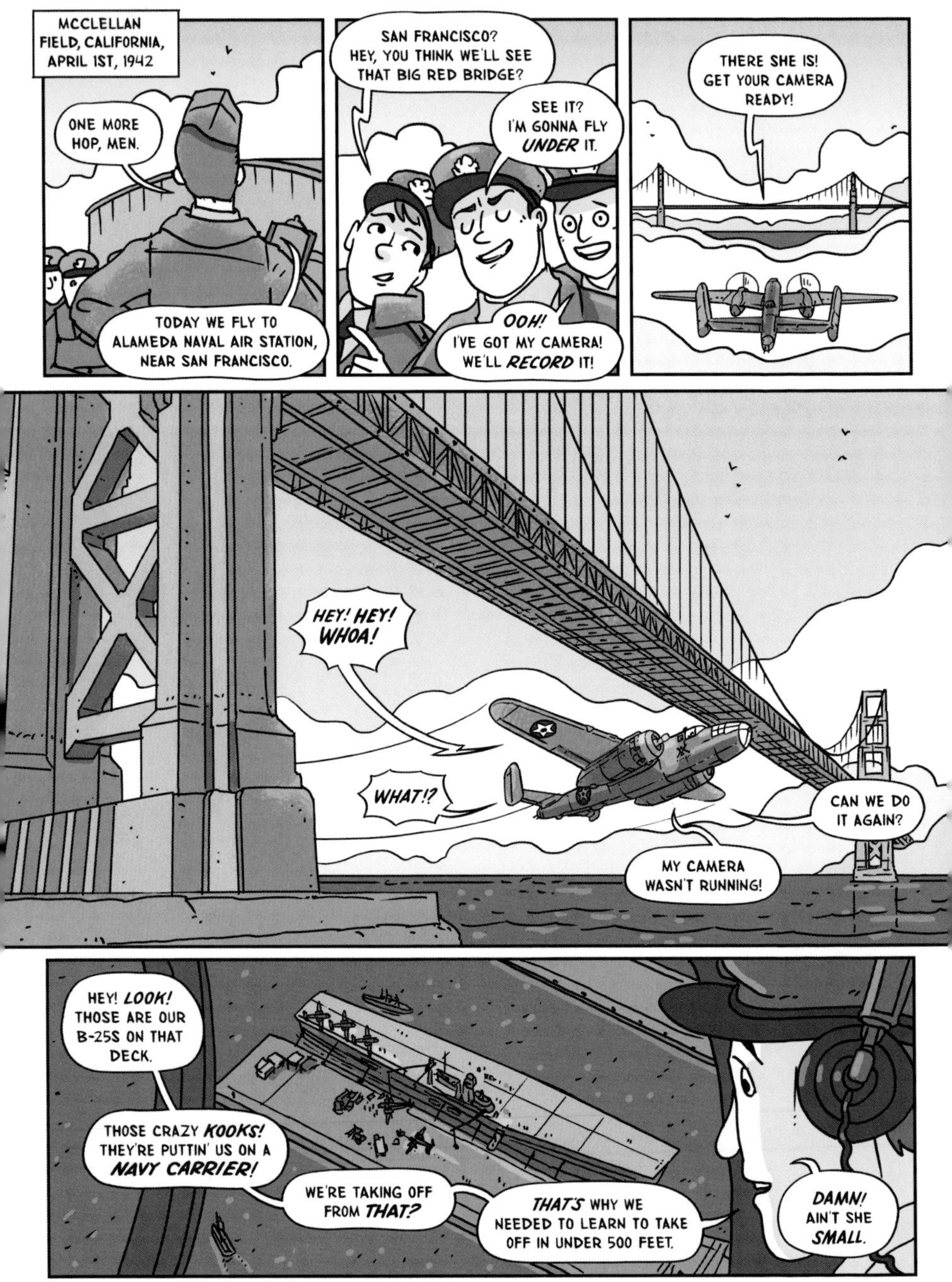
MCCLELLAN FIELD, CALIFORNIA, APRIL 1ST, 1942
ONE MORE HOP, MEN.
TODAY WE FLY TO ALAMEDA NAVAL AIR STATION, NEAR SAN FRANCISCO.
SAN FRANCISCO? HEY, YOU THINK WE'LL SEE THAT BIG RED BRIDGE?
SEE IT? I'M GONNA FLY UNDER IT.
OOH! I'VE GOT MY CAMERA! WE'LL RECORD IT!
THERE SHE IS! GET YOUR CAMERA READY!
HEY! HEY! WHOA!
WHAT!?
CAN WE DO IT AGAIN?
MY CAMERA WASN'T RUNNING!
HEY! LOOK! THOSE ARE OUR B-25S ON THAT DECK.
THOSE CRAZY KOOKS! THEY'RE PUTTIN' US ON A NAVY CARRIER!
WE'RE TAKING OFF FROM THAT?
THAT'S WHY WE NEEDED TO LEARN TO TAKE OFF IN UNDER 500 FEET.
DAMN! AIN'T SHE SMALL.

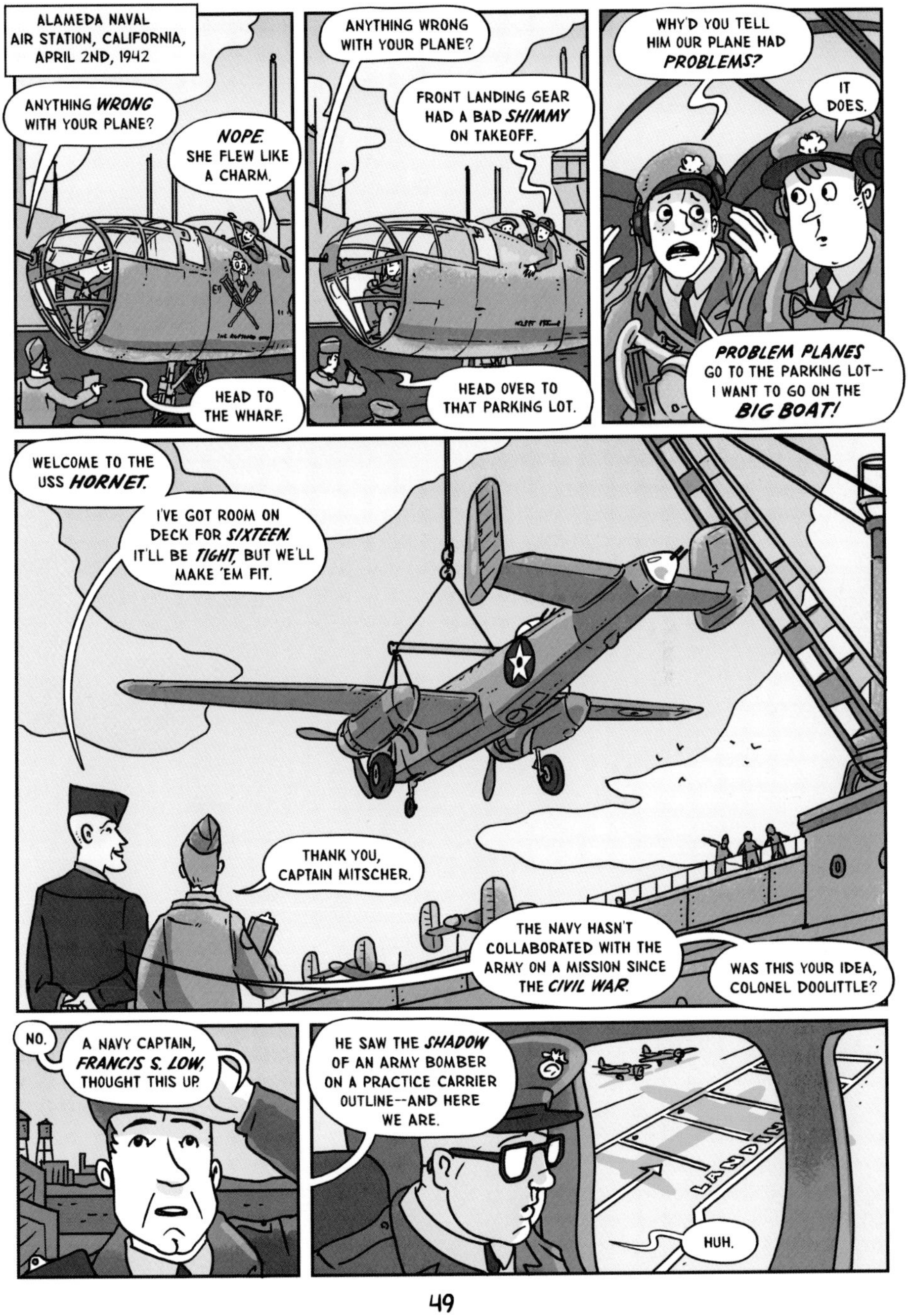
ALAMEDA NAVAL AIR STATION, CALIFORNIA, APRIL 2ND, 1942
ANYTHING WRONG WITH YOUR PLANE?
NOPE. SHE FLEW LIKE A CHARM.
HEAD TO THE WHARF.
ANYTHING WRONG WITH YOUR PLANE?
FRONT LANDING GEAR HAD A BAD SHIMMY ON TAKEOFF.
HEAD OVER TO THAT PARKING LOT.
WHY'D YOU TELL HIM OUR PLANE HAD PROBLEMS?
IT DOES.
PROBLEM PLANES GO TO THE PARKING LOT-- I WANT TO GO ON THE BIG BOAT!
WELCOME TO THE USS HORNET.
I'VE GOT ROOM ON DECK FOR SIXTEEN. IT'LL BE TIGHT, BUT WE'LL MAKE 'EM FIT.
THANK YOU, CAPTAIN MITSCHER.
THE NAVY HASN'T COLLABORATED WITH THE ARMY ON A MISSION SINCE THE CIVIL WAR.
WAS THIS YOUR IDEA, COLONEL DOOLITTLE?
NO.
A NAVY CAPTAIN, FRANCIS S. LOW, THOUGHT THIS UP.
HE SAW THE SHADOW OF AN ARMY BOMBER ON A PRACTICE CARRIER OUTLINE--AND HERE WE ARE.
LANDIN
HUH.

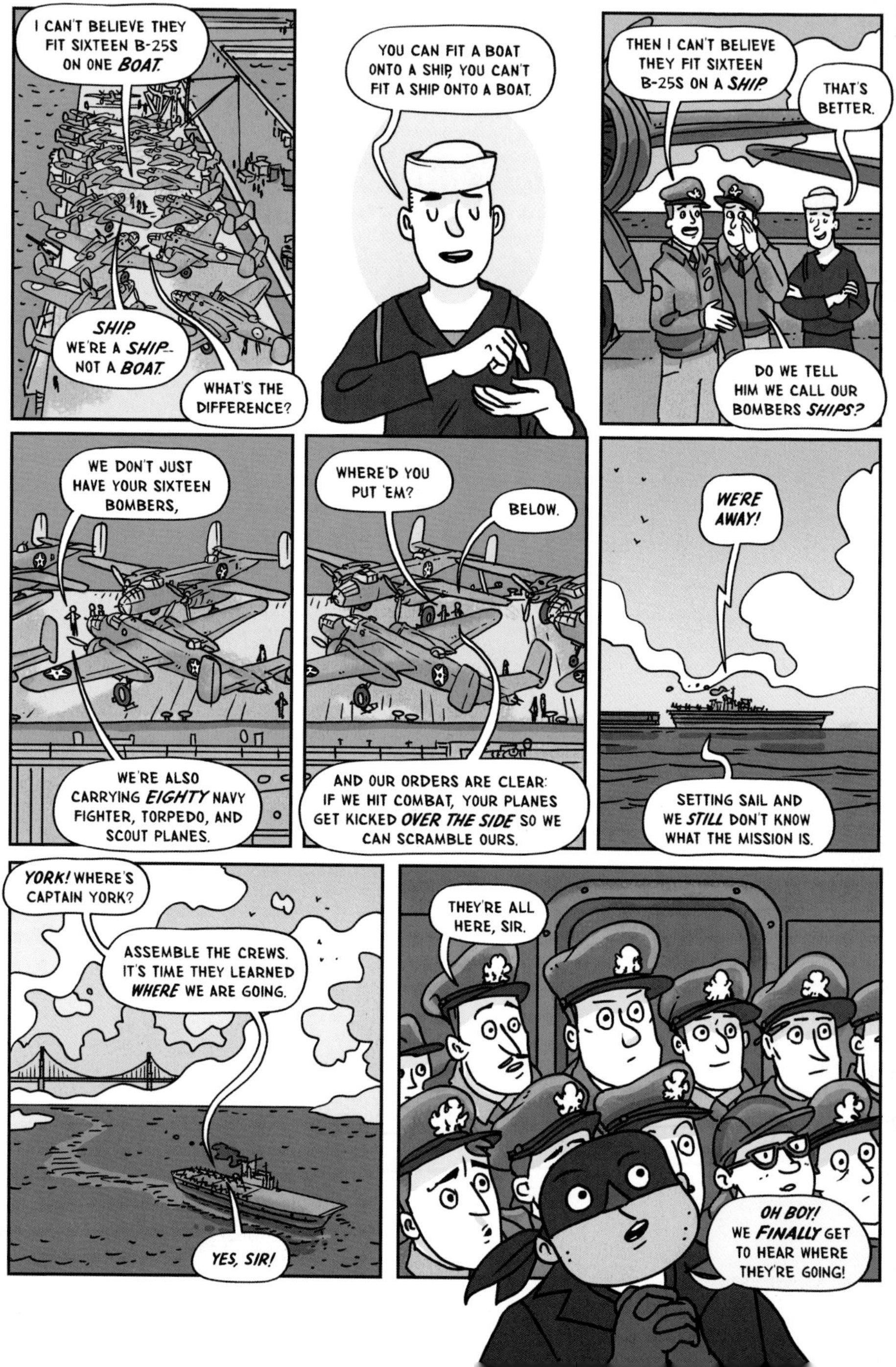
I CAN'T BELIEVE THEY FIT SIXTEEN B-25S ON ONE BOAT.
SHIP. WE'RE A SHIP-- NOT A BOAT.
WHAT'S THE DIFFERENCE?
YOU CAN FIT A BOAT ONTO A SHIP, YOU CAN'T FIT A SHIP ONTO A BOAT.
THEN I CAN'T BELIEVE THEY FIT SIXTEEN B-25S ON A SHIP.
THAT'S BETTER.
DO WE TELL HIM WE CALL OUR BOMBERS SHIPS?
WE DON'T JUST HAVE YOUR SIXTEEN BOMBERS,
WE'RE ALSO CARRYING EIGHTY NAVY FIGHTER, TORPEDO, AND SCOUT PLANES.
WHERE'D YOU PUT 'EM?
BELOW.
AND OUR ORDERS ARE CLEAR: IF WE HIT COMBAT, YOUR PLANES GET KICKED OVER THE SIDE SO WE CAN SCRAMBLE OURS.
WE'RE AWAY!
SETTING SAIL AND WE STILL DON'T KNOW WHAT THE MISSION IS.
YORK! WHERE'S CAPTAIN YORK?
ASSEMBLE THE CREWS. IT'S TIME THEY LEARNED WHERE WE ARE GOING.
YES, SIR!
THEY'RE ALL HERE, SIR.
OH BOY! WE FINALLY GET TO HEAR WHERE THEY'RE GOING!

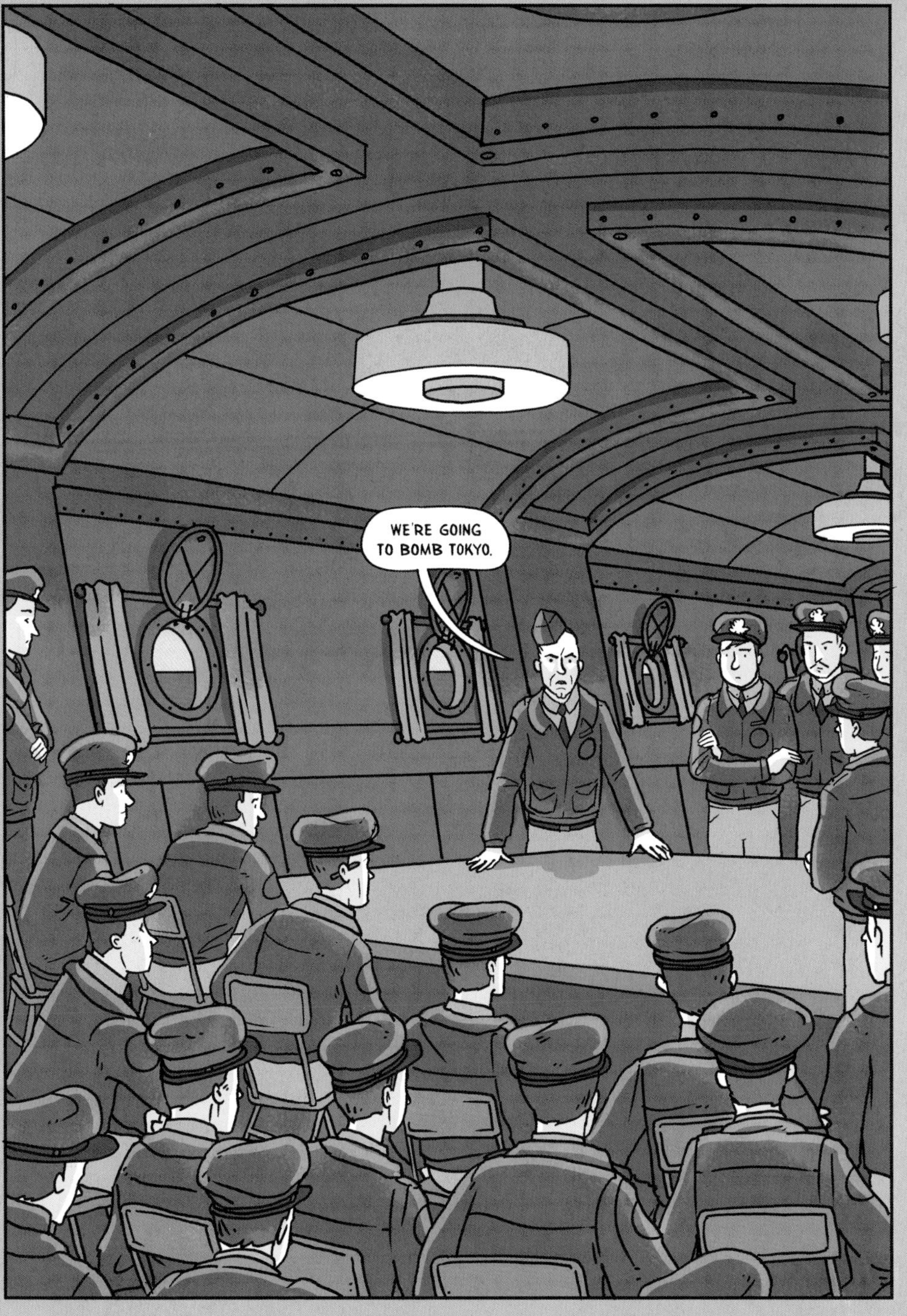
WE'RE GOING TO BOMB TOKYO.

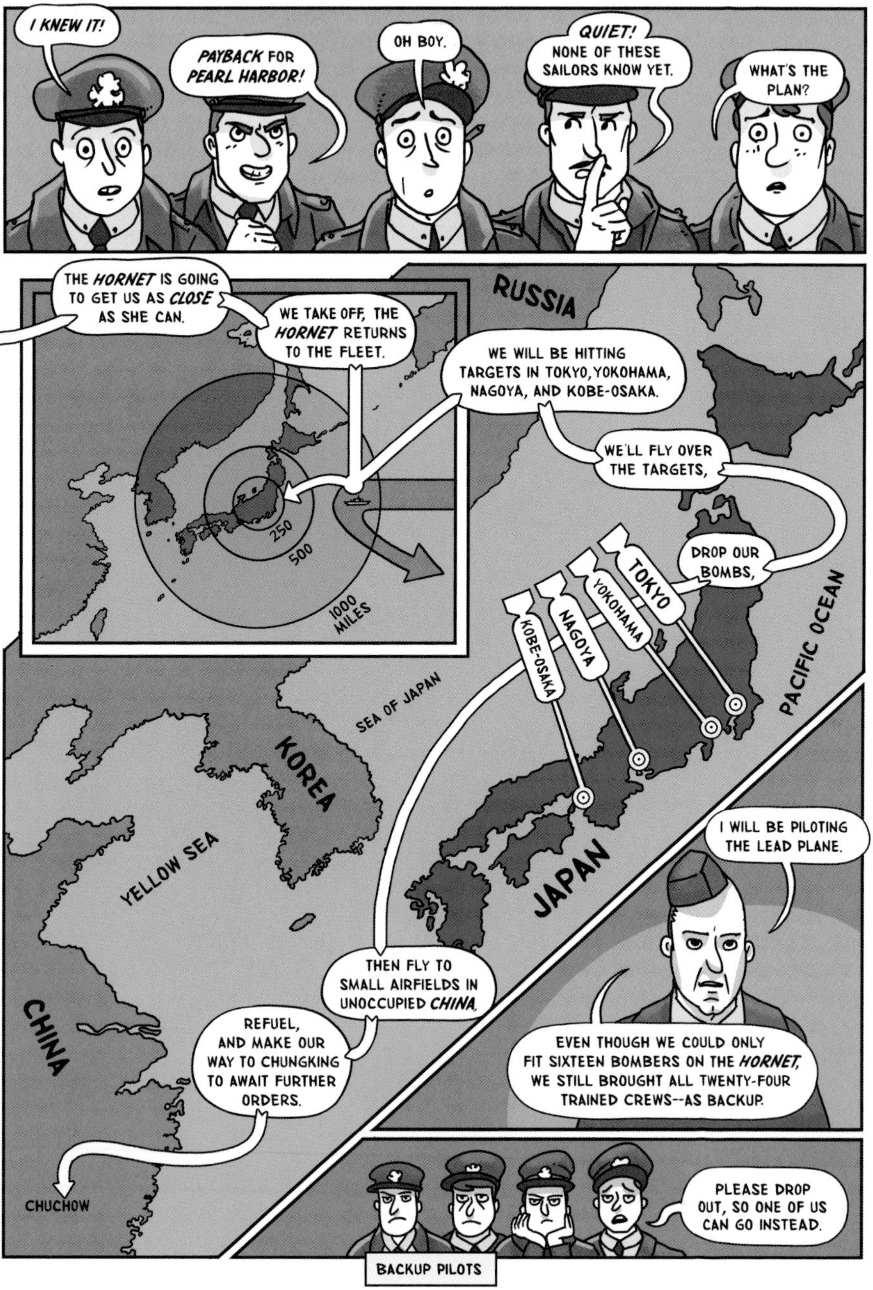
I KNEW IT!
PAYBACK FOR PEARL HARBOR!
OH BOY.
QUIET! NONE OF THESE SAILORS KNOW YET.
WHAT'S THE PLAN?
THE HORNET IS GOING TO GET US AS CLOSE AS SHE CAN.
WE TAKE OFF, THE HORNET RETURNS TO THE FLEET.
RUSSIA
250
500
1000 MILES
WE WILL BE HITTING TARGETS IN TOKYO, YOKOHAMA, NAGOYA, AND KOBE-OSAKA.
WE'LL FLY OVER THE TARGETS,
DROP OUR BOMBS,
TOKYO
YOKOHAMA
NAGOYA
KOBE-OSAKA
PACIFIC OCEAN
SEA OF JAPAN
KOREA
YELLOW SEA
JAPAN
CHINA
THEN FLY TO SMALL AIRFIELDS IN UNOCCUPIED CHINA,
REFUEL, AND MAKE OUR WAY TO CHUNGKING TO AWAIT FURTHER ORDERS.
CHUCHOW
I WILL BE PILOTING THE LEAD PLANE.
EVEN THOUGH WE COULD ONLY FIT SIXTEEN BOMBERS ON THE HORNET, WE STILL BROUGHT ALL TWENTY-FOUR TRAINED CREWS--AS BACKUP.
PLEASE DROP OUT, SO ONE OF US CAN GO INSTEAD.
BACKUP PILOTS

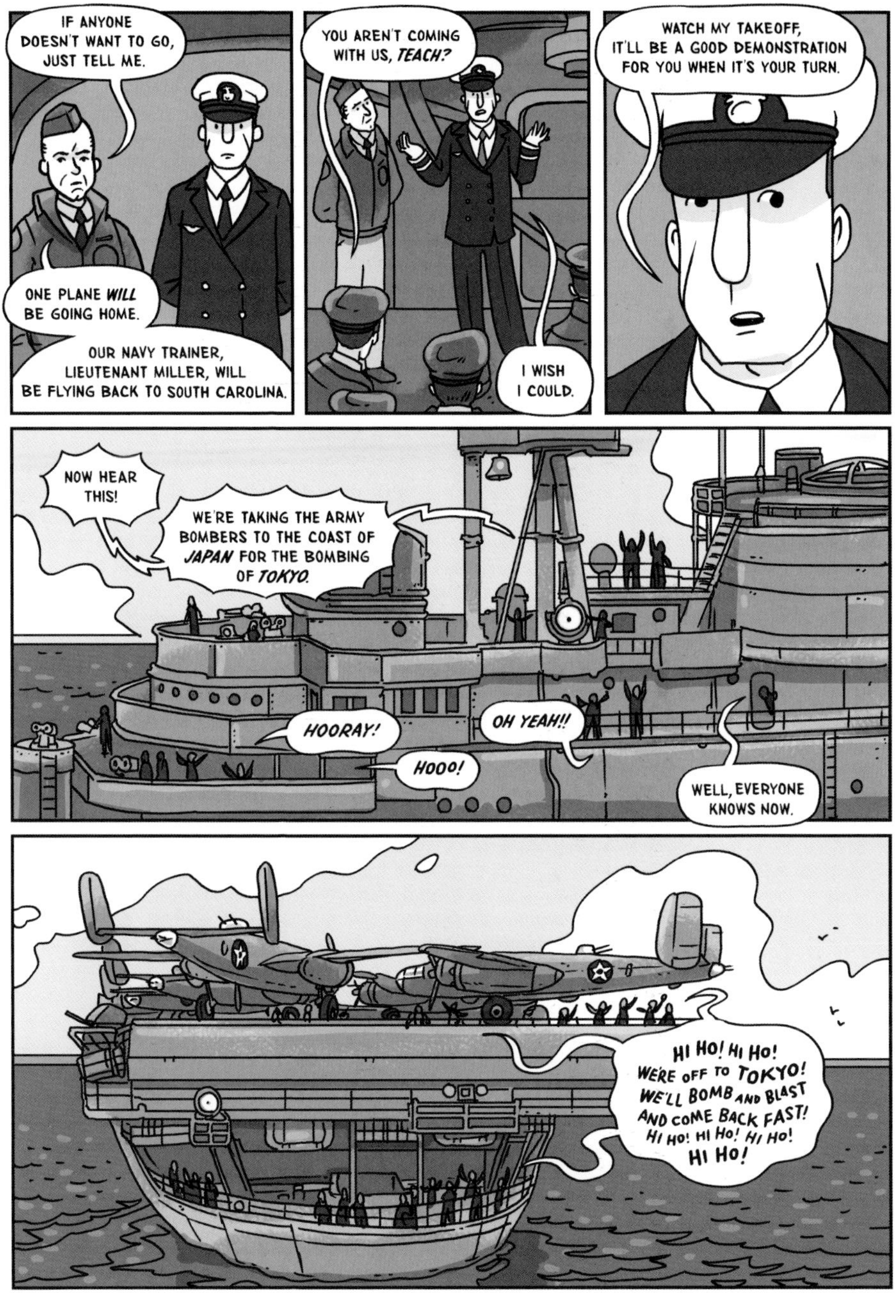

IF ANYONE DOESN'T WANT TO GO, JUST TELL ME.
ONE PLANE *WILL* BE GOING HOME.
OUR NAVY TRAINER, LIEUTENANT MILLER, WILL BE FLYING BACK TO SOUTH CAROLINA.
YOU AREN'T COMING WITH US, *TEACH?*
I WISH I COULD.
WATCH MY TAKEOFF, IT'LL BE A GOOD DEMONSTRATION FOR YOU WHEN IT'S YOUR TURN.
NOW HEAR THIS!
WE'RE TAKING THE ARMY BOMBERS TO THE COAST OF *JAPAN* FOR THE BOMBING OF *TOKYO.*
HOORAY!
OH YEAH!!
HOOO!
WELL, EVERYONE KNOWS NOW.
HI HO! HI HO! WE'RE OFF TO TOKYO! WE'LL BOMB AND BLAST AND COME BACK FAST! HI HO! HI HO! HI HO! HI HO!

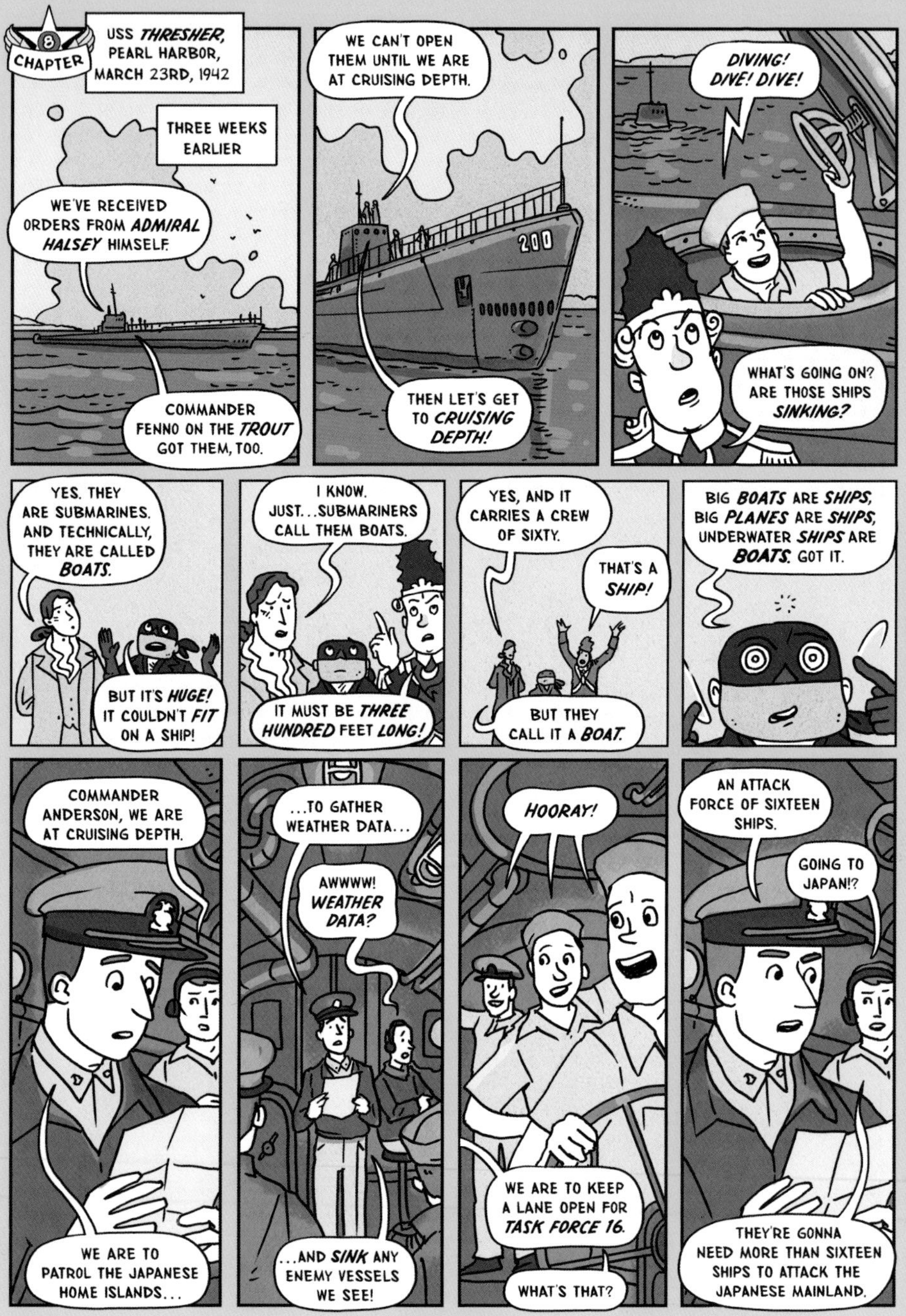
8
CHAPTER
USS *THRESHER,*
PEARL HARBOR,
MARCH 23RD, 1942
THREE WEEKS
EARLIER
WE'VE RECEIVED ORDERS FROM *ADMIRAL HALSEY* HIMSELF.
COMMANDER FENNO ON THE *TROUT* GOT THEM, TOO.
WE CAN'T OPEN THEM UNTIL WE ARE AT CRUISING DEPTH.
200
THEN LET'S GET TO *CRUISING DEPTH!*
DIVING! DIVE! DIVE!
WHAT'S GOING ON? ARE THOSE SHIPS *SINKING?*
YES. THEY ARE SUBMARINES. AND TECHNICALLY, THEY ARE CALLED *BOATS.*
BUT IT'S *HUGE!* IT COULDN'T *FIT* ON A SHIP!
I KNOW. JUST...SUBMARINERS CALL THEM BOATS.
IT MUST BE *THREE HUNDRED* FEET *LONG!*
YES, AND IT CARRIES A CREW OF SIXTY.
THAT'S A *SHIP!*
BUT THEY CALL IT A *BOAT.*
BIG *BOATS* ARE *SHIPS,* BIG *PLANES* ARE *SHIPS,* UNDERWATER *SHIPS* ARE *BOATS.* GOT IT.
COMMANDER ANDERSON, WE ARE AT CRUISING DEPTH.
WE ARE TO PATROL THE JAPANESE HOME ISLANDS...
...TO GATHER WEATHER DATA...
AWWWW! *WEATHER DATA?*
...AND *SINK* ANY ENEMY VESSELS WE SEE!
HOORAY!
WE ARE TO KEEP A LANE OPEN FOR *TASK FORCE 16.*
WHAT'S THAT?
AN ATTACK FORCE OF SIXTEEN SHIPS.
GOING TO JAPAN!?
THEY'RE GONNA NEED MORE THAN SIXTEEN SHIPS TO ATTACK THE JAPANESE MAINLAND.

USS *HORNET*, PACIFIC, APRIL 10TH, 1942

THERE'S THE ADMIRAL.

WHOA! I DIDN'T REALIZE OUR ESCORT WOULD INCLUDE ANOTHER *CARRIER!*

NOT JUST ANY CARRIER, THAT'S THE "*BIG E*"--USS *ENTERPRISE* --WITH A FULL COMPLEMENT OF *NINETY* NAVY ATTACK PLANES.

TASK FORCE 16

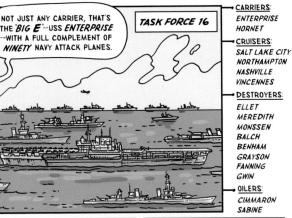

CARRIERS:
ENTERPRISE
HORNET

CRUISERS:
SALT LAKE CITY
NORTHAMPTON
NASHVILLE
VINCENNES

DESTROYERS:
ELLET
MEREDITH
MONSSEN
BALCH
BENHAM
GRAYSON
FANNING
GWIN

OILERS:
CIMMARON
SABINE

TASK FORCE 16, SIXTEEN SHIPS, CARRYING SIXTEEN BOMBERS.

FIFTEEN. MILLER WILL BE FLYING ONE HOME.

NOPE. I'M GONNA STAY ON THE *HORNET.* YOU'LL HAVE ALL SIXTEEN BOMBERS.

EVERY PILOT I'VE GOT IS EITHER *SEASICK* OR *BROKE* FROM PLAYING CRAPS.

SOME ARE SICK *AND* BROKE!

I'M NOT SICK, SIR.

GOOD MAN, BIRCH. SEE THAT EVERYONE STAYS ON TOP OF THEIR MAINTENANCE.

THESE PLANES NEED TO BE IN *TIP-TOP* SHAPE FOR LAUNCH.

HE DOESN'T NEED TO REMIND OUR ENGINEER, MANSKE.

KID SLEEPS ON DECK WITH OUR PLANE.

HEY, MANSKE!

HUH?

MY GLASSES!!!

SORRY, BUDDY!

IF YOU CAN'T SEE, YOU CAN'T GO! I'LL BE YOUR REPLACEMENT!

I CAN SEE FINE.

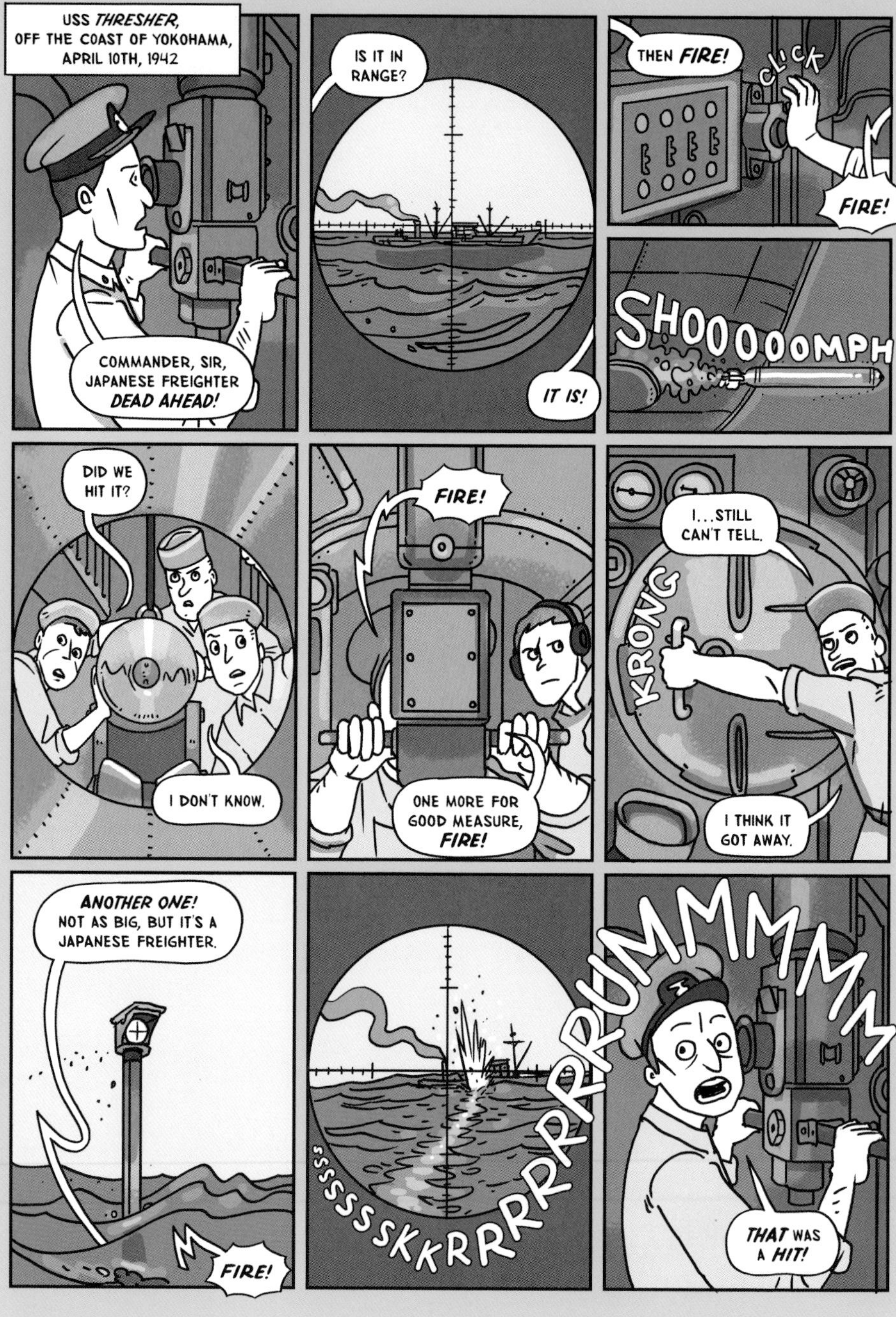
USS THRESHER, OFF THE COAST OF YOKOHAMA, APRIL 10TH, 1942
COMMANDER, SIR, JAPANESE FREIGHTER DEAD AHEAD!
IS IT IN RANGE?
IT IS!
THEN FIRE!
CLICK
FIRE!
SHOOOOOOMPH
DID WE HIT IT?
I DON'T KNOW.
FIRE!
ONE MORE FOR GOOD MEASURE, FIRE!
I...STILL CAN'T TELL.
KRONG
I THINK IT GOT AWAY.
ANOTHER ONE! NOT AS BIG, BUT IT'S A JAPANESE FREIGHTER.
FIRE!
SSSSSSSKKRRRRRRRRUMMMMMM
THAT WAS A HIT!

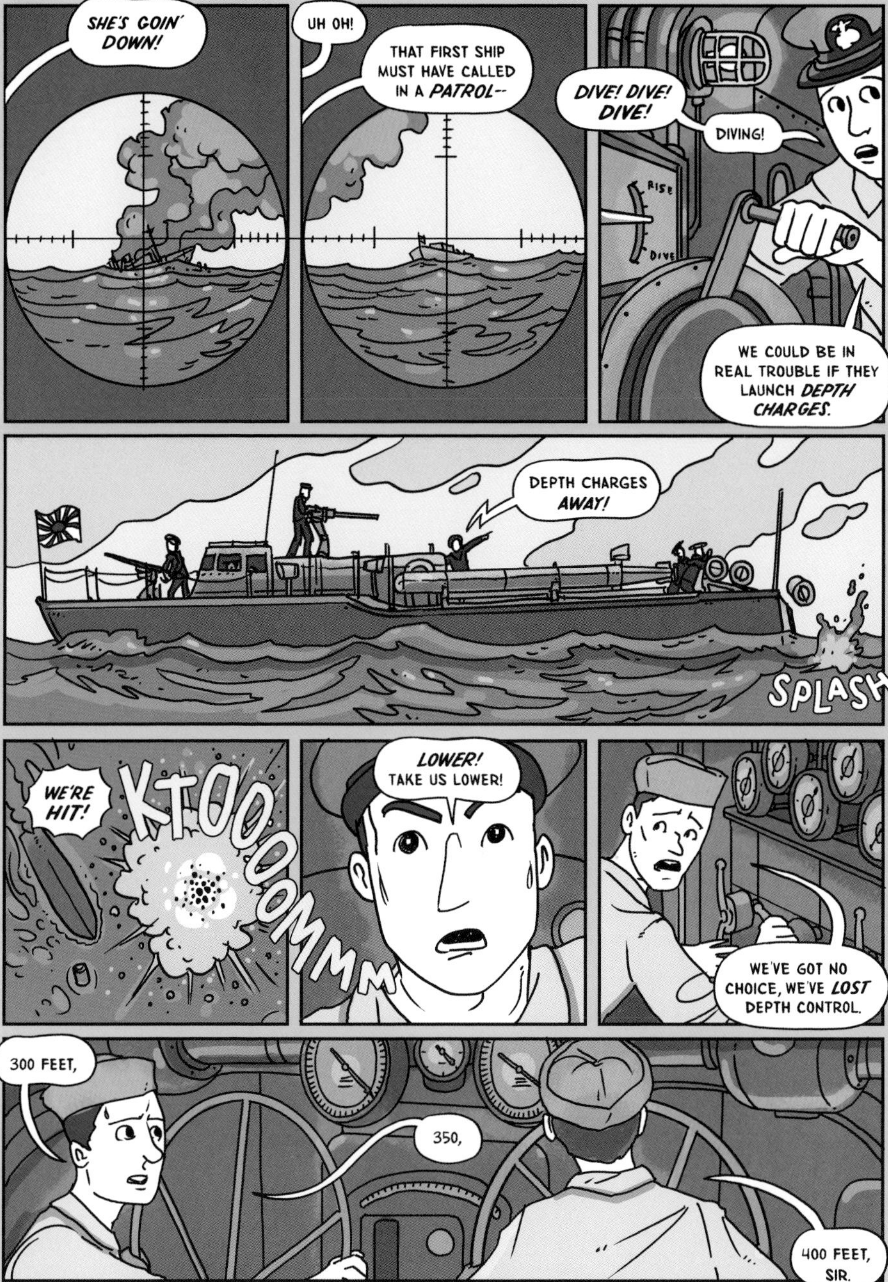

SHE'S GOIN' DOWN!
UH OH!
THAT FIRST SHIP MUST HAVE CALLED IN A *PATROL*--
DIVE! DIVE! DIVE!
DIVING!
RISE
DIVE
WE COULD BE IN REAL TROUBLE IF THEY LAUNCH *DEPTH CHARGES*.
DEPTH CHARGES *AWAY!*
SPLASH
WE'RE HIT!
KTOOOOOMMMM
LOWER! TAKE US LOWER!
WE'VE GOT NO CHOICE, WE'VE *LOST* DEPTH CONTROL.
300 FEET,
350,
400 FEET, SIR.

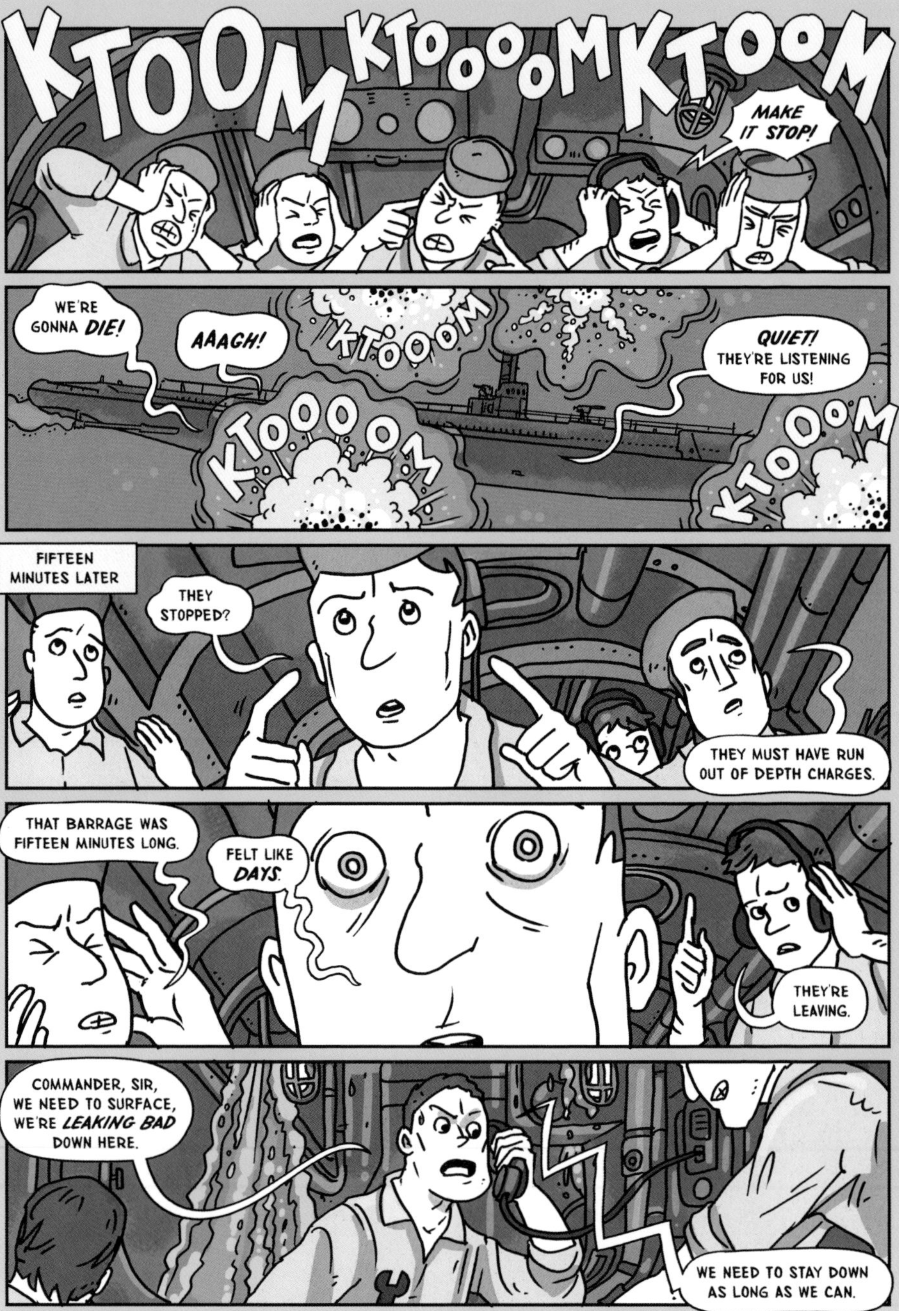
KTOOM KTOOOOOM KTOOM
MAKE IT STOP!
WE'RE GONNA DIE!
AAAGH!
KTOOOM
KTOOOOM
QUIET! THEY'RE LISTENING FOR US!
KTOOOM
FIFTEEN MINUTES LATER
THEY STOPPED?
THEY MUST HAVE RUN OUT OF DEPTH CHARGES.
THAT BARRAGE WAS FIFTEEN MINUTES LONG.
FELT LIKE DAYS.
THEY'RE LEAVING.
COMMANDER, SIR, WE NEED TO SURFACE, WE'RE LEAKING BAD DOWN HERE.
WE NEED TO STAY DOWN AS LONG AS WE CAN.

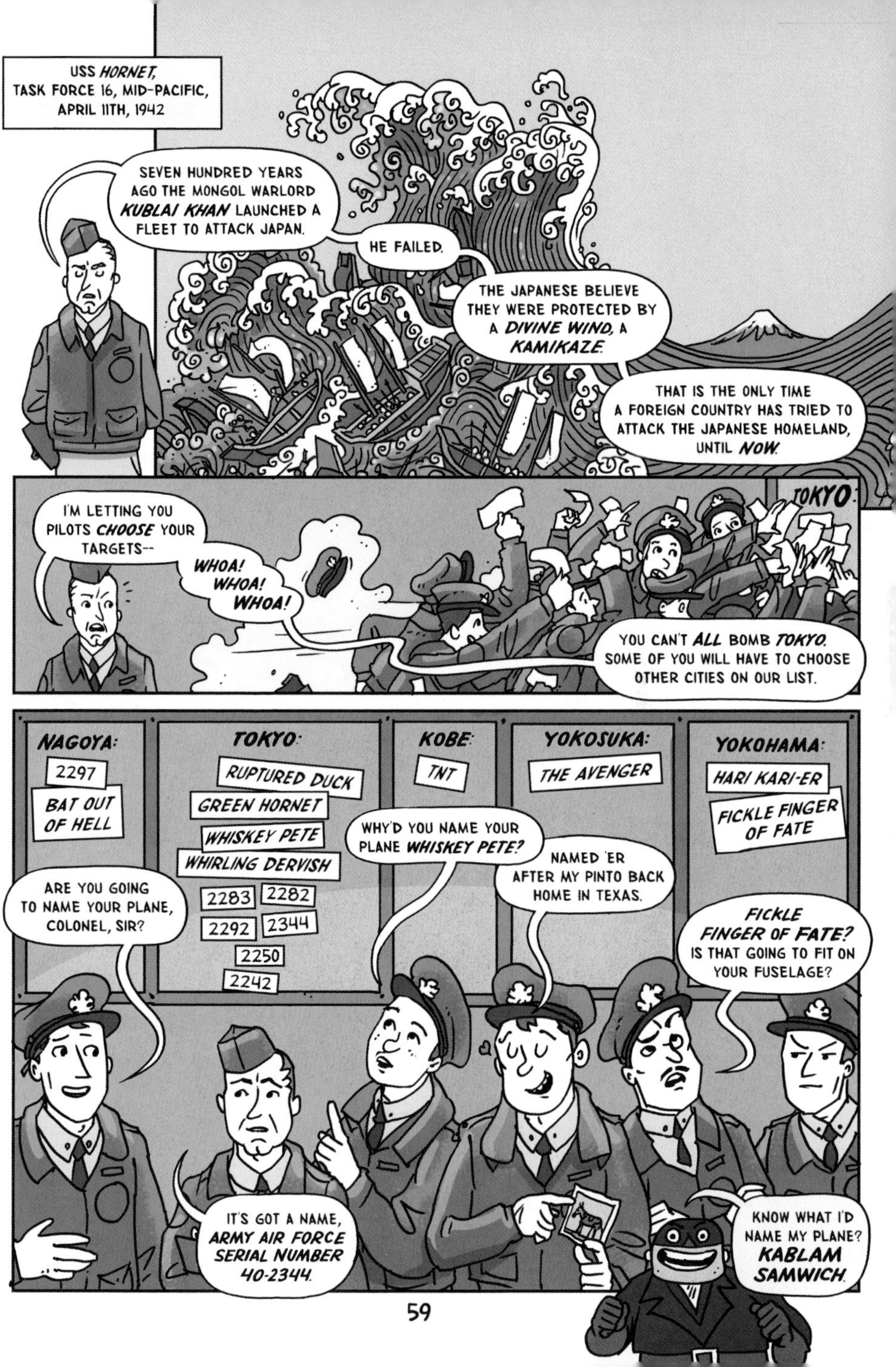

USS *HORNET*, TASK FORCE 16, MID-PACIFIC, APRIL 11TH, 1942
SEVEN HUNDRED YEARS AGO THE MONGOL WARLORD ***KUBLAI KHAN*** LAUNCHED A FLEET TO ATTACK JAPAN.
HE FAILED.
THE JAPANESE BELIEVE THEY WERE PROTECTED BY A ***DIVINE WIND***, A ***KAMIKAZE***.
THAT IS THE ONLY TIME A FOREIGN COUNTRY HAS TRIED TO ATTACK THE JAPANESE HOMELAND, UNTIL ***NOW***.
TOKYO:
I'M LETTING YOU PILOTS ***CHOOSE*** YOUR TARGETS--
WHOA! WHOA! WHOA!
YOU CAN'T ***ALL*** BOMB ***TOKYO***. SOME OF YOU WILL HAVE TO CHOOSE OTHER CITIES ON OUR LIST.
NAGOYA: 2297 BAT OUT OF HELL
TOKYO: RUPTURED DUCK GREEN HORNET WHISKEY PETE WHIRLING DERVISH 2283 2282 2292 2344 2250 2242
KOBE: TNT
YOKOSUKA: THE AVENGER
YOKOHAMA: HARI KARI-ER FICKLE FINGER OF FATE
ARE YOU GOING TO NAME YOUR PLANE, COLONEL, SIR?
IT'S GOT A NAME, ***ARMY AIR FORCE SERIAL NUMBER 40-2344***.
WHY'D YOU NAME YOUR PLANE ***WHISKEY PETE?***
NAMED 'ER AFTER MY PINTO BACK HOME IN TEXAS.
FICKLE FINGER OF FATE? IS THAT GOING TO FIT ON YOUR FUSELAGE?
KNOW WHAT I'D NAME MY PLANE? ***KABLAM SAMWICH***.

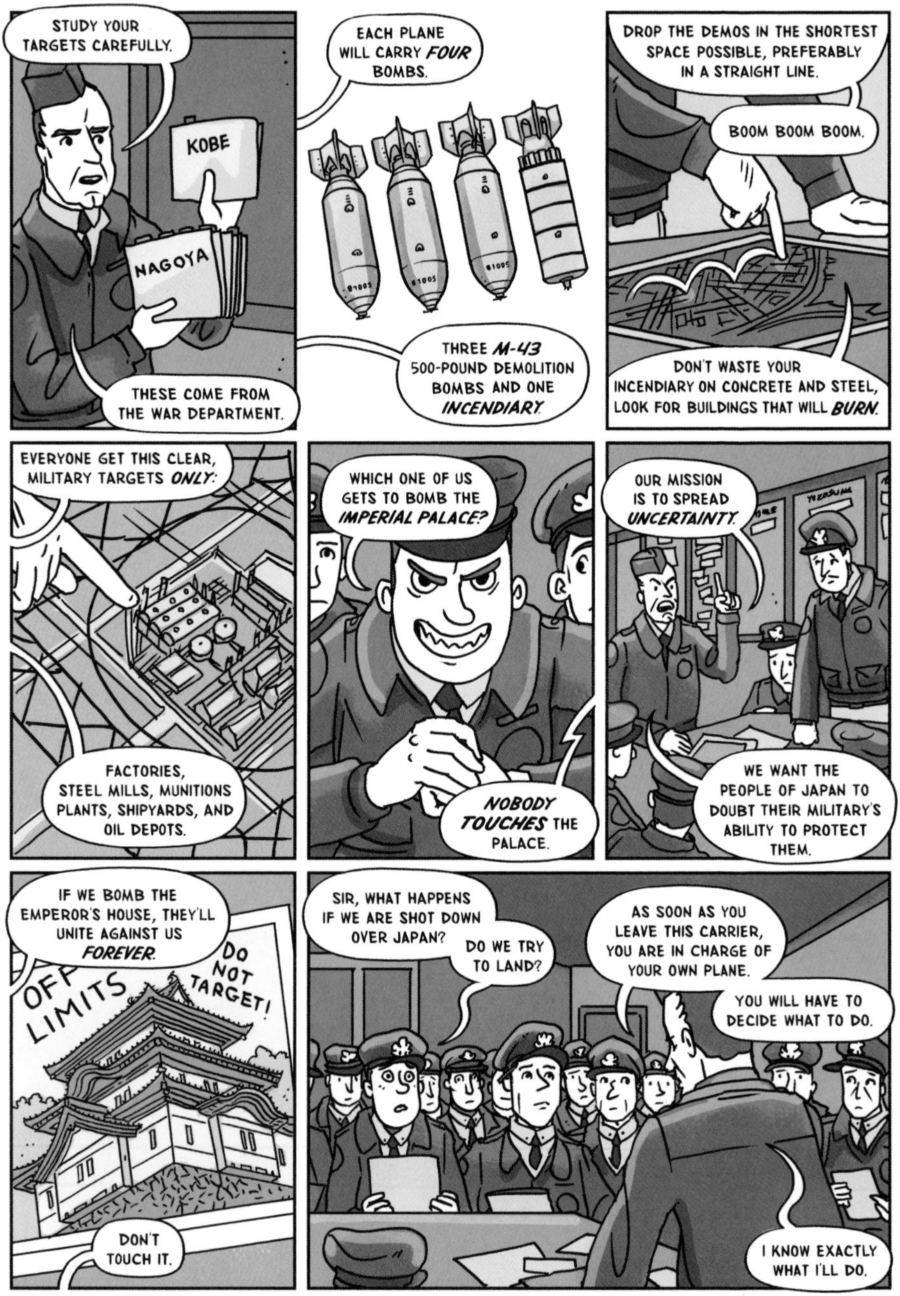
STUDY YOUR TARGETS CAREFULLY.
KOBE
NAGOYA
THESE COME FROM THE WAR DEPARTMENT.
EACH PLANE WILL CARRY *FOUR* BOMBS.
THREE *M-43* 500-POUND DEMOLITION BOMBS AND ONE *INCENDIARY*.
DROP THE DEMOS IN THE SHORTEST SPACE POSSIBLE, PREFERABLY IN A STRAIGHT LINE.
BOOM BOOM BOOM.
DON'T WASTE YOUR INCENDIARY ON CONCRETE AND STEEL, LOOK FOR BUILDINGS THAT WILL *BURN*.
EVERYONE GET THIS CLEAR, MILITARY TARGETS *ONLY*:
FACTORIES, STEEL MILLS, MUNITIONS PLANTS, SHIPYARDS, AND OIL DEPOTS.
WHICH ONE OF US GETS TO BOMB THE *IMPERIAL PALACE?*
NOBODY TOUCHES THE PALACE.
OUR MISSION IS TO SPREAD *UNCERTAINTY*.
WE WANT THE PEOPLE OF JAPAN TO DOUBT THEIR MILITARY'S ABILITY TO PROTECT THEM.
IF WE BOMB THE EMPEROR'S HOUSE, THEY'LL UNITE AGAINST US *FOREVER*.
OFF LIMITS
DO NOT TARGET!
DON'T TOUCH IT.
SIR, WHAT HAPPENS IF WE ARE SHOT DOWN OVER JAPAN?
DO WE TRY TO LAND?
AS SOON AS YOU LEAVE THIS CARRIER, YOU ARE IN CHARGE OF YOUR OWN PLANE.
YOU WILL HAVE TO DECIDE WHAT TO DO.
I KNOW EXACTLY WHAT I'LL DO.

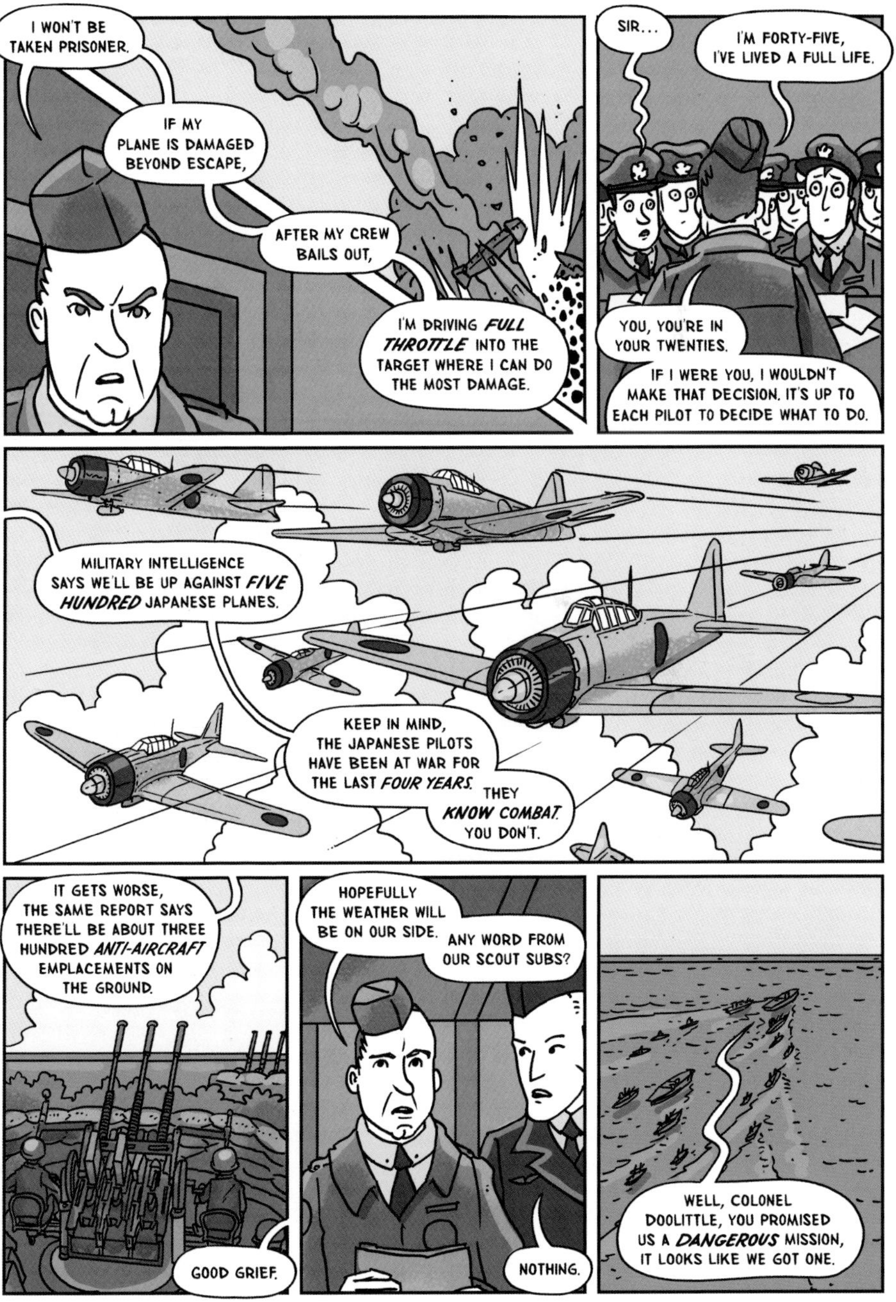
I WON'T BE TAKEN PRISONER.
IF MY PLANE IS DAMAGED BEYOND ESCAPE,
AFTER MY CREW BAILS OUT,
I'M DRIVING FULL THROTTLE INTO THE TARGET WHERE I CAN DO THE MOST DAMAGE.
SIR...
I'M FORTY-FIVE, I'VE LIVED A FULL LIFE.
YOU, YOU'RE IN YOUR TWENTIES.
IF I WERE YOU, I WOULDN'T MAKE THAT DECISION. IT'S UP TO EACH PILOT TO DECIDE WHAT TO DO.
MILITARY INTELLIGENCE SAYS WE'LL BE UP AGAINST FIVE HUNDRED JAPANESE PLANES.
KEEP IN MIND, THE JAPANESE PILOTS HAVE BEEN AT WAR FOR THE LAST FOUR YEARS.
THEY KNOW COMBAT. YOU DON'T.
IT GETS WORSE, THE SAME REPORT SAYS THERE'LL BE ABOUT THREE HUNDRED ANTI-AIRCRAFT EMPLACEMENTS ON THE GROUND.
GOOD GRIEF.
HOPEFULLY THE WEATHER WILL BE ON OUR SIDE.
ANY WORD FROM OUR SCOUT SUBS?
NOTHING.
WELL, COLONEL DOOLITTLE, YOU PROMISED US A DANGEROUS MISSION, IT LOOKS LIKE WE GOT ONE.

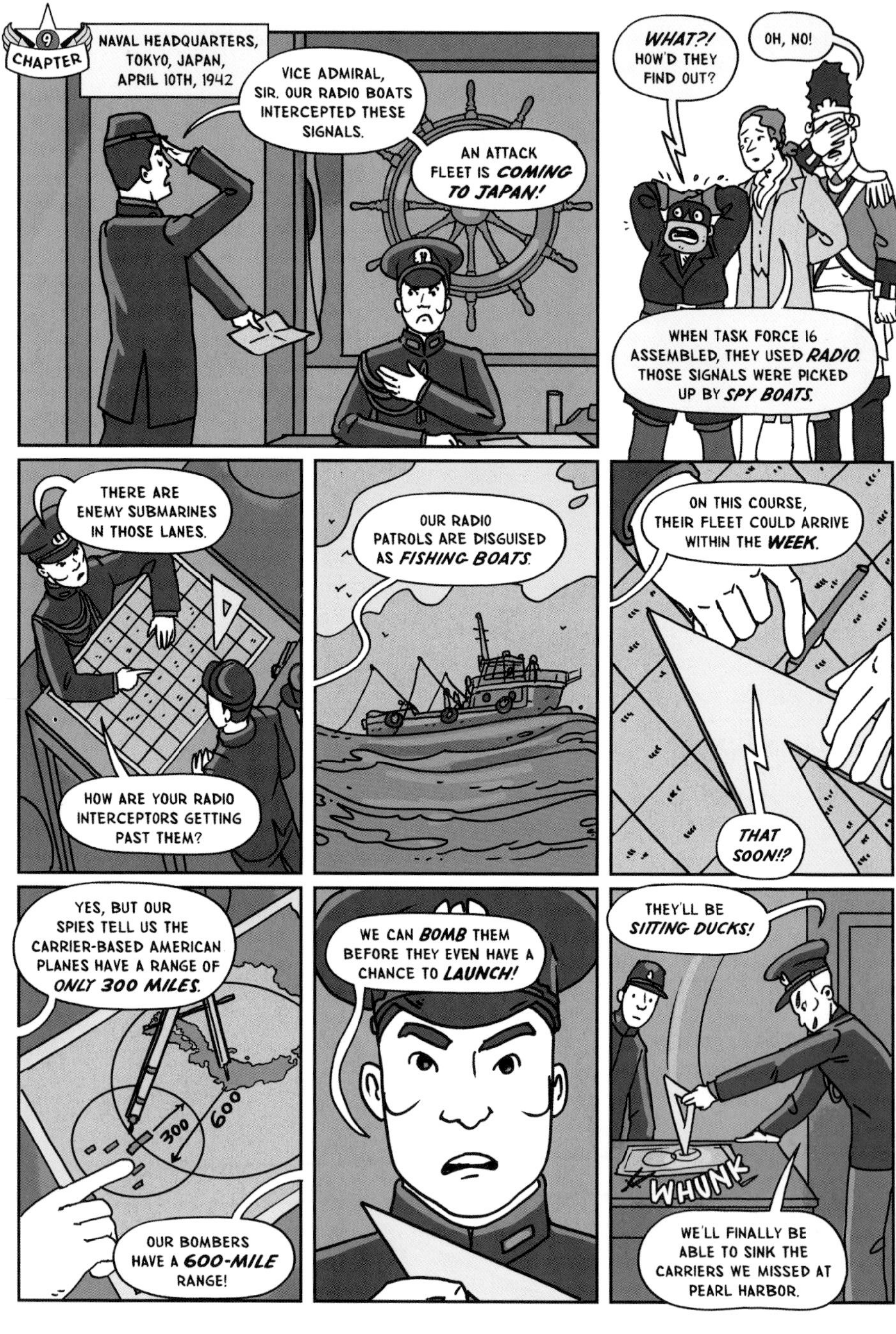
9 CHAPTER
NAVAL HEADQUARTERS, TOKYO, JAPAN, APRIL 10TH, 1942
VICE ADMIRAL, SIR. OUR RADIO BOATS INTERCEPTED THESE SIGNALS.
AN ATTACK FLEET IS COMING TO JAPAN!
WHAT?! HOW'D THEY FIND OUT?
OH, NO!
WHEN TASK FORCE 16 ASSEMBLED, THEY USED RADIO. THOSE SIGNALS WERE PICKED UP BY SPY BOATS.
THERE ARE ENEMY SUBMARINES IN THOSE LANES.
HOW ARE YOUR RADIO INTERCEPTORS GETTING PAST THEM?
OUR RADIO PATROLS ARE DISGUISED AS FISHING BOATS.
ON THIS COURSE, THEIR FLEET COULD ARRIVE WITHIN THE WEEK.
THAT SOON!?
YES, BUT OUR SPIES TELL US THE CARRIER-BASED AMERICAN PLANES HAVE A RANGE OF ONLY 300 MILES.
300
600
OUR BOMBERS HAVE A 600-MILE RANGE!
WE CAN BOMB THEM BEFORE THEY EVEN HAVE A CHANCE TO LAUNCH!
THEY'LL BE SITTING DUCKS!
WHUNK
WE'LL FINALLY BE ABLE TO SINK THE CARRIERS WE MISSED AT PEARL HARBOR.

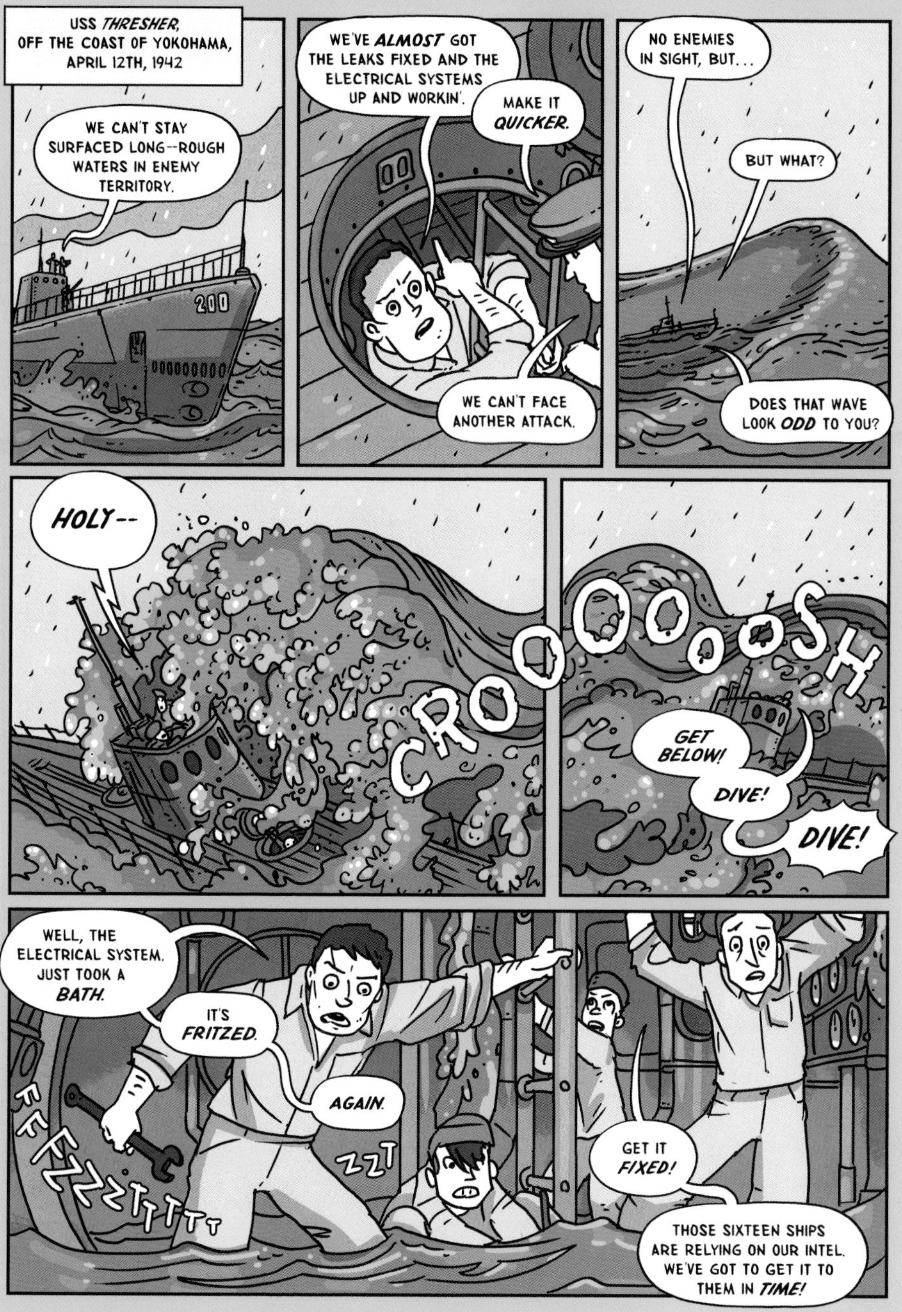
USS *THRESHER*, OFF THE COAST OF YOKOHAMA, APRIL 12TH, 1942
WE CAN'T STAY SURFACED LONG--ROUGH WATERS IN ENEMY TERRITORY.
200
WE'VE *ALMOST* GOT THE LEAKS FIXED AND THE ELECTRICAL SYSTEMS UP AND WORKIN'.
MAKE IT *QUICKER*.
WE CAN'T FACE ANOTHER ATTACK.
NO ENEMIES IN SIGHT, BUT...
BUT WHAT?
DOES THAT WAVE LOOK *ODD* TO YOU?
HOLY--
CROOOOOOSH
GET BELOW!
DIVE!
DIVE!
WELL, THE ELECTRICAL SYSTEM. JUST TOOK A *BATH*.
IT'S *FRITZED*.
AGAIN.
FFFZZZTTTTTT
ZZZT
GET IT *FIXED!*
THOSE SIXTEEN SHIPS ARE RELYING ON OUR INTEL. WE'VE GOT TO GET IT TO THEM IN *TIME!*

USS *HORNET*, MID-PACIFIC, APRIL 15TH, 1942

1 WE WILL *REFUEL* ONE THOUSAND MILES FROM TOKYO.

2 THE OILERS AND DESTROYERS WILL *STAY* AT THE 1000-MILE RANGE.

3 THE CARRIERS AND CRUISERS WILL SPEED INTO THE 500-MILE RANGE,

4 *LAUNCH* THE BOMBERS,

5 THEN RETURN AND REGROUP.

JAPAN

TOKYO

1000

500

SIGNAL THE PLAN TO THE REST OF THE ATTACK GROUP.

WHAT'S THAT GUY DOING?

FLAG SEMAPHORE, IT'S A WAY OF COMMUNICATING SHIP TO SHIP WITHOUT RADIO.

WHY WEREN'T THEY USING THAT *BEFORE!?*

ADMIRAL MITSCHER USED RADIO *ONCE*, TO SIGNAL ADMIRAL HALSEY AND JOIN TASK FORCE 16.

AND THE SPY BOATS HEARD IT.

SCOUT PLANES HAVE SEEN NO SIGN OF ENEMY VESSELS. NO SIGN OF THE *THRESHER* OR THE *TROUT.*

I WISH THEY'D HURRY. WE *REALLY NEED* THAT WEATHER REPORT.

I'LL GIVE YOU A WEATHER REPORT, SIR: IT LOOKS *BAD.*

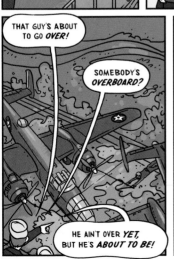

THAT GUY'S ABOUT TO GO *OVER!*

SOMEBODY'S *OVERBOARD?*

HE AIN'T OVER *YET,* BUT HE'S *ABOUT TO BE!*

HEEEELLLP!

KID, YOU *GOTTA* QUIT SLEEPING BY YOUR PLANE!

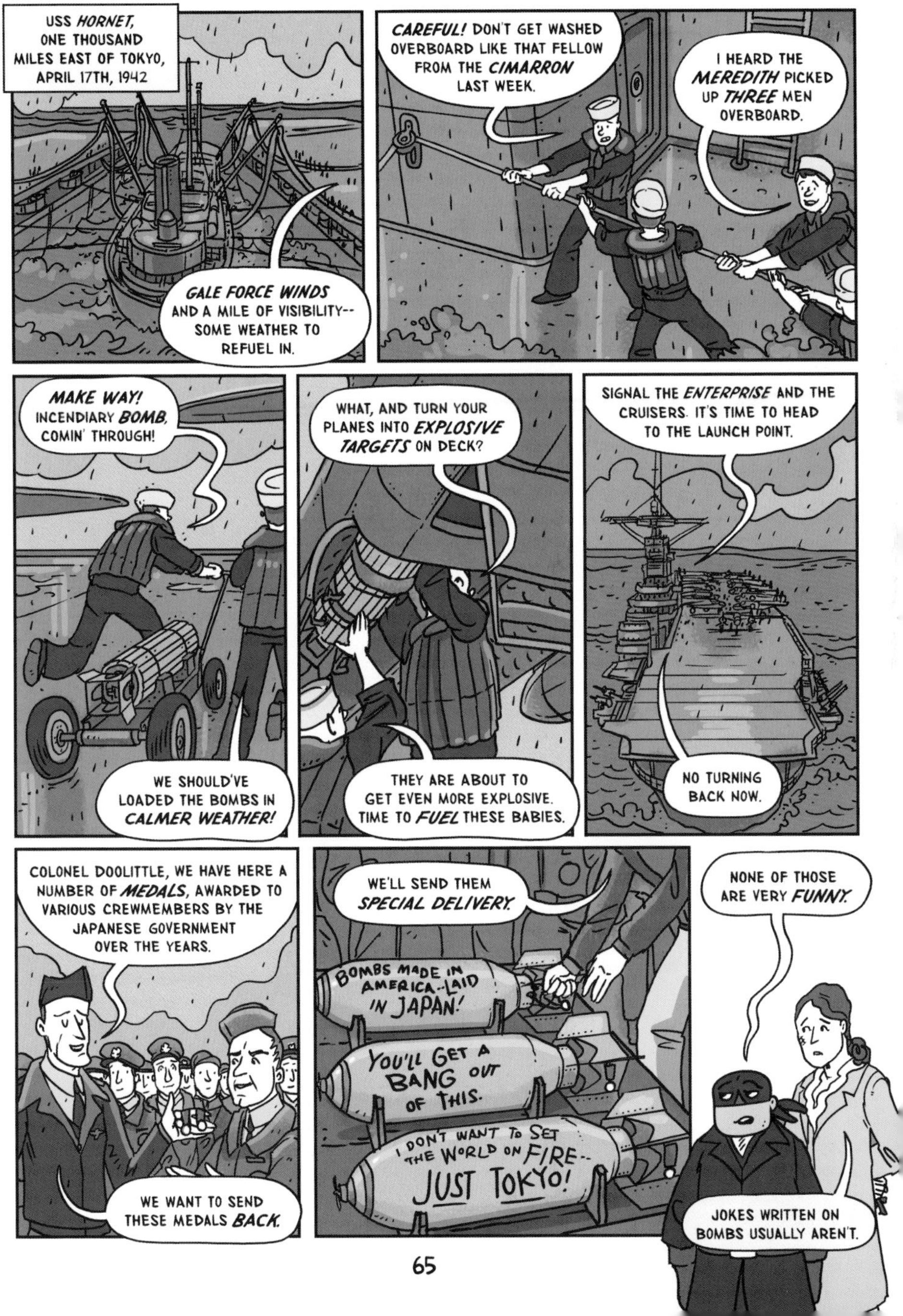
USS *HORNET*, ONE THOUSAND MILES EAST OF TOKYO, APRIL 17TH, 1942
GALE FORCE WINDS AND A MILE OF VISIBILITY-- SOME WEATHER TO REFUEL IN.
CAREFUL! DON'T GET WASHED OVERBOARD LIKE THAT FELLOW FROM THE *CIMARRON* LAST WEEK.
I HEARD THE *MEREDITH* PICKED UP *THREE* MEN OVERBOARD.
MAKE WAY! INCENDIARY *BOMB*, COMIN' THROUGH!
WE SHOULD'VE LOADED THE BOMBS IN *CALMER WEATHER!*
WHAT, AND TURN YOUR PLANES INTO *EXPLOSIVE TARGETS* ON DECK?
THEY ARE ABOUT TO GET EVEN MORE EXPLOSIVE. TIME TO *FUEL* THESE BABIES.
SIGNAL THE *ENTERPRISE* AND THE CRUISERS. IT'S TIME TO HEAD TO THE LAUNCH POINT.
NO TURNING BACK NOW.
COLONEL DOOLITTLE, WE HAVE HERE A NUMBER OF *MEDALS*, AWARDED TO VARIOUS CREWMEMBERS BY THE JAPANESE GOVERNMENT OVER THE YEARS.
WE WANT TO SEND THESE MEDALS *BACK*.
WE'LL SEND THEM *SPECIAL DELIVERY*.
BOMBS MADE IN AMERICA--LAID IN JAPAN!
YOU'LL GET A BANG OUT OF THIS.
I DON'T WANT TO SET THE WORLD ON FIRE-- JUST TOKYO!
NONE OF THOSE ARE VERY *FUNNY*.
JOKES WRITTEN ON BOMBS USUALLY AREN'T.

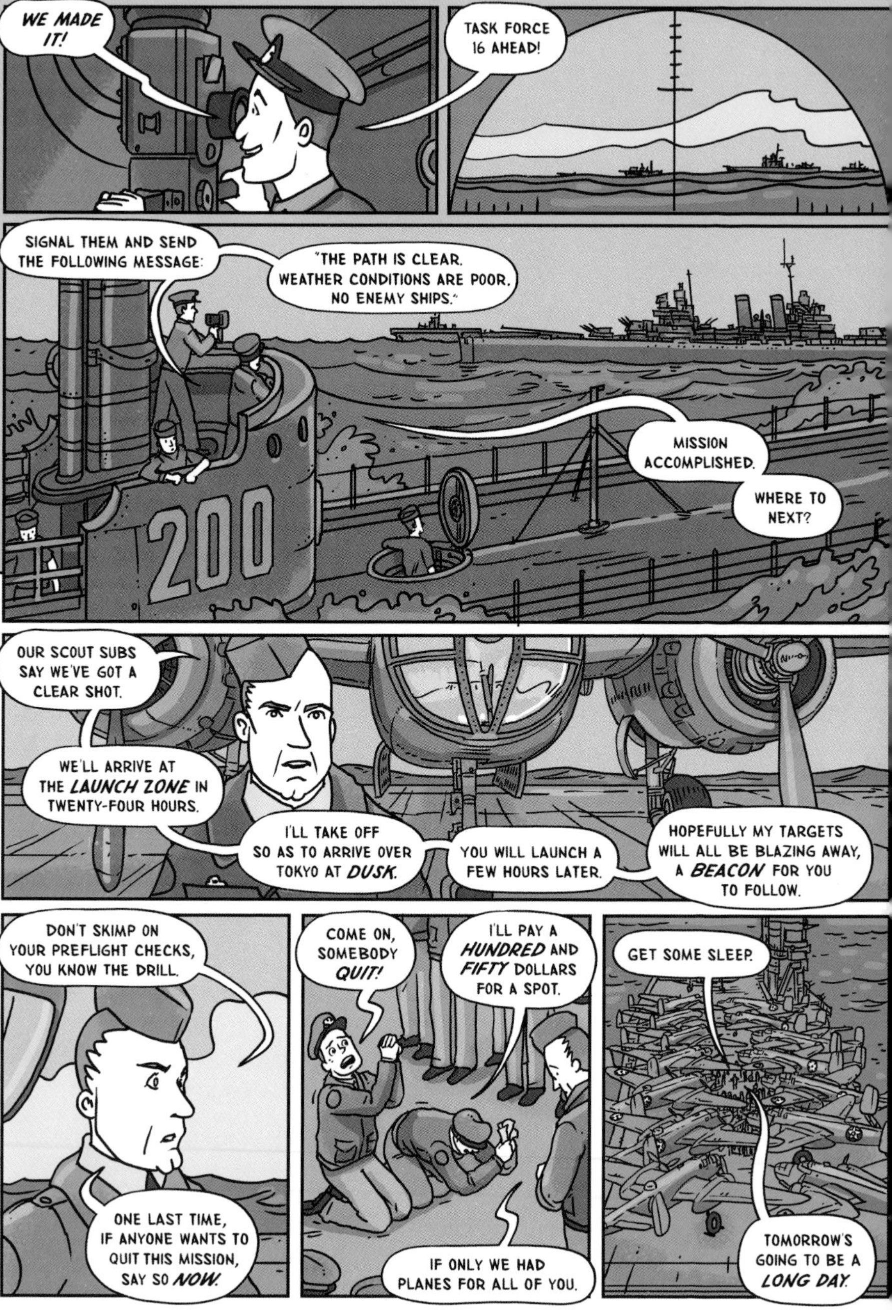
WE MADE IT!
TASK FORCE 16 AHEAD!
SIGNAL THEM AND SEND THE FOLLOWING MESSAGE:
"THE PATH IS CLEAR. WEATHER CONDITIONS ARE POOR. NO ENEMY SHIPS."
200
MISSION ACCOMPLISHED.
WHERE TO NEXT?
OUR SCOUT SUBS SAY WE'VE GOT A CLEAR SHOT.
WE'LL ARRIVE AT THE LAUNCH ZONE IN TWENTY-FOUR HOURS.
I'LL TAKE OFF SO AS TO ARRIVE OVER TOKYO AT DUSK.
YOU WILL LAUNCH A FEW HOURS LATER.
HOPEFULLY MY TARGETS WILL ALL BE BLAZING AWAY, A BEACON FOR YOU TO FOLLOW.
DON'T SKIMP ON YOUR PREFLIGHT CHECKS, YOU KNOW THE DRILL.
ONE LAST TIME, IF ANYONE WANTS TO QUIT THIS MISSION, SAY SO NOW.
COME ON, SOMEBODY QUIT!
I'LL PAY A HUNDRED AND FIFTY DOLLARS FOR A SPOT.
IF ONLY WE HAD PLANES FOR ALL OF YOU.
GET SOME SLEEP.
TOMORROW'S GOING TO BE A LONG DAY.

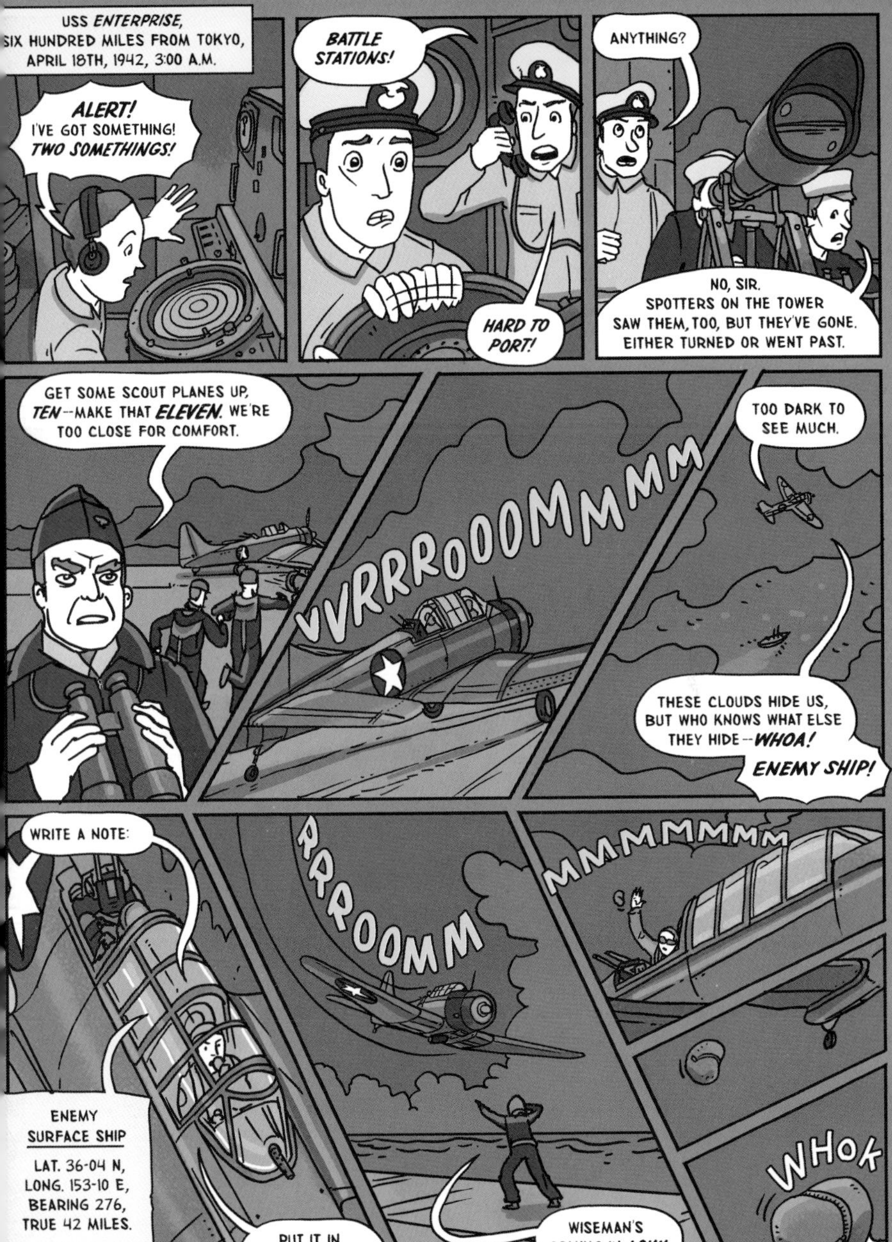
USS ENTERPRISE, SIX HUNDRED MILES FROM TOKYO, APRIL 18TH, 1942, 3:00 A.M.
ALERT! I'VE GOT SOMETHING! TWO SOMETHINGS!
BATTLE STATIONS!
HARD TO PORT!
ANYTHING?
NO, SIR. SPOTTERS ON THE TOWER SAW THEM, TOO, BUT THEY'VE GONE. EITHER TURNED OR WENT PAST.
GET SOME SCOUT PLANES UP, TEN--MAKE THAT ELEVEN. WE'RE TOO CLOSE FOR COMFORT.
VVRRROOOMMMMM
TOO DARK TO SEE MUCH.
THESE CLOUDS HIDE US, BUT WHO KNOWS WHAT ELSE THEY HIDE--WHOA!
ENEMY SHIP!
WRITE A NOTE:
ENEMY SURFACE SHIP
LAT. 36-04 N, LONG. 153-10 E, BEARING 276, TRUE 42 MILES.
BELIEVED SEEN BY THE ENEMY.
PUT IT IN THE BEANBAG-- IT'S FASTER!
RRROOMM
MMMMMMMM
WISEMAN'S COMING IN LOW!
WHOK

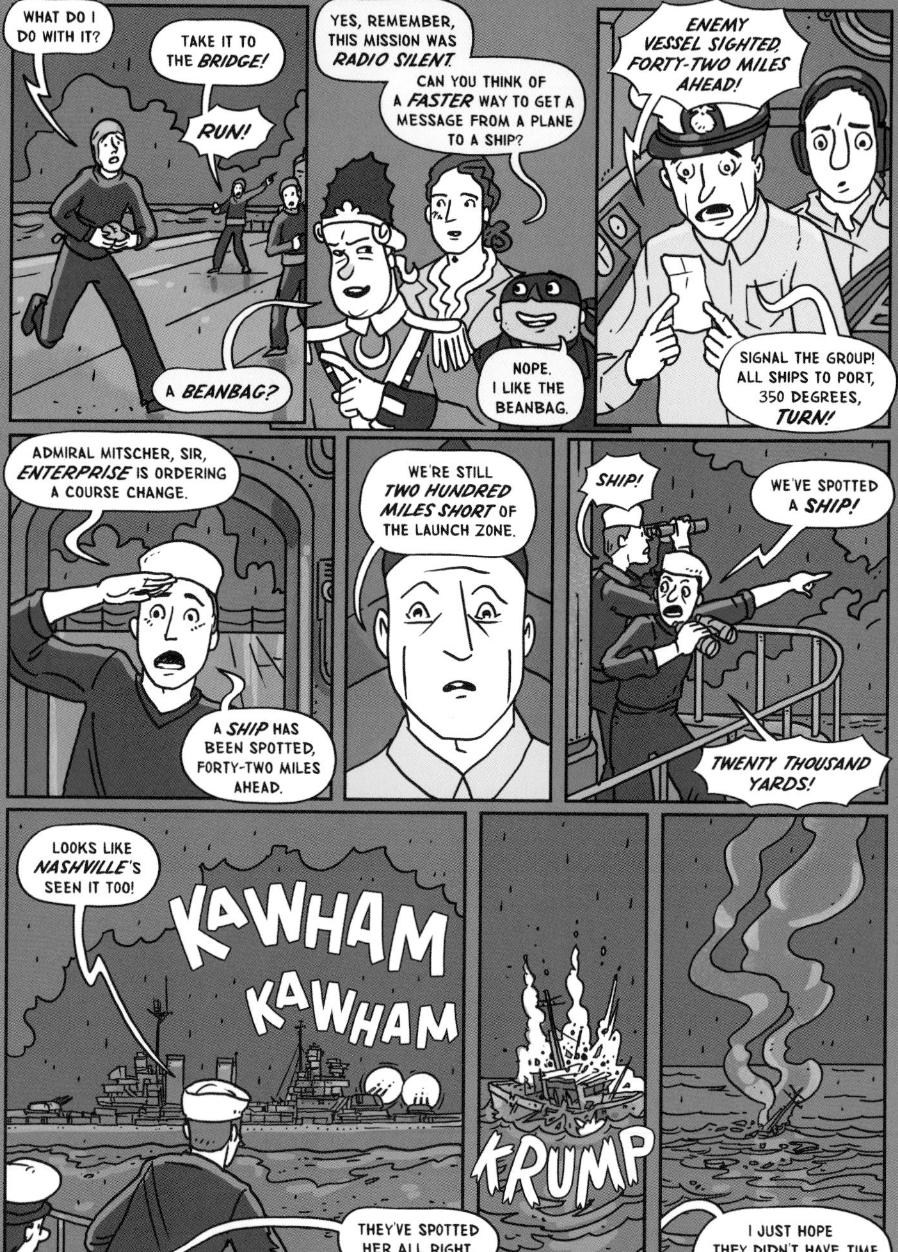
WHAT DO I DO WITH IT?
TAKE IT TO THE BRIDGE!
RUN!
A BEANBAG?
YES, REMEMBER, THIS MISSION WAS RADIO SILENT.
CAN YOU THINK OF A FASTER WAY TO GET A MESSAGE FROM A PLANE TO A SHIP?
NOPE. I LIKE THE BEANBAG.
ENEMY VESSEL SIGHTED, FORTY-TWO MILES AHEAD!
SIGNAL THE GROUP! ALL SHIPS TO PORT, 350 DEGREES, TURN!
ADMIRAL MITSCHER, SIR, ENTERPRISE IS ORDERING A COURSE CHANGE.
A SHIP HAS BEEN SPOTTED, FORTY-TWO MILES AHEAD.
WE'RE STILL TWO HUNDRED MILES SHORT OF THE LAUNCH ZONE.
SHIP!
WE'VE SPOTTED A SHIP!
TWENTY THOUSAND YARDS!
LOOKS LIKE NASHVILLE'S SEEN IT TOO!
KAWHAM
KAWHAM
THEY'VE SPOTTED HER ALL RIGHT.
KRUMP
I JUST HOPE THEY DIDN'T HAVE TIME TO REPORT US.

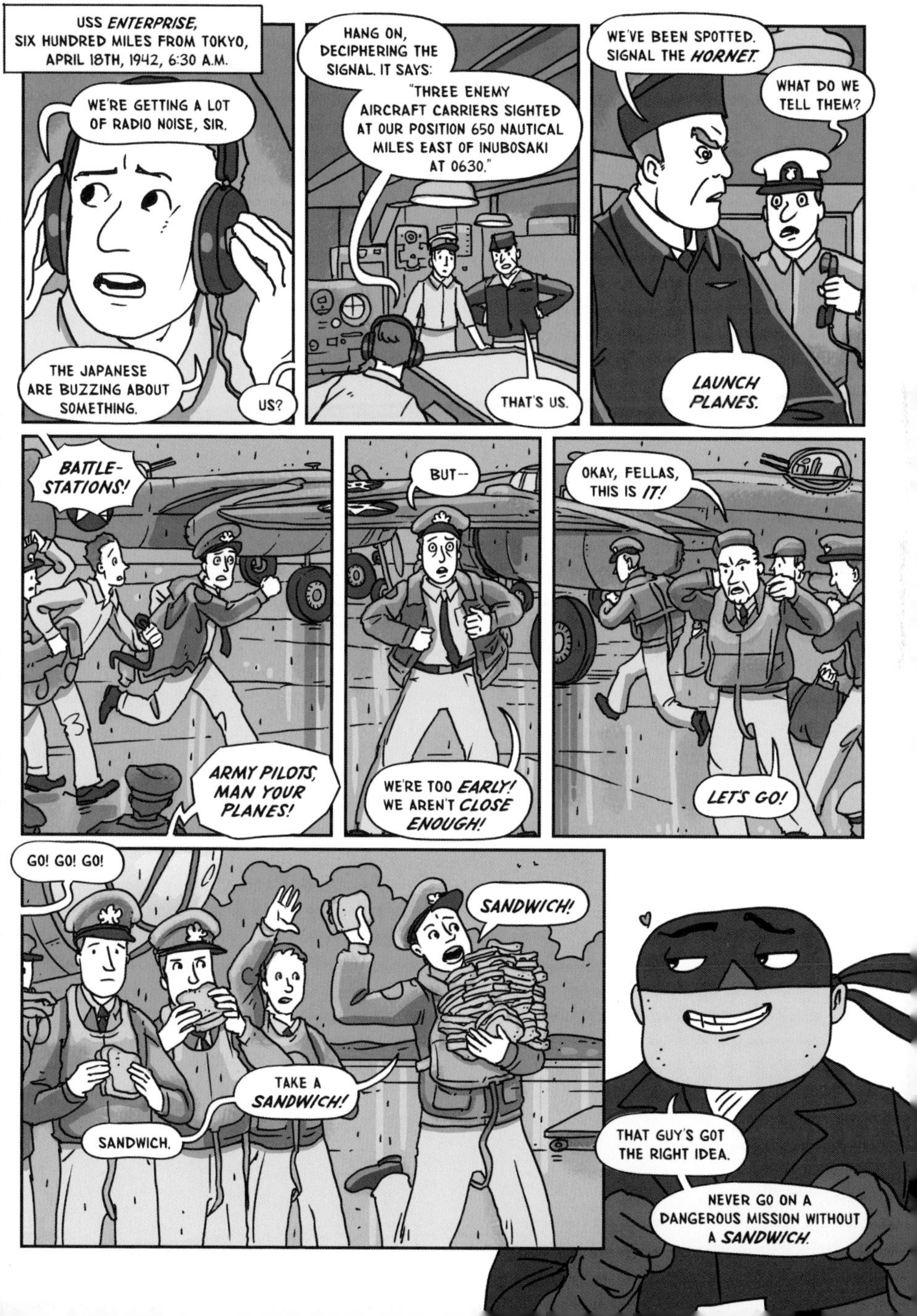

USS *ENTERPRISE*, SIX HUNDRED MILES FROM TOKYO, APRIL 18TH, 1942, 6:30 A.M.
WE'RE GETTING A LOT OF RADIO NOISE, SIR.
THE JAPANESE ARE BUZZING ABOUT SOMETHING.
US?
HANG ON, DECIPHERING THE SIGNAL. IT SAYS:
"THREE ENEMY AIRCRAFT CARRIERS SIGHTED AT OUR POSITION 650 NAUTICAL MILES EAST OF INUBOSAKI AT 0630."
THAT'S US.
WE'VE BEEN SPOTTED. SIGNAL THE *HORNET*.
WHAT DO WE TELL THEM?
LAUNCH PLANES.
BATTLE-STATIONS!
ARMY PILOTS, MAN YOUR PLANES!
BUT--
WE'RE TOO *EARLY!* WE AREN'T *CLOSE ENOUGH!*
OKAY, FELLAS, THIS IS *IT!*
LET'S GO!
GO! GO! GO!
SANDWICH!
TAKE A *SANDWICH!*
SANDWICH.
THAT GUY'S GOT THE RIGHT IDEA.
NEVER GO ON A DANGEROUS MISSION WITHOUT A *SANDWICH.*

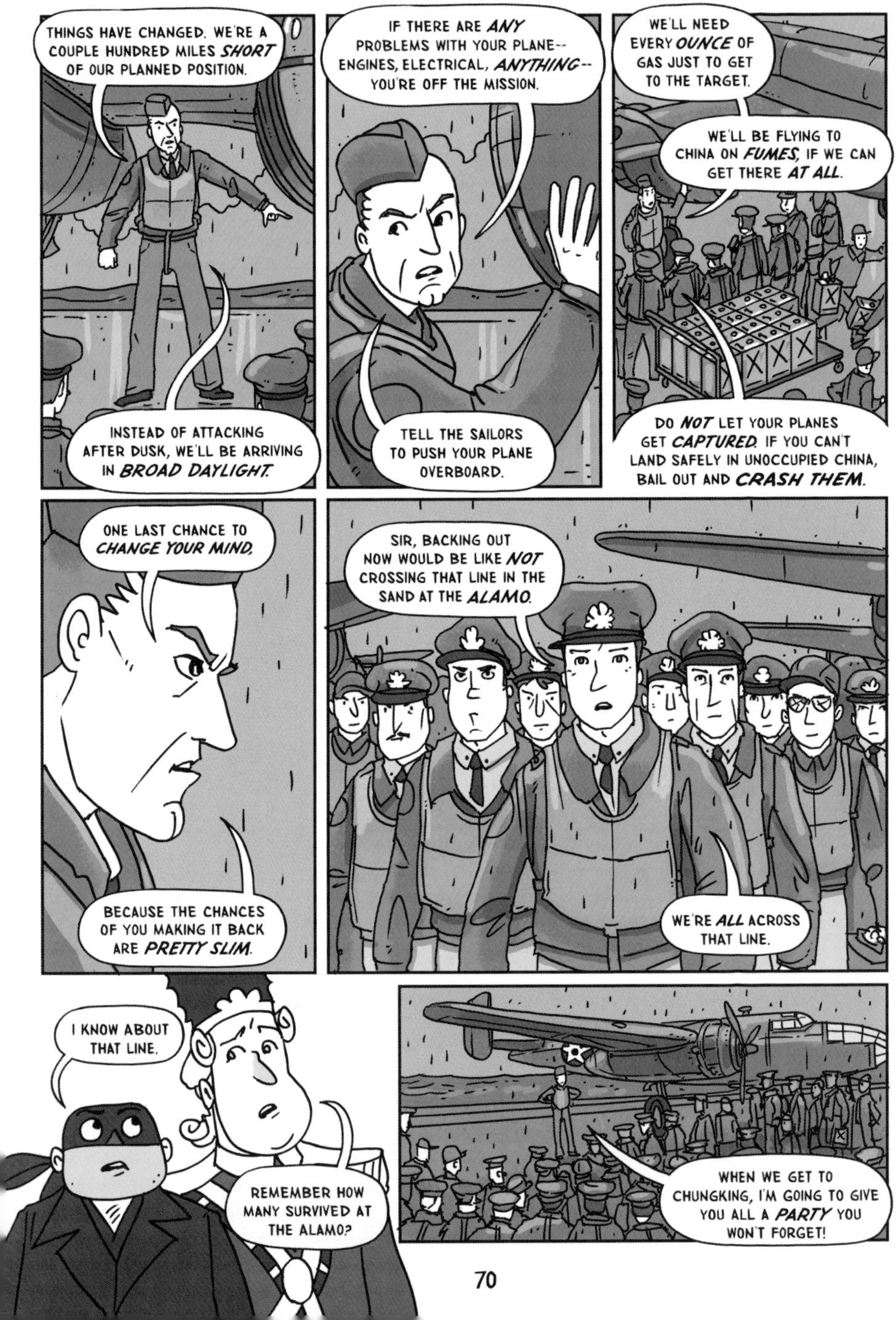
THINGS HAVE CHANGED. WE'RE A COUPLE HUNDRED MILES SHORT OF OUR PLANNED POSITION.
INSTEAD OF ATTACKING AFTER DUSK, WE'LL BE ARRIVING IN BROAD DAYLIGHT.
IF THERE ARE ANY PROBLEMS WITH YOUR PLANE-- ENGINES, ELECTRICAL, ANYTHING-- YOU'RE OFF THE MISSION.
TELL THE SAILORS TO PUSH YOUR PLANE OVERBOARD.
WE'LL NEED EVERY OUNCE OF GAS JUST TO GET TO THE TARGET.
WE'LL BE FLYING TO CHINA ON FUMES, IF WE CAN GET THERE AT ALL.
DO NOT LET YOUR PLANES GET CAPTURED. IF YOU CAN'T LAND SAFELY IN UNOCCUPIED CHINA, BAIL OUT AND CRASH THEM.
ONE LAST CHANCE TO CHANGE YOUR MIND.
BECAUSE THE CHANCES OF YOU MAKING IT BACK ARE PRETTY SLIM.
SIR, BACKING OUT NOW WOULD BE LIKE NOT CROSSING THAT LINE IN THE SAND AT THE ALAMO.
WE'RE ALL ACROSS THAT LINE.
I KNOW ABOUT THAT LINE.
REMEMBER HOW MANY SURVIVED AT THE ALAMO?
WHEN WE GET TO CHUNGKING, I'M GOING TO GIVE YOU ALL A PARTY YOU WON'T FORGET!

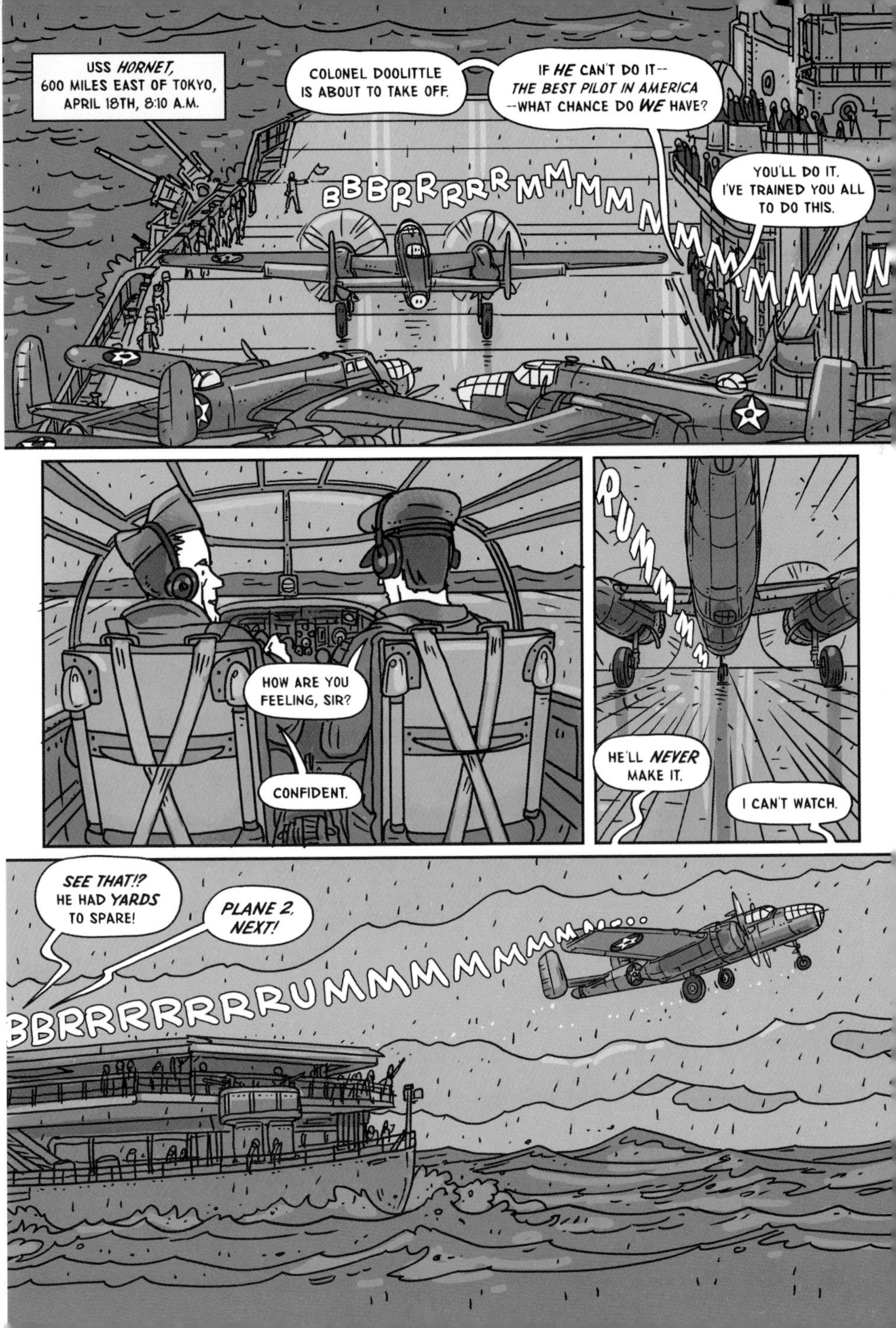
USS *HORNET,*
600 MILES EAST OF TOKYO,
APRIL 18TH, 8:10 A.M.
COLONEL DOOLITTLE IS ABOUT TO TAKE OFF.
IF ***HE*** CAN'T DO IT-- *THE BEST PILOT IN AMERICA* --WHAT CHANCE DO ***WE*** HAVE?
BBBRRRRRRMMMMMMMMMMMMMMMM
YOU'LL DO IT. I'VE TRAINED YOU ALL TO DO THIS.
HOW ARE YOU FEELING, SIR?
CONFIDENT.
RUMMMMM
HE'LL ***NEVER*** MAKE IT.
I CAN'T WATCH.
SEE THAT!? HE HAD ***YARDS*** TO SPARE!
PLANE 2, NEXT!
BBRRRRRRRRUMMMMMMMMMM...

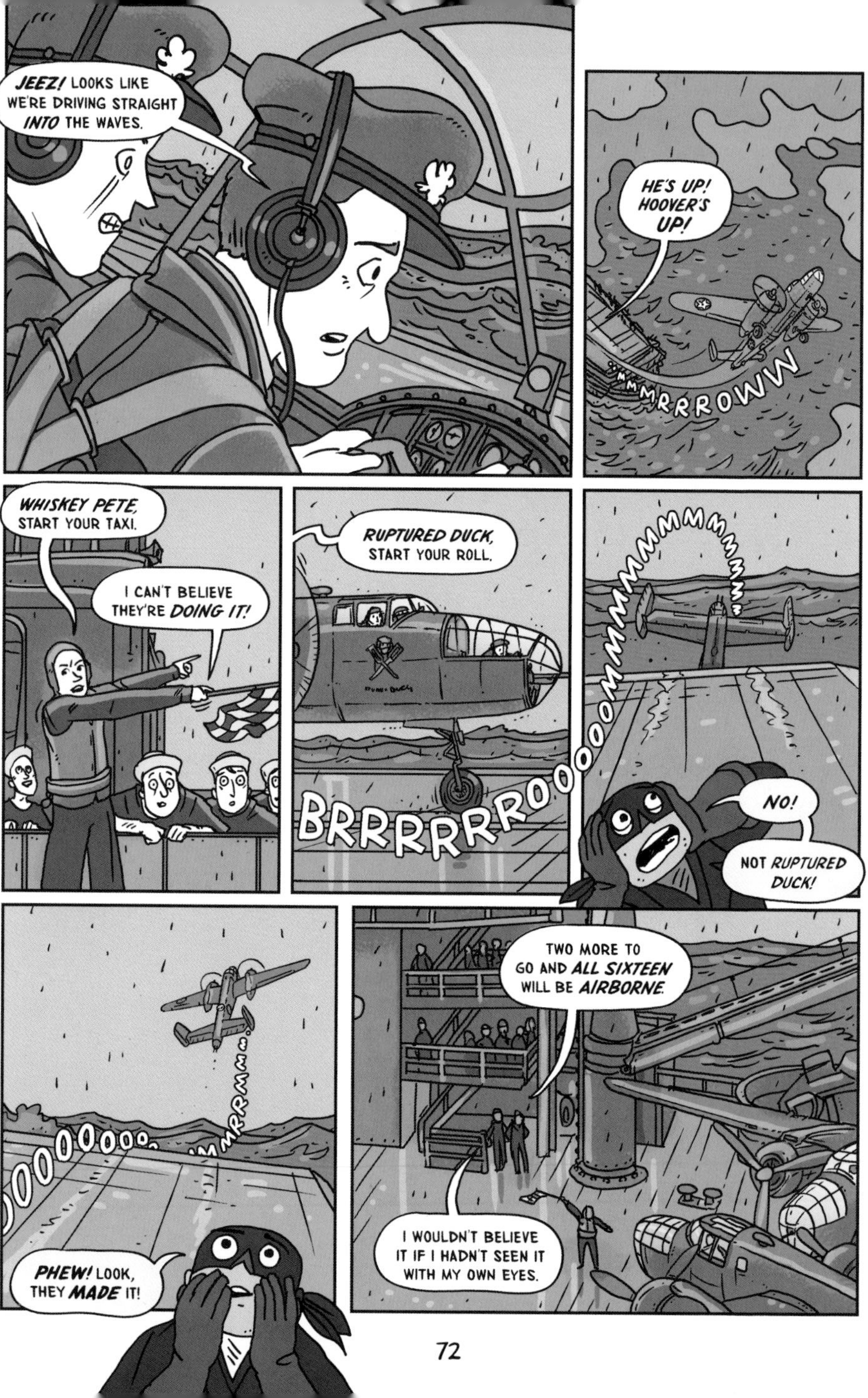
JEEZ! LOOKS LIKE WE'RE DRIVING STRAIGHT INTO THE WAVES.
HE'S UP! HOOVER'S UP!
MMMRRROWW
WHISKEY PETE, START YOUR TAXI.
I CAN'T BELIEVE THEY'RE DOING IT!
RUPTURED DUCK, START YOUR ROLL.
BRRRRRRROOOOOOMMMMMMMMMMMMMMMMMM
NO!
NOT RUPTURED DUCK!
OOOOOOOO...MMRRMMM...
PHEW! LOOK, THEY MADE IT!
TWO MORE TO GO AND ALL SIXTEEN WILL BE AIRBORNE.
I WOULDN'T BELIEVE IT IF I HADN'T SEEN IT WITH MY OWN EYES.

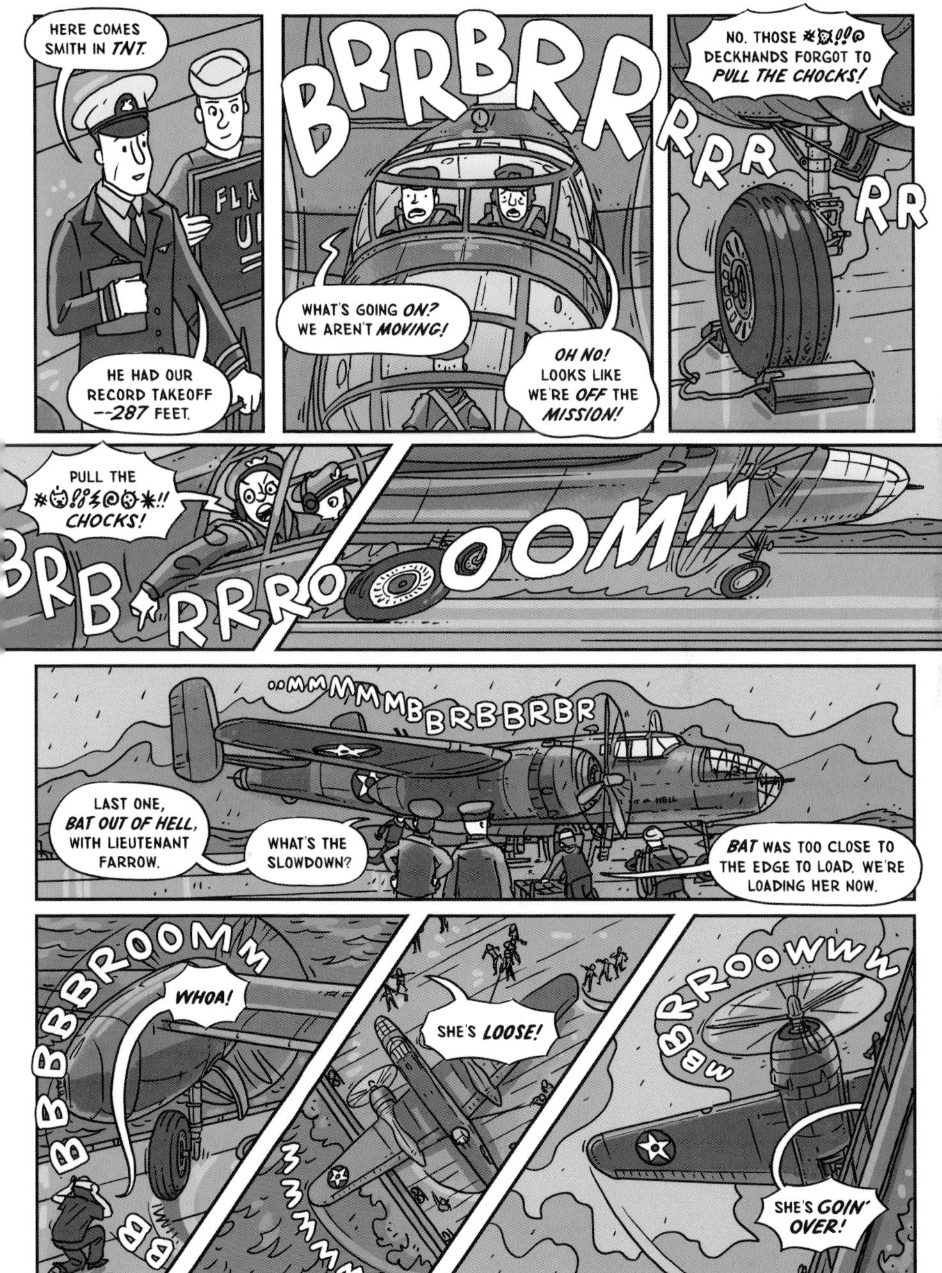
HERE COMES SMITH IN *TNT.*
HE HAD OUR RECORD TAKEOFF --287 FEET.
BRRBRR RRR RR
WHAT'S GOING *ON?* WE AREN'T *MOVING!*
OH NO! LOOKS LIKE WE'RE *OFF* THE *MISSION!*
NO. THOSE *☠!?@ DECKHANDS FORGOT TO *PULL THE CHOCKS!*
PULL THE *☺!?$@☺*!! *CHOCKS!*
BRBRRROOOMM
..MMMMMBBRBBRBR
LAST ONE, *BAT OUT OF HELL,* WITH LIEUTENANT FARROW.
WHAT'S THE SLOWDOWN?
BAT WAS TOO CLOSE TO THE EDGE TO LOAD. WE'RE LOADING HER NOW.
BBBBBBROOMM
WHOA!
SHE'S *LOOSE!*
MMMMMMM
MBBRROOWWW
SHE'S *GOIN' OVER!*

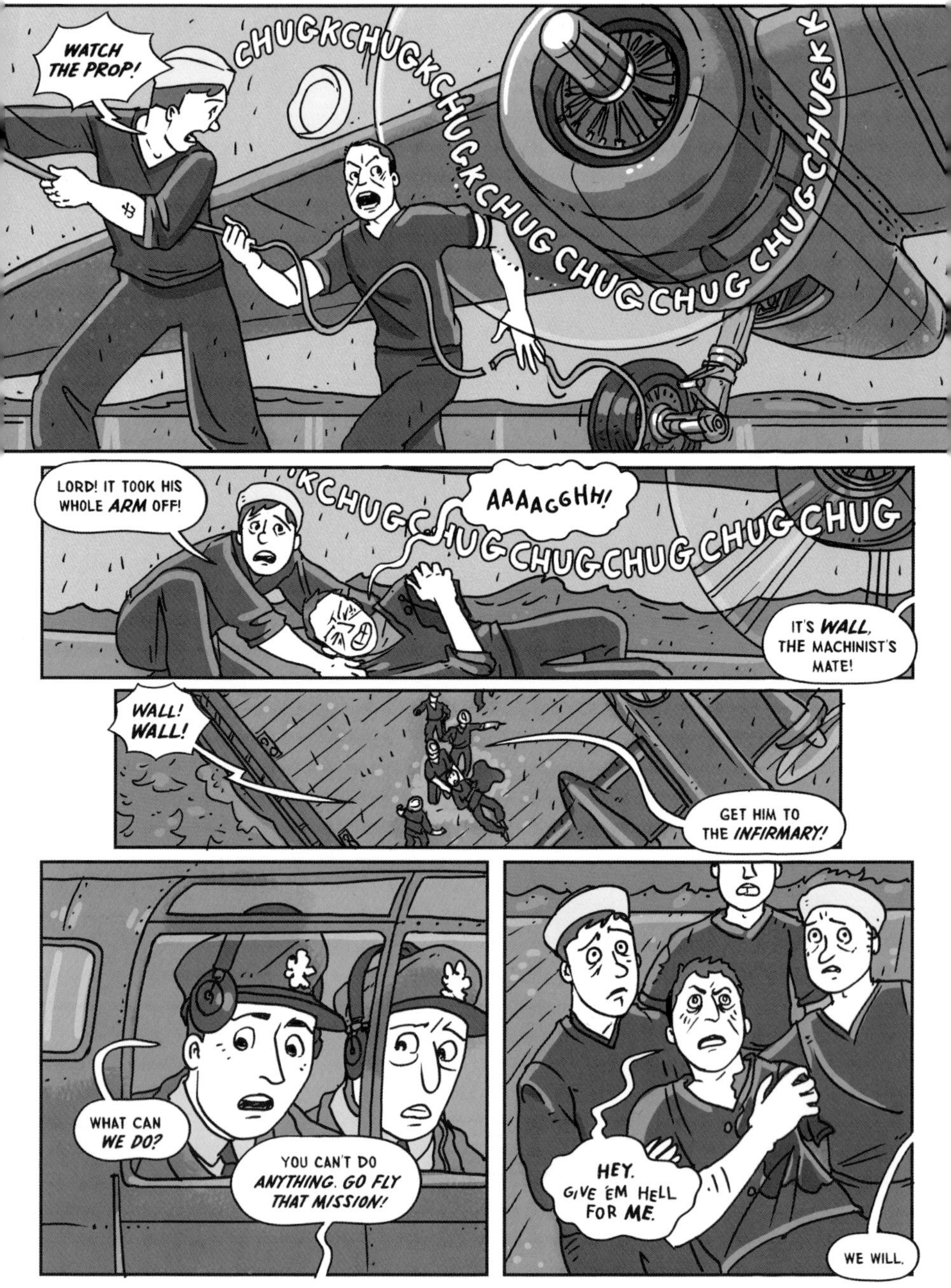
WATCH THE PROP!
CHUGKCHUGKCHUGKCHUGCHUGCHUGCHUGCHUGCHUGKK
LORD! IT TOOK HIS WHOLE ARM OFF!
'KCHUGCHUGCHUGCHUGCHUGCHUG
AAAAGGHH!
IT'S WALL, THE MACHINIST'S MATE!
WALL! WALL!
GET HIM TO THE INFIRMARY!
WHAT CAN WE DO?
YOU CAN'T DO ANYTHING. GO FLY THAT MISSION!
HEY. GIVE 'EM HELL FOR ME.
WE WILL.

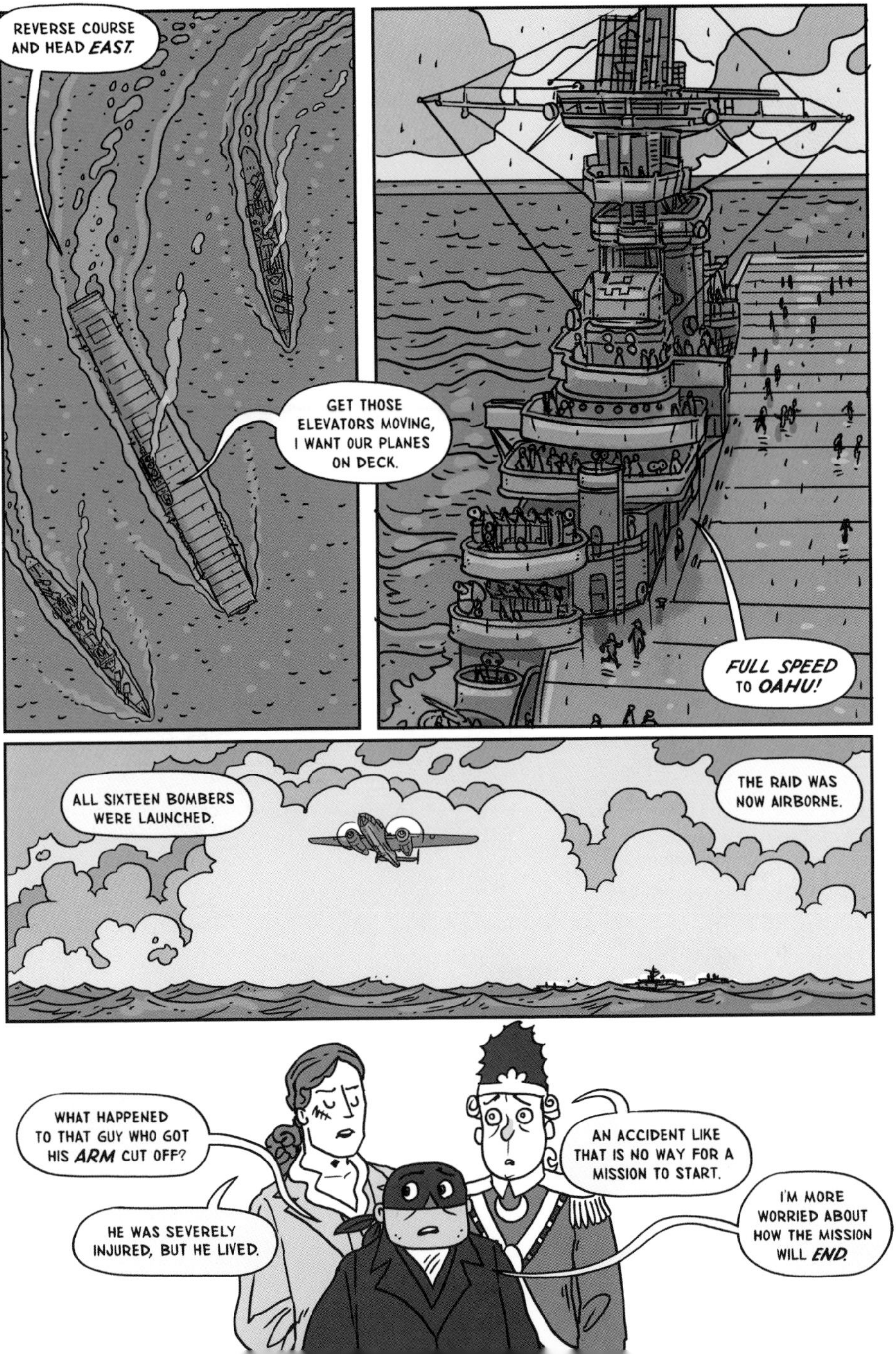
REVERSE COURSE AND HEAD *EAST.*
GET THOSE ELEVATORS MOVING, I WANT OUR PLANES ON DECK.
FULL SPEED TO ***OAHU!***
ALL SIXTEEN BOMBERS WERE LAUNCHED.
THE RAID WAS NOW AIRBORNE.
WHAT HAPPENED TO THAT GUY WHO GOT HIS ***ARM*** CUT OFF?
HE WAS SEVERELY INJURED, BUT HE LIVED.
AN ACCIDENT LIKE THAT IS NO WAY FOR A MISSION TO START.
I'M MORE WORRIED ABOUT HOW THE MISSION WILL ***END.***

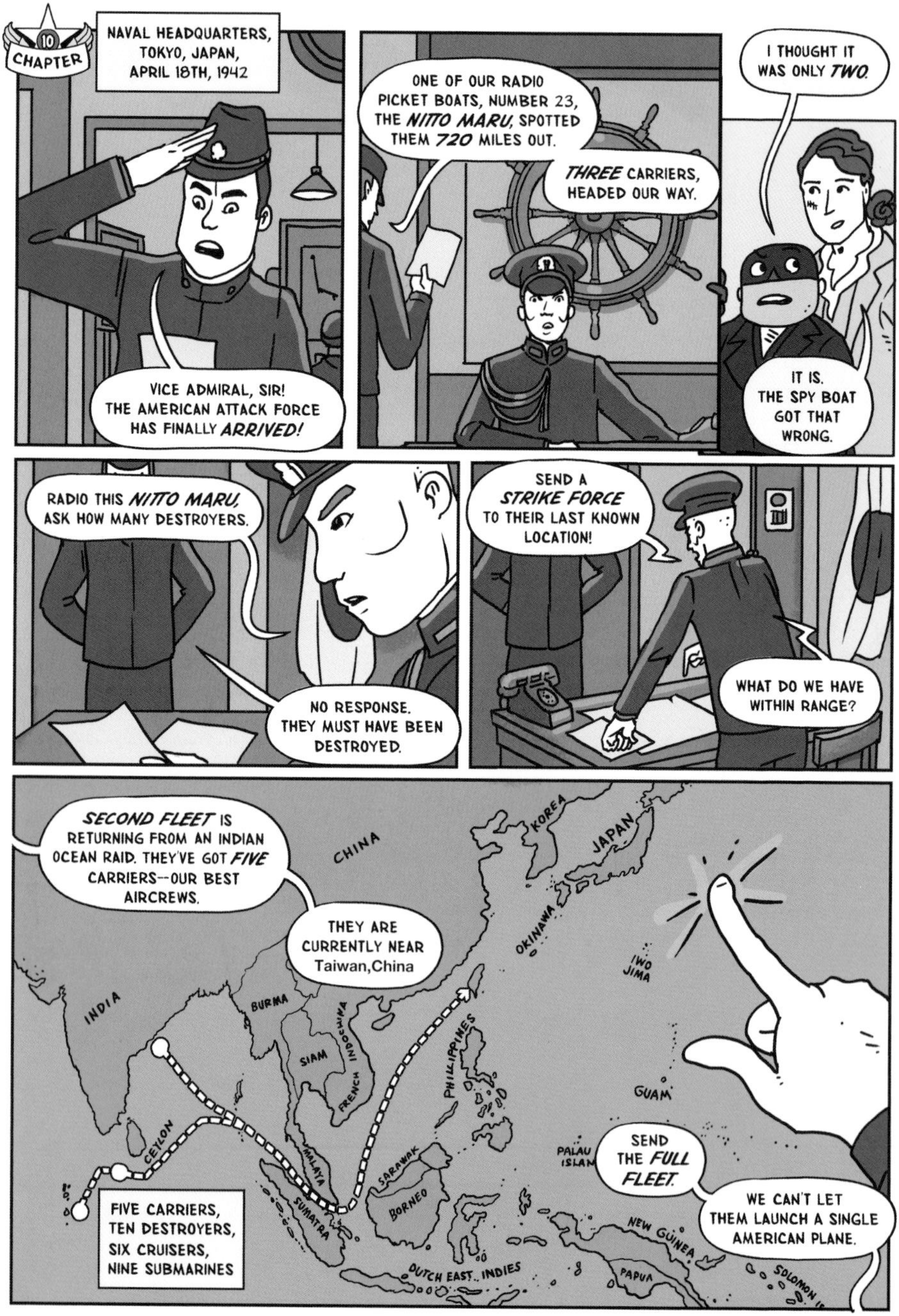

10
CHAPTER
NAVAL HEADQUARTERS, TOKYO, JAPAN, APRIL 18TH, 1942
VICE ADMIRAL, SIR! THE AMERICAN ATTACK FORCE HAS FINALLY *ARRIVED!*
ONE OF OUR RADIO PICKET BOATS, NUMBER 23, THE *NITTO MARU,* SPOTTED THEM *720* MILES OUT.
THREE CARRIERS, HEADED OUR WAY.
I THOUGHT IT WAS ONLY *TWO.*
IT IS. THE SPY BOAT GOT THAT WRONG.
RADIO THIS *NITTO MARU,* ASK HOW MANY DESTROYERS.
NO RESPONSE. THEY MUST HAVE BEEN DESTROYED.
SEND A *STRIKE FORCE* TO THEIR LAST KNOWN LOCATION!
WHAT DO WE HAVE WITHIN RANGE?
SECOND FLEET IS RETURNING FROM AN INDIAN OCEAN RAID. THEY'VE GOT *FIVE* CARRIERS--OUR BEST AIRCREWS.
THEY ARE CURRENTLY NEAR Taiwan,China
CHINA
KOREA
JAPAN
OKINAWA
IWO JIMA
INDIA
BURMA
SIAM
FRENCH INDOCHINA
PHILIPPINES
GUAM
CEYLON
MALAYA
SUMATRA
SARAWAK
BORNEO
PALAU
NEW GUINEA
PAPUA
DUTCH EAST INDIES
SOLOMON
FIVE CARRIERS, TEN DESTROYERS, SIX CRUISERS, NINE SUBMARINES
SEND THE *FULL FLEET.*
WE CAN'T LET THEM LAUNCH A SINGLE AMERICAN PLANE.

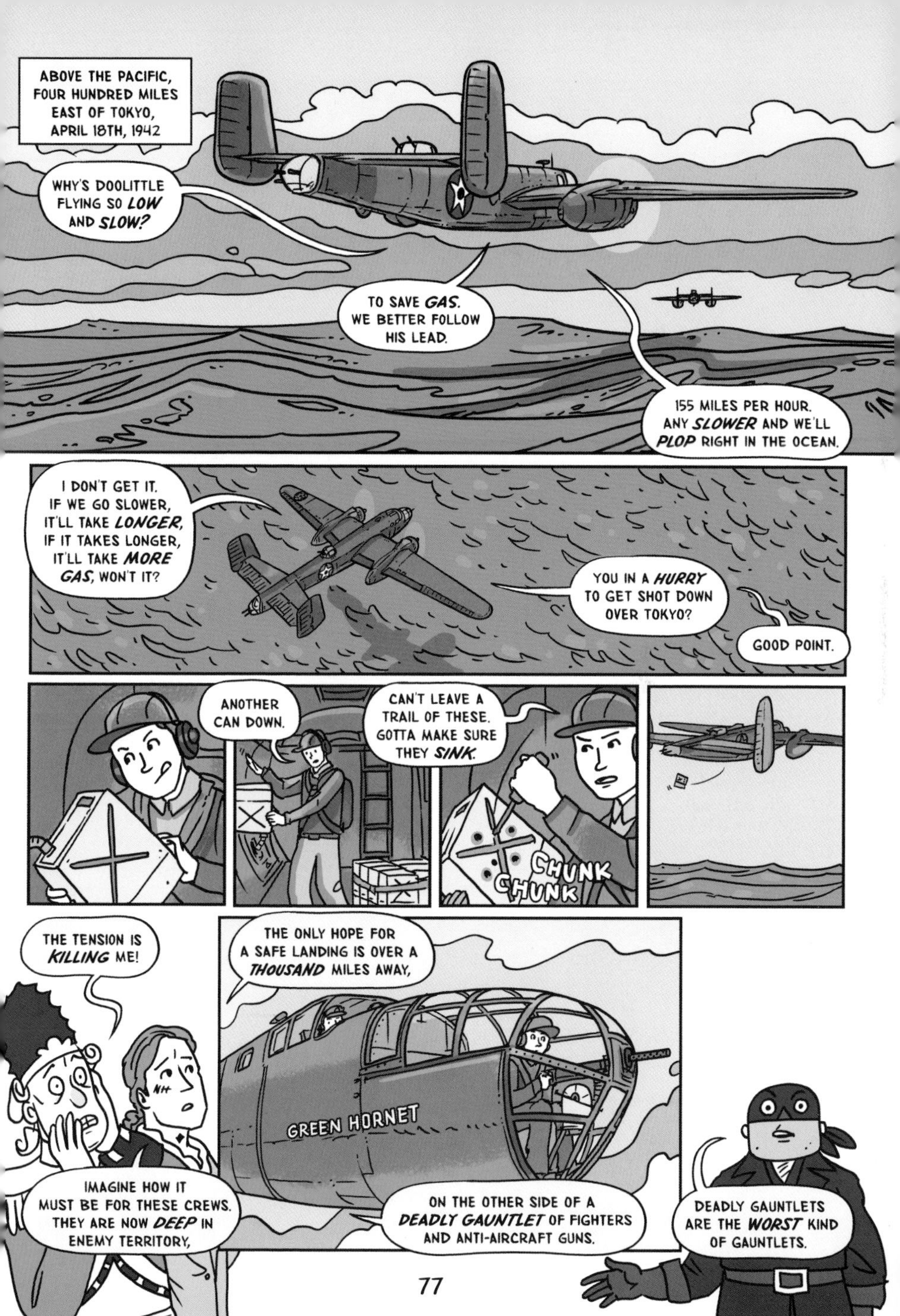
ABOVE THE PACIFIC, FOUR HUNDRED MILES EAST OF TOKYO, APRIL 18TH, 1942
WHY'S DOOLITTLE FLYING SO *LOW* AND *SLOW?*
TO SAVE *GAS.* WE BETTER FOLLOW HIS LEAD.
155 MILES PER HOUR. ANY *SLOWER* AND WE'LL *PLOP* RIGHT IN THE OCEAN.
I DON'T GET IT. IF WE GO SLOWER, IT'LL TAKE *LONGER,* IF IT TAKES LONGER, IT'LL TAKE *MORE GAS,* WON'T IT?
YOU IN A *HURRY* TO GET SHOT DOWN OVER TOKYO?
GOOD POINT.
ANOTHER CAN DOWN.
CAN'T LEAVE A TRAIL OF THESE. GOTTA MAKE SURE THEY *SINK.*
CHUNK
CHUNK
THE TENSION IS *KILLING* ME!
THE ONLY HOPE FOR A SAFE LANDING IS OVER A *THOUSAND* MILES AWAY,
GREEN HORNET
IMAGINE HOW IT MUST BE FOR THESE CREWS. THEY ARE NOW *DEEP* IN ENEMY TERRITORY,
ON THE OTHER SIDE OF A *DEADLY GAUNTLET* OF FIGHTERS AND ANTI-AIRCRAFT GUNS.
DEADLY GAUNTLETS ARE THE *WORST* KIND OF GAUNTLETS.

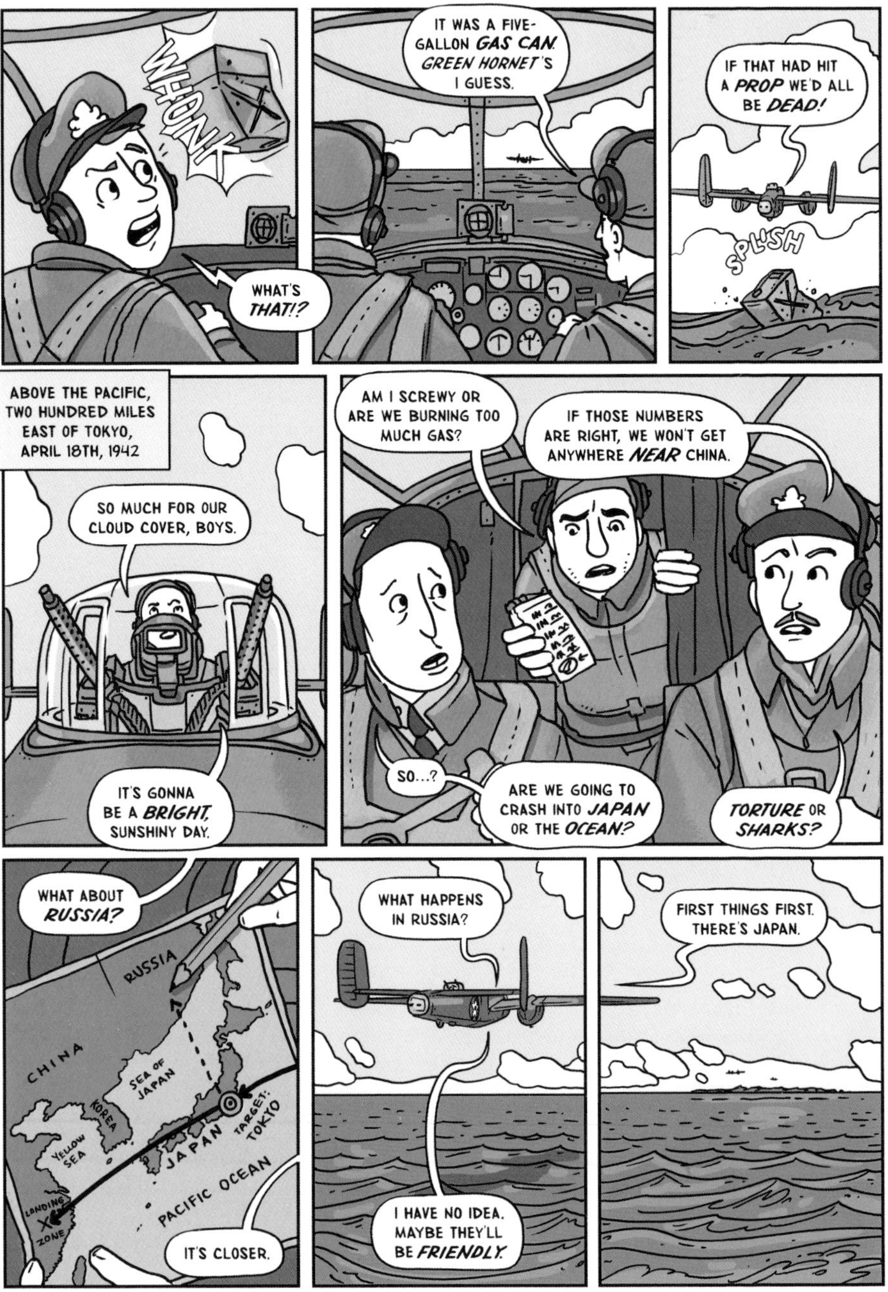
WHONK
WHAT'S THAT!?
IT WAS A FIVE-GALLON GAS CAN. GREEN HORNET'S I GUESS.
IF THAT HAD HIT A PROP WE'D ALL BE DEAD!
SPLUSH
ABOVE THE PACIFIC, TWO HUNDRED MILES EAST OF TOKYO, APRIL 18TH, 1942
SO MUCH FOR OUR CLOUD COVER, BOYS.
IT'S GONNA BE A BRIGHT, SUNSHINY DAY.
AM I SCREWY OR ARE WE BURNING TOO MUCH GAS?
IF THOSE NUMBERS ARE RIGHT, WE WON'T GET ANYWHERE NEAR CHINA.
SO...?
ARE WE GOING TO CRASH INTO JAPAN OR THE OCEAN?
TORTURE OR SHARKS?
WHAT ABOUT RUSSIA?
RUSSIA
CHINA
SEA OF JAPAN
KOREA
YELLOW SEA
JAPAN
TARGET: TOKYO
PACIFIC OCEAN
LANDING ZONE
IT'S CLOSER.
WHAT HAPPENS IN RUSSIA?
I HAVE NO IDEA. MAYBE THEY'LL BE FRIENDLY.
FIRST THINGS FIRST. THERE'S JAPAN.

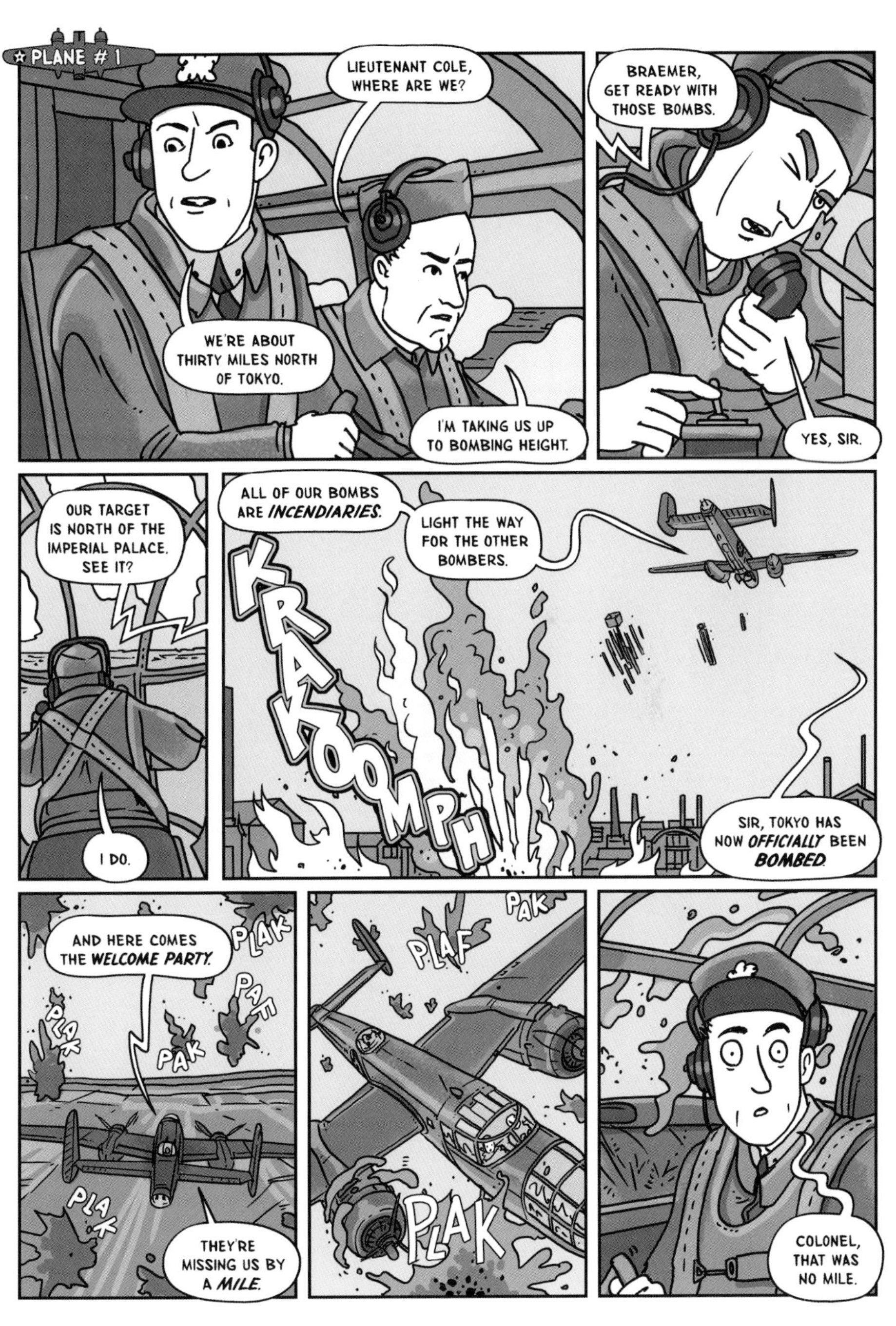
PLANE # 1
LIEUTENANT COLE, WHERE ARE WE?
WE'RE ABOUT THIRTY MILES NORTH OF TOKYO.
I'M TAKING US UP TO BOMBING HEIGHT.
BRAEMER, GET READY WITH THOSE BOMBS.
YES, SIR.
OUR TARGET IS NORTH OF THE IMPERIAL PALACE. SEE IT?
I DO.
ALL OF OUR BOMBS ARE *INCENDIARIES.*
LIGHT THE WAY FOR THE OTHER BOMBERS.
KRAKOOMPH
SIR, TOKYO HAS NOW *OFFICIALLY* BEEN ***BOMBED.***
AND HERE COMES THE ***WELCOME PARTY.***
PLAK
PAF
PLAK
PAK
PLAK
THEY'RE MISSING US BY A *MILE.*
PAK
PLAF
PLAK
COLONEL, THAT WAS NO MILE.

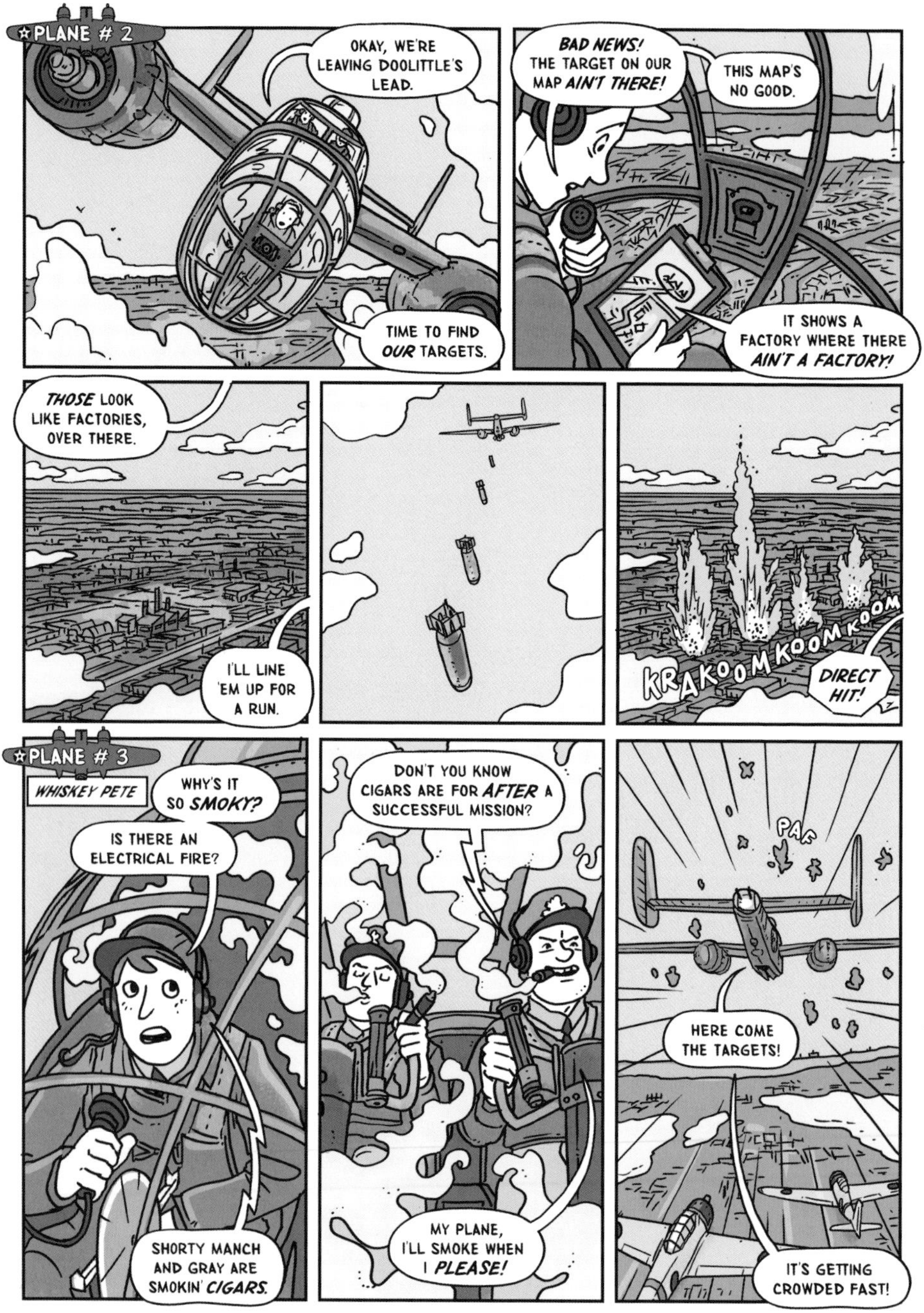
PLANE # 2
OKAY, WE'RE LEAVING DOOLITTLE'S LEAD.
TIME TO FIND OUR TARGETS.
BAD NEWS! THE TARGET ON OUR MAP AIN'T THERE!
THIS MAP'S NO GOOD.
IT SHOWS A FACTORY WHERE THERE AIN'T A FACTORY!
THOSE LOOK LIKE FACTORIES, OVER THERE.
I'LL LINE 'EM UP FOR A RUN.
KRAKOOMKOOMKOOM
DIRECT HIT!
PLANE # 3
WHISKEY PETE
WHY'S IT SO SMOKY?
IS THERE AN ELECTRICAL FIRE?
SHORTY MANCH AND GRAY ARE SMOKIN' CIGARS.
DON'T YOU KNOW CIGARS ARE FOR AFTER A SUCCESSFUL MISSION?
MY PLANE, I'LL SMOKE WHEN I PLEASE!
PAF
HERE COME THE TARGETS!
IT'S GETTING CROWDED FAST!

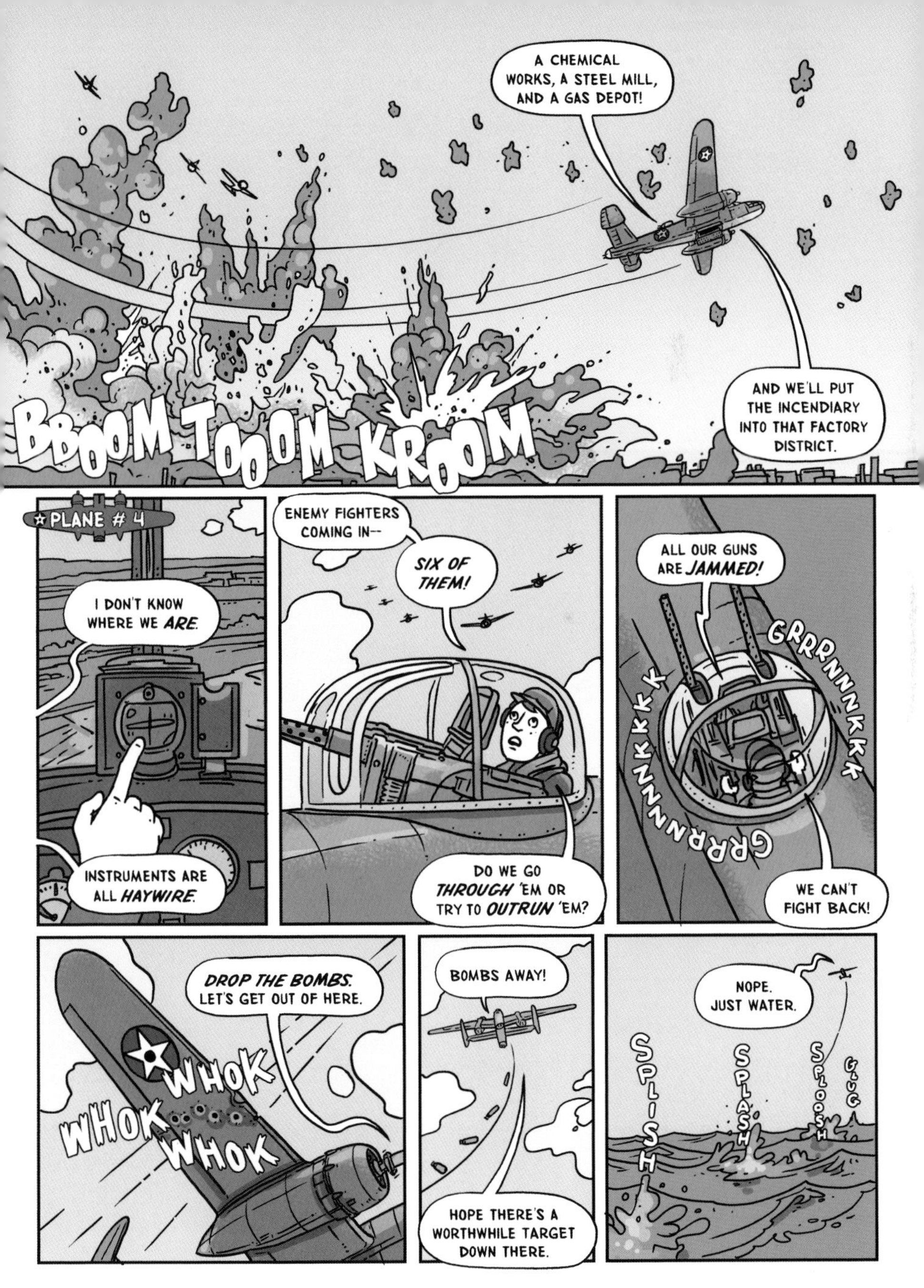
A CHEMICAL WORKS, A STEEL MILL, AND A GAS DEPOT!
AND WE'LL PUT THE INCENDIARY INTO THAT FACTORY DISTRICT.
BBOOM TOOOM KROOM
PLANE # 4
I DON'T KNOW WHERE WE *ARE*.
INSTRUMENTS ARE ALL *HAYWIRE*.
ENEMY FIGHTERS COMING IN--
SIX OF THEM!
DO WE GO *THROUGH* 'EM OR TRY TO *OUTRUN* 'EM?
ALL OUR GUNS ARE *JAMMED!*
GRRRNNNKKK
GRRRNNNNKKKK
WE CAN'T FIGHT BACK!
DROP THE BOMBS. LET'S GET OUT OF HERE.
WHOK
WHOK
WHOK
BOMBS AWAY!
HOPE THERE'S A WORTHWHILE TARGET DOWN THERE.
NOPE. JUST WATER.
SPLISH
SPLASH
SPLOOSH
GLUG

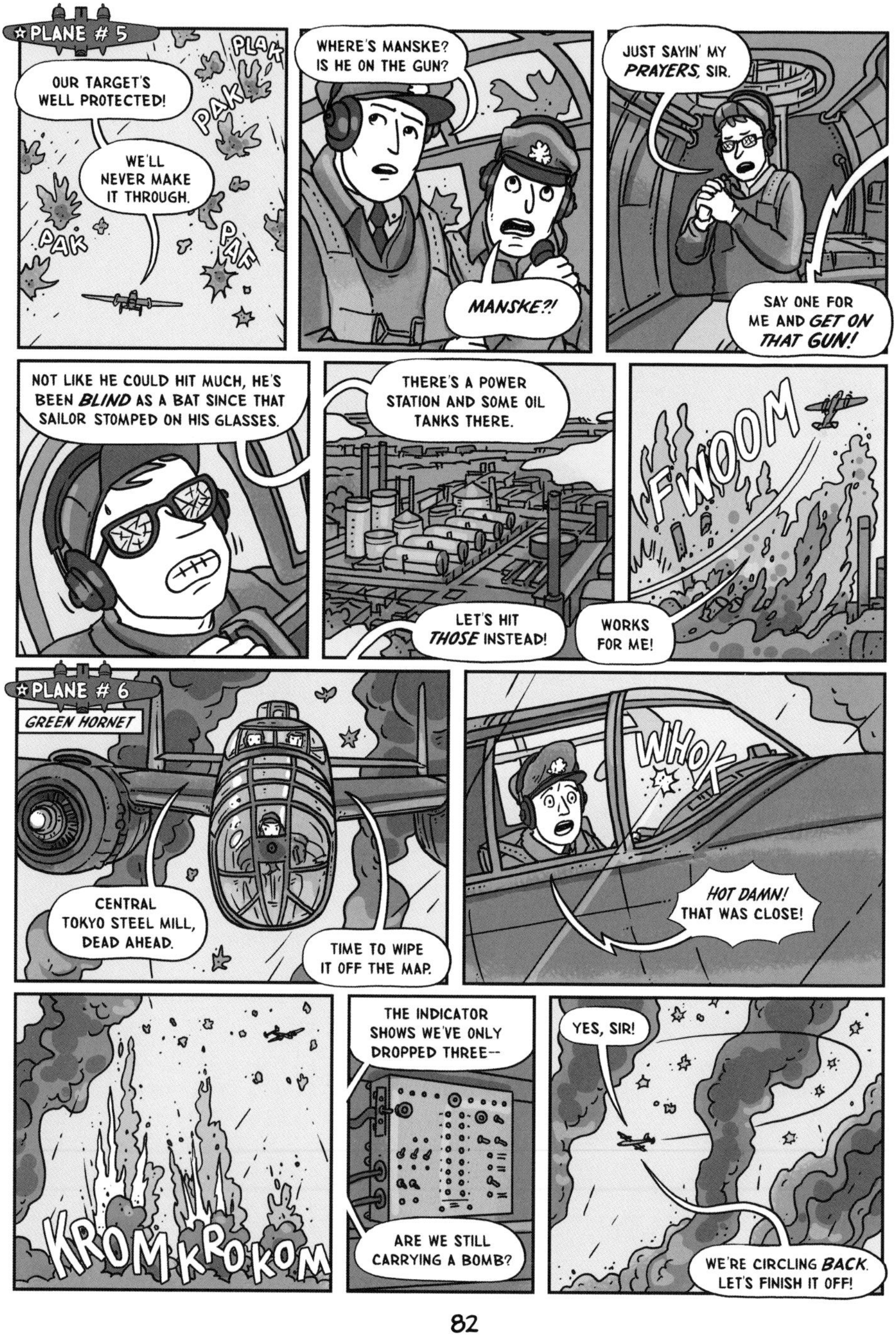
PLANE # 5
OUR TARGET'S WELL PROTECTED!
WE'LL NEVER MAKE IT THROUGH.
PLAK
PAK
PAK
PAF
WHERE'S MANSKE? IS HE ON THE GUN?
MANSKE?!
JUST SAYIN' MY PRAYERS, SIR.
SAY ONE FOR ME AND GET ON THAT GUN!
NOT LIKE HE COULD HIT MUCH, HE'S BEEN BLIND AS A BAT SINCE THAT SAILOR STOMPED ON HIS GLASSES.
THERE'S A POWER STATION AND SOME OIL TANKS THERE.
LET'S HIT THOSE INSTEAD!
FWOOM
WORKS FOR ME!
PLANE # 6
GREEN HORNET
CENTRAL TOKYO STEEL MILL, DEAD AHEAD.
TIME TO WIPE IT OFF THE MAP.
WHOK
HOT DAMN! THAT WAS CLOSE!
KROMKROKOM
THE INDICATOR SHOWS WE'VE ONLY DROPPED THREE--
ARE WE STILL CARRYING A BOMB?
YES, SIR!
WE'RE CIRCLING BACK. LET'S FINISH IT OFF!

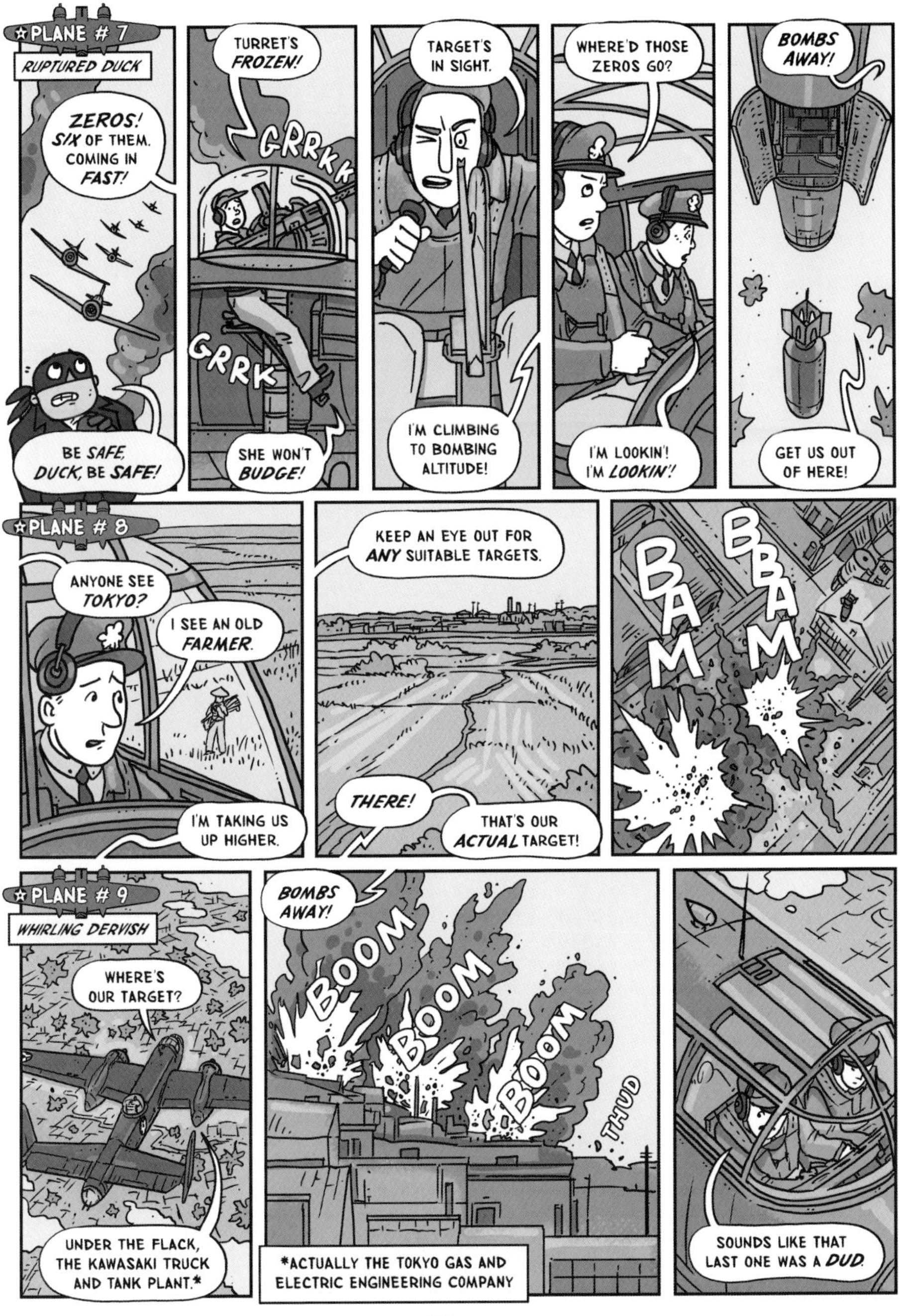

PLANE # 7
RUPTURED DUCK
ZEROS! SIX OF THEM. COMING IN FAST!
BE SAFE, DUCK, BE SAFE!
TURRET'S FROZEN!
GRRKK
GRRK
SHE WON'T BUDGE!
TARGET'S IN SIGHT.
I'M CLIMBING TO BOMBING ALTITUDE!
WHERE'D THOSE ZEROS GO?
I'M LOOKIN'! I'M LOOKIN'!
BOMBS AWAY!
GET US OUT OF HERE!
PLANE # 8
ANYONE SEE TOKYO?
I SEE AN OLD FARMER.
I'M TAKING US UP HIGHER.
KEEP AN EYE OUT FOR ANY SUITABLE TARGETS.
THERE!
THAT'S OUR ACTUAL TARGET!
BAM
BAM
PLANE # 9
WHIRLING DERVISH
WHERE'S OUR TARGET?
UNDER THE FLACK, THE KAWASAKI TRUCK AND TANK PLANT.*
BOMBS AWAY!
BOOM
BOOM
BOOM
THUD
*ACTUALLY THE TOKYO GAS AND ELECTRIC ENGINEERING COMPANY
SOUNDS LIKE THAT LAST ONE WAS A DUD.

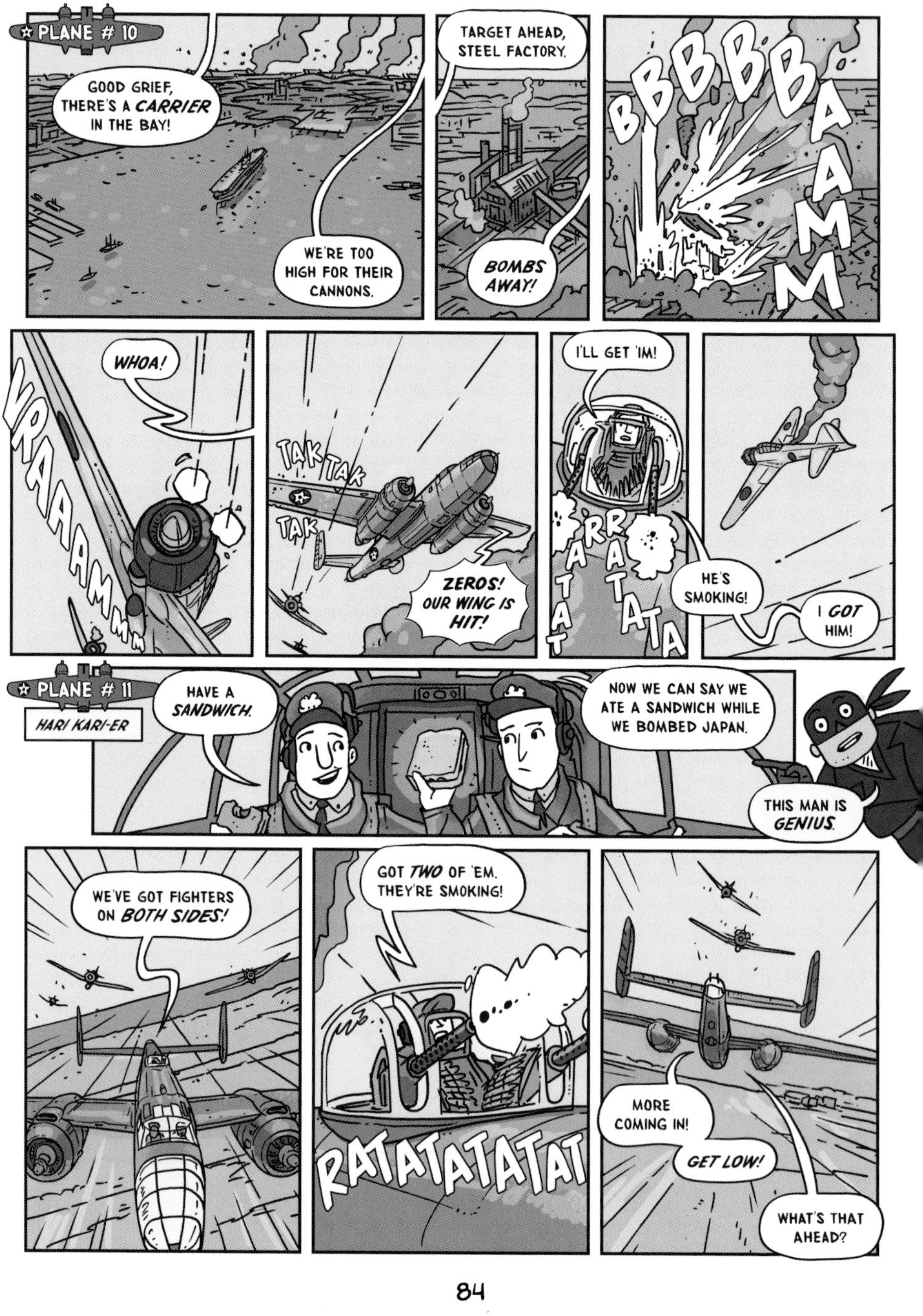

PLANE # 10
GOOD GRIEF, THERE'S A *CARRIER* IN THE BAY!
WE'RE TOO HIGH FOR THEIR CANNONS.
TARGET AHEAD, STEEL FACTORY.
BOMBS AWAY!
BBBBBAAMM
WHOA!
VRAAAAMMMM
TAK TAK TAK
ZEROS! OUR WING IS HIT!
I'LL GET 'IM!
TATAT RATATATA
HE'S SMOKING!
I *GOT* HIM!
PLANE # 11
HARI KARI-ER
HAVE A *SANDWICH.*
NOW WE CAN SAY WE ATE A SANDWICH WHILE WE BOMBED JAPAN.
THIS MAN IS *GENIUS.*
WE'VE GOT FIGHTERS ON *BOTH SIDES!*
GOT *TWO* OF 'EM. THEY'RE SMOKING!
RATATATATAT
MORE COMING IN!
GET LOW!
WHAT'S THAT AHEAD?

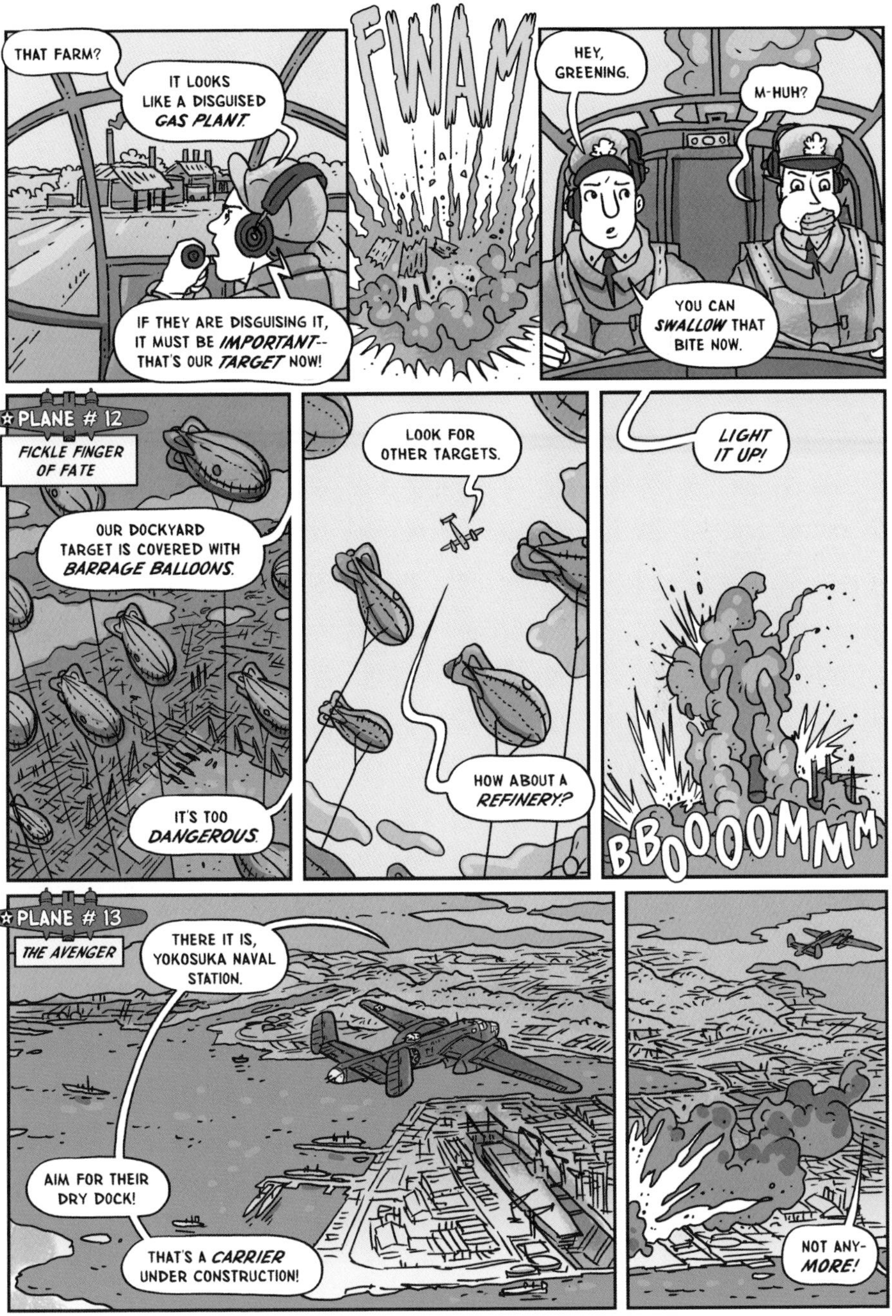
THAT FARM?
IT LOOKS LIKE A DISGUISED GAS PLANT.
IF THEY ARE DISGUISING IT, IT MUST BE IMPORTANT-- THAT'S OUR TARGET NOW!
FWAM
HEY, GREENING.
M-HUH?
YOU CAN SWALLOW THAT BITE NOW.
PLANE # 12
FICKLE FINGER OF FATE
OUR DOCKYARD TARGET IS COVERED WITH BARRAGE BALLOONS.
IT'S TOO DANGEROUS.
LOOK FOR OTHER TARGETS.
HOW ABOUT A REFINERY?
LIGHT IT UP!
BBOOOOMMM
PLANE # 13
THE AVENGER
THERE IT IS, YOKOSUKA NAVAL STATION.
AIM FOR THEIR DRY DOCK!
THAT'S A CARRIER UNDER CONSTRUCTION!
NOT ANY-MORE!

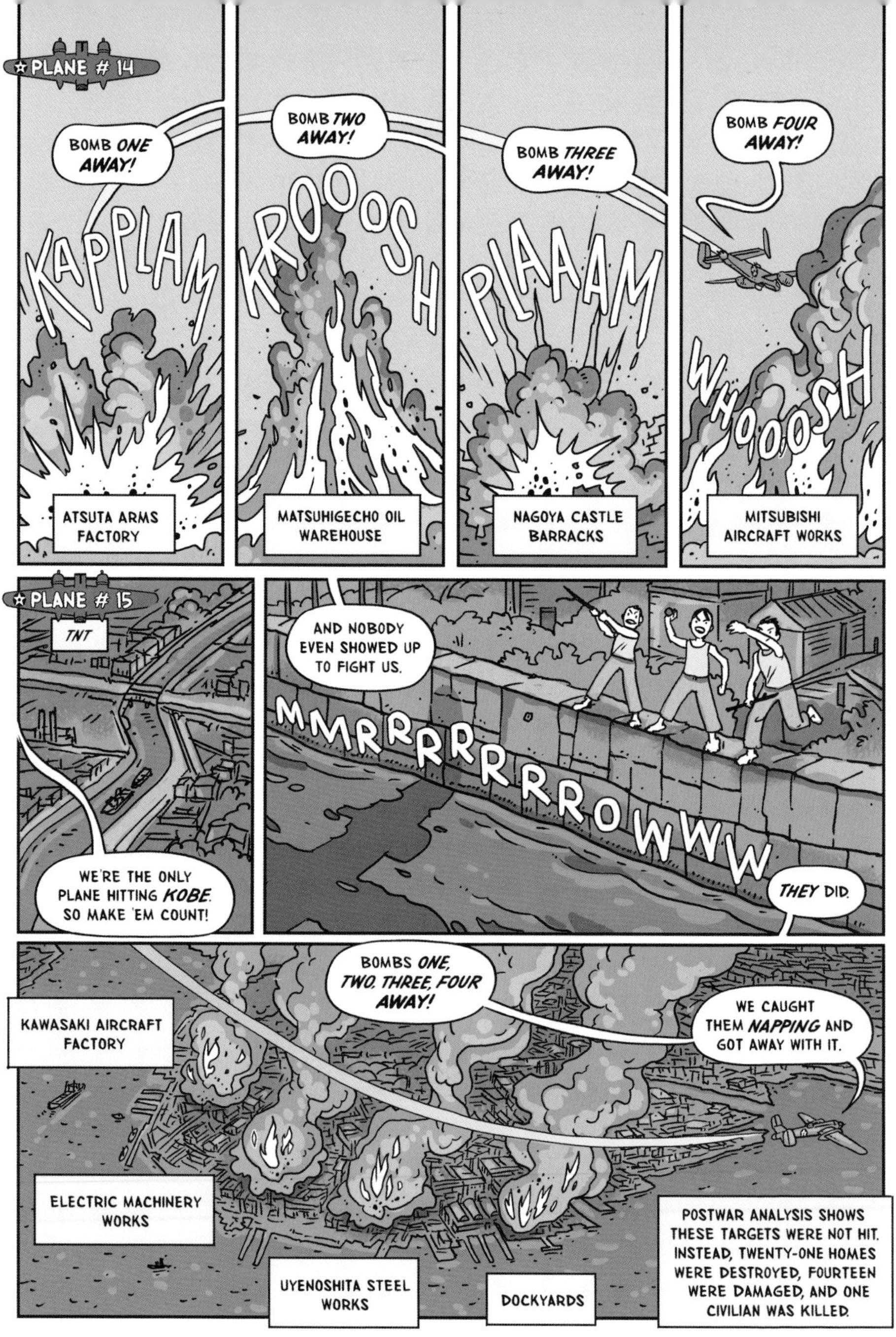
PLANE # 14
BOMB ONE AWAY!
KAPPLAM
ATSUTA ARMS FACTORY
BOMB TWO AWAY!
KROOOSH
MATSUHIGECHO OIL WAREHOUSE
BOMB THREE AWAY!
PLAAAAM
NAGOYA CASTLE BARRACKS
BOMB FOUR AWAY!
WHOOOOSH
MITSUBISHI AIRCRAFT WORKS
PLANE # 15
TNT
WE'RE THE ONLY PLANE HITTING KOBE. SO MAKE 'EM COUNT!
AND NOBODY EVEN SHOWED UP TO FIGHT US.
MMRRRRRRROWWW
THEY DID.
KAWASAKI AIRCRAFT FACTORY
BOMBS ONE, TWO, THREE, FOUR AWAY!
WE CAUGHT THEM NAPPING AND GOT AWAY WITH IT.
ELECTRIC MACHINERY WORKS
UYENOSHITA STEEL WORKS
DOCKYARDS
POSTWAR ANALYSIS SHOWS THESE TARGETS WERE NOT HIT. INSTEAD, TWENTY-ONE HOMES WERE DESTROYED, FOURTEEN WERE DAMAGED, AND ONE CIVILIAN WAS KILLED.

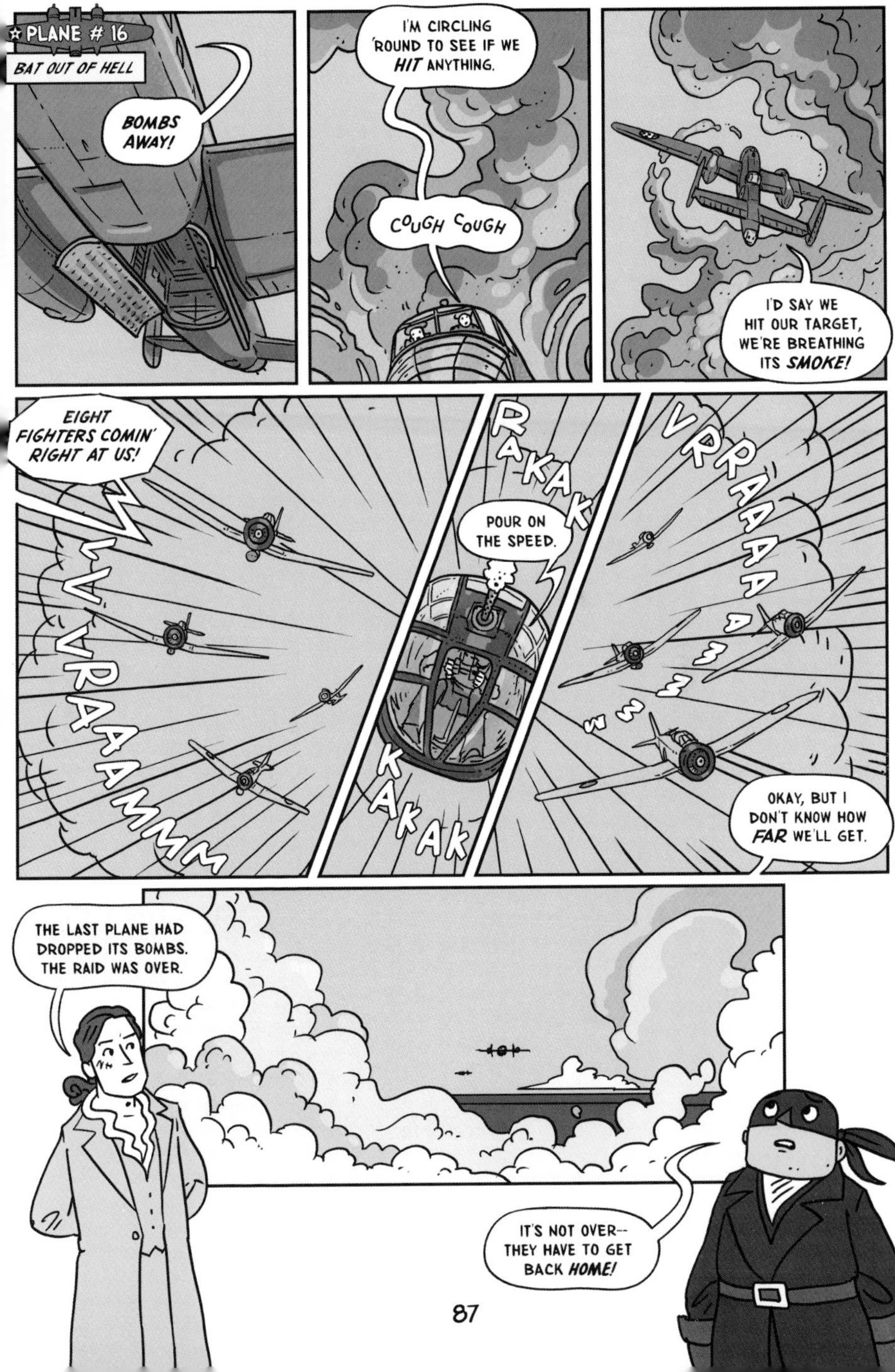
PLANE # 16
BAT OUT OF HELL
BOMBS AWAY!
I'M CIRCLING 'ROUND TO SEE IF WE HIT ANYTHING.
COUGH COUGH
I'D SAY WE HIT OUR TARGET, WE'RE BREATHING ITS SMOKE!
EIGHT FIGHTERS COMIN' RIGHT AT US!
VVRAAAMMM
RAKAKAK
POUR ON THE SPEED.
KAKAK
VRRAAAAAMMMM
OKAY, BUT I DON'T KNOW HOW FAR WE'LL GET.
THE LAST PLANE HAD DROPPED ITS BOMBS. THE RAID WAS OVER.
IT'S NOT OVER-- THEY HAVE TO GET BACK HOME!

CHAPTER 11

★ PLANE # 16

BAT OUT OF HELL

WE LOST THOSE FIGHTERS, BUT WE ARE *ALL* OUT OF GAS.

THAT'S *CHINA* DOWN THERE, *NANCHANG.*

THEN LET'S *JUMP!*

NANCHANG IS UNDER *JAPANESE* CONTROL.

WE DON'T REALLY HAVE A *CHOICE.*

REMEMBER: PUSH *AWAY* FROM THE PLANE, COUNT TO *TEN*, AND *PULL* THE CORD.

SO LONG, *BAT!*

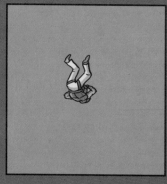

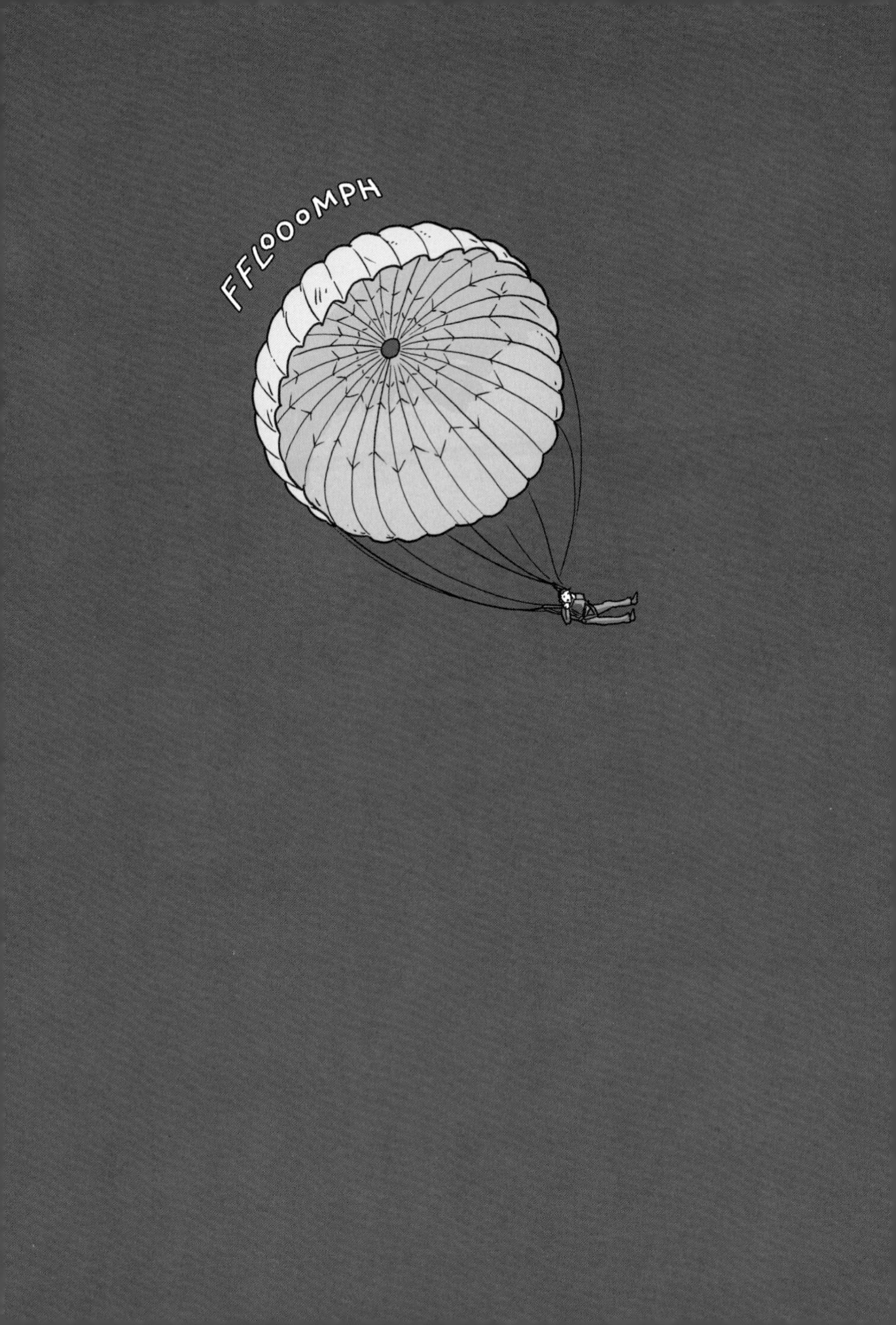
FFLOOOOMPH

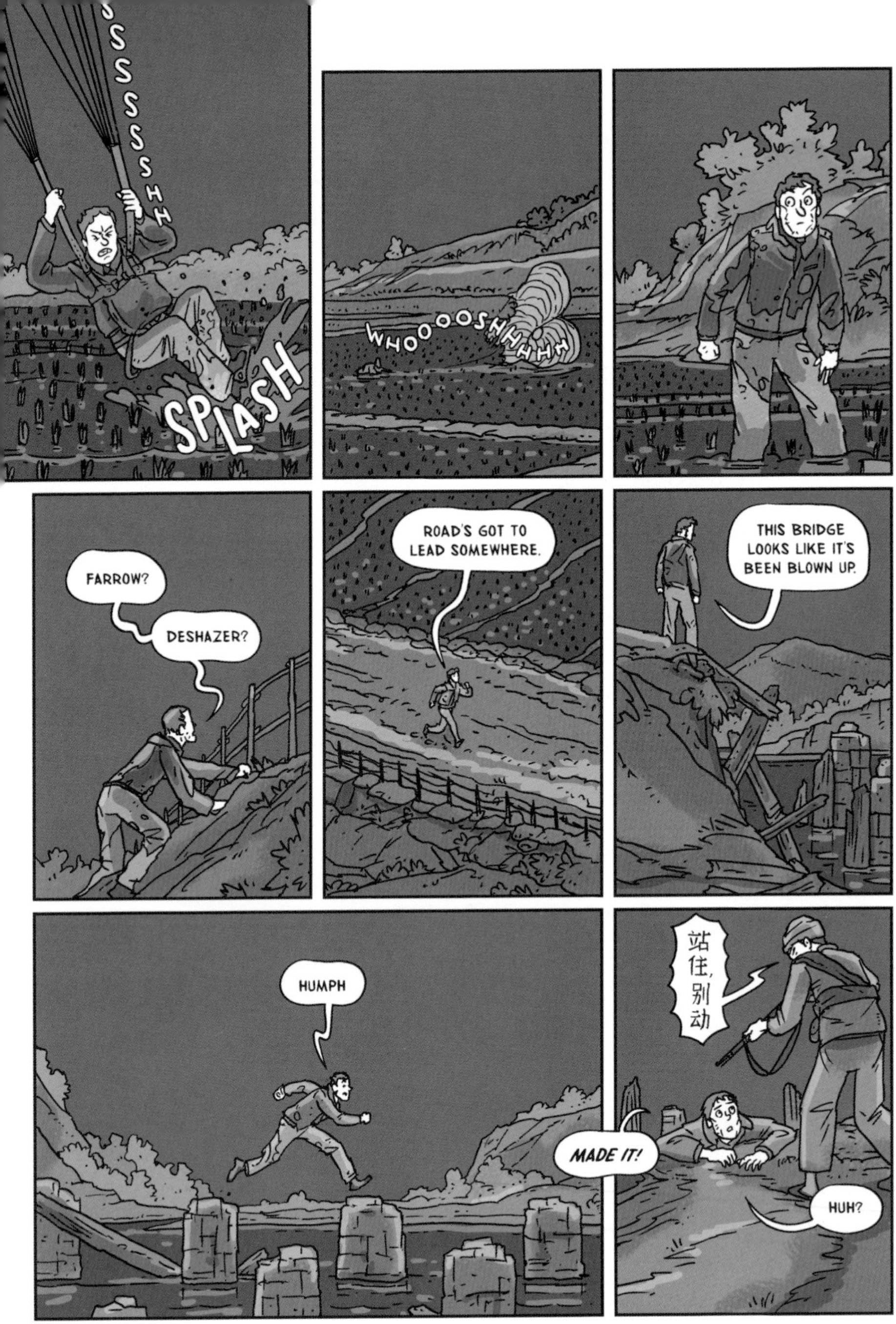
SSSSSSHH
SPLASH
WHOOOOSHHHHH
FARROW?
DESHAZER?
ROAD'S GOT TO LEAD SOMEWHERE.
THIS BRIDGE LOOKS LIKE IT'S BEEN BLOWN UP.
HUMPH
站住,别动
MADE IT!
HUH?

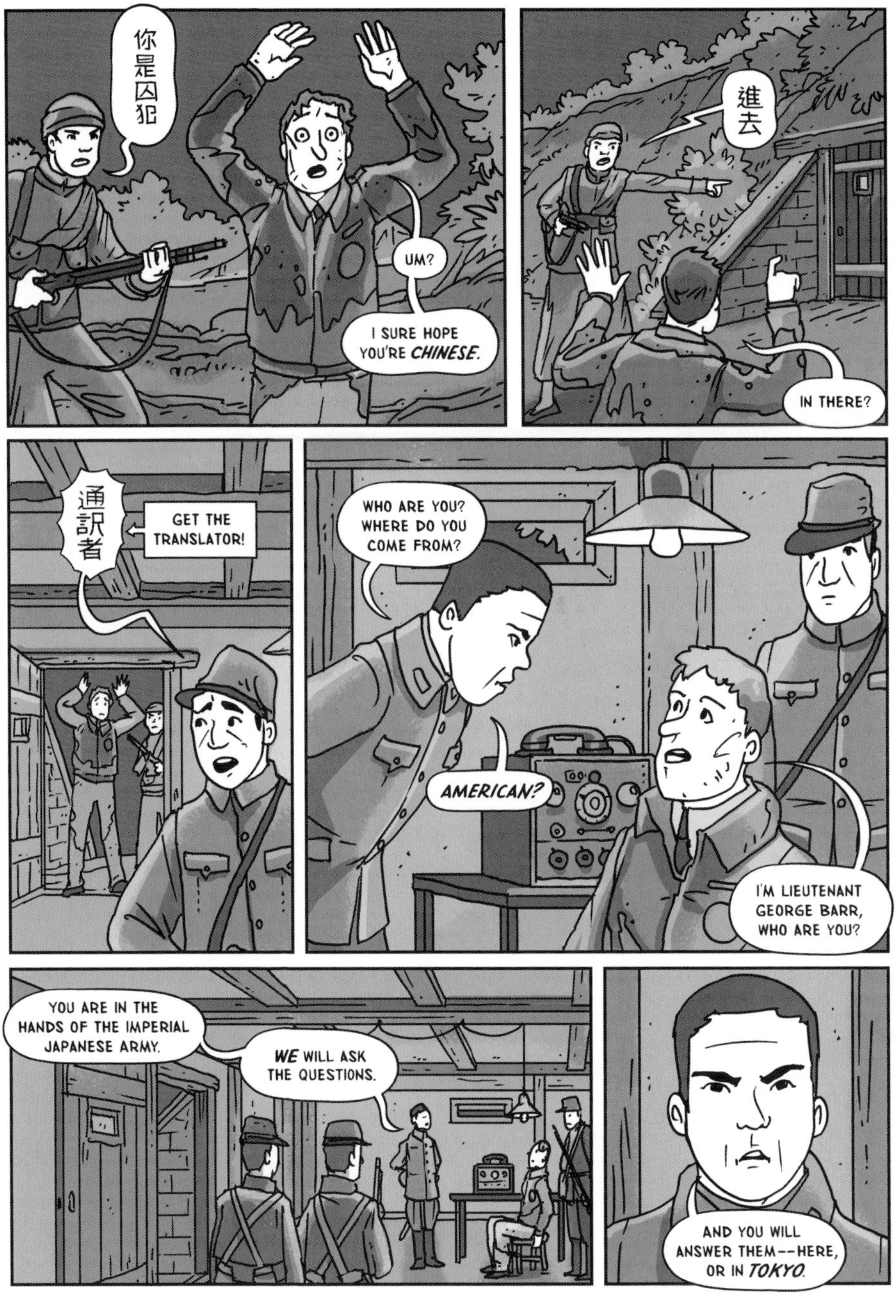

你是囚犯
UM?
I SURE HOPE YOU'RE *CHINESE*.
進去
IN THERE?
通訳者
GET THE TRANSLATOR!
WHO ARE YOU? WHERE DO YOU COME FROM?
AMERICAN?
I'M LIEUTENANT GEORGE BARR, WHO ARE YOU?
YOU ARE IN THE HANDS OF THE IMPERIAL JAPANESE ARMY.
WE WILL ASK THE QUESTIONS.
AND YOU WILL ANSWER THEM--HERE, OR IN *TOKYO*.

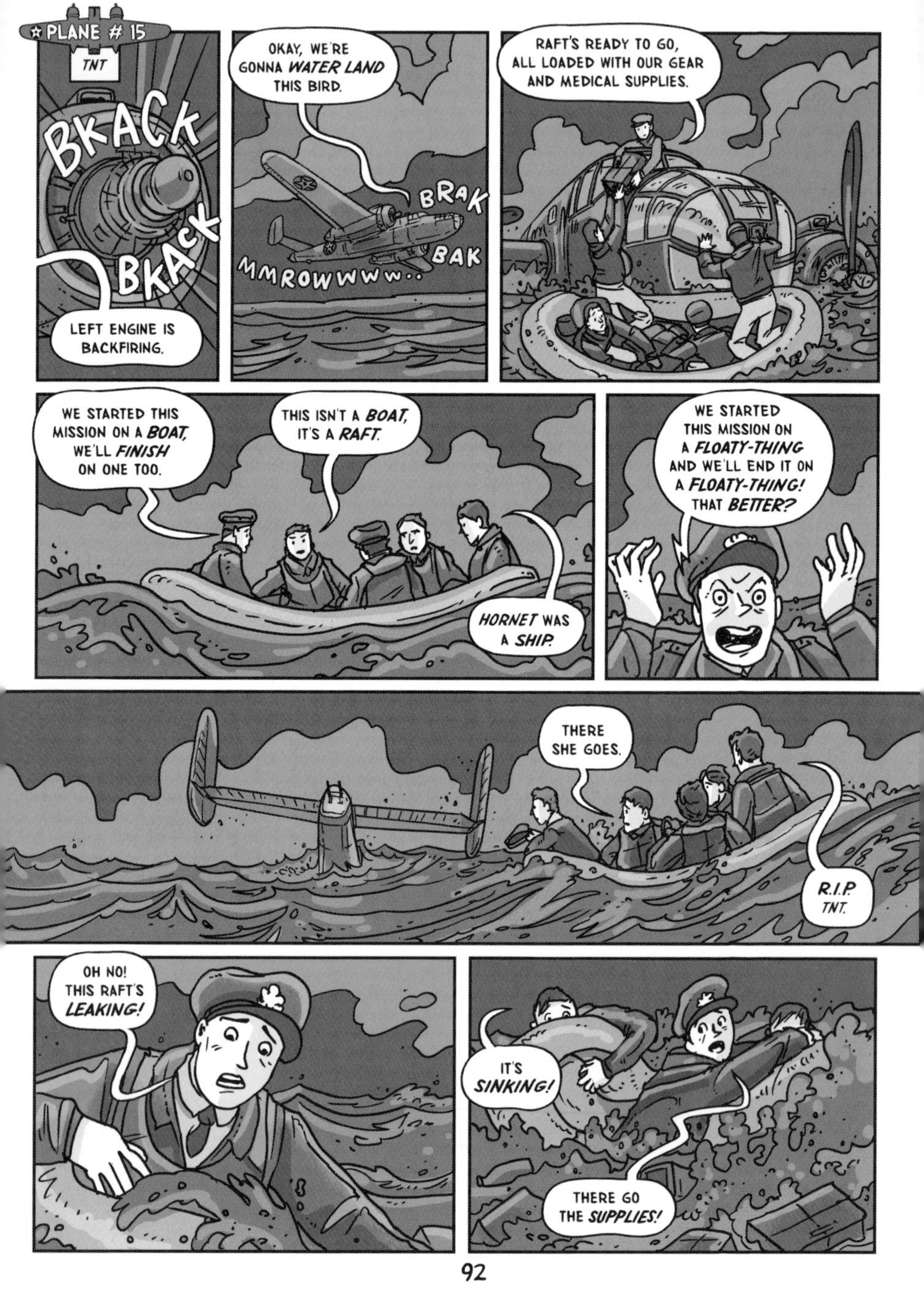
PLANE # 15
TNT
BKACK
BKACK
LEFT ENGINE IS BACKFIRING.
OKAY, WE'RE GONNA *WATER LAND* THIS BIRD.
BRAK
BAK
MMROWWWW..
RAFT'S READY TO GO, ALL LOADED WITH OUR GEAR AND MEDICAL SUPPLIES.
WE STARTED THIS MISSION ON A *BOAT*, WE'LL *FINISH* ON ONE TOO.
THIS ISN'T A *BOAT*, IT'S A *RAFT*.
HORNET WAS A *SHIP*.
WE STARTED THIS MISSION ON A *FLOATY-THING* AND WE'LL END IT ON A *FLOATY-THING!* THAT *BETTER?*
THERE SHE GOES.
R.I.P. TNT.
OH NO! THIS RAFT'S *LEAKING!*
IT'S *SINKING!*
THERE GO THE *SUPPLIES!*

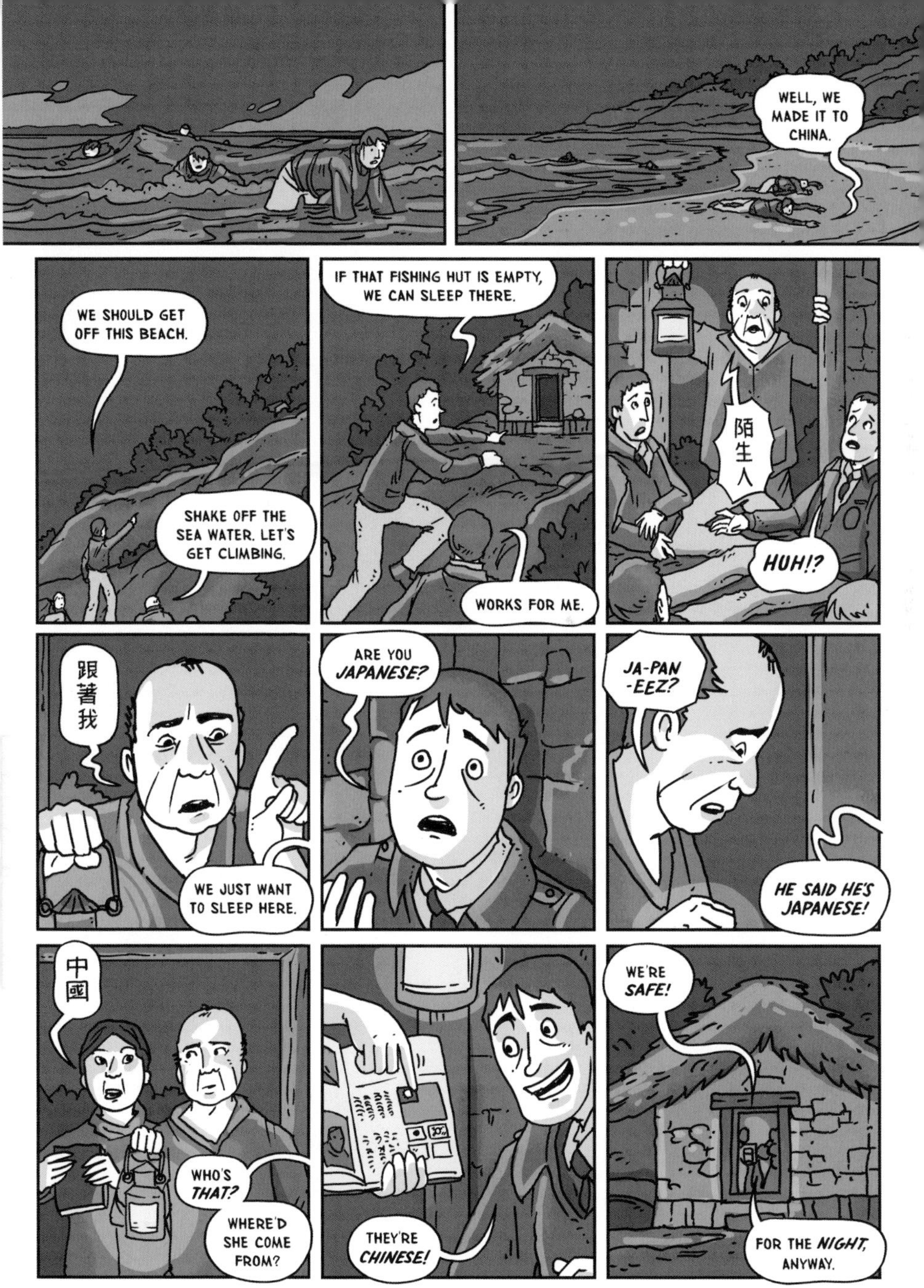
WELL, WE MADE IT TO CHINA.
WE SHOULD GET OFF THIS BEACH.
SHAKE OFF THE SEA WATER. LET'S GET CLIMBING.
IF THAT FISHING HUT IS EMPTY, WE CAN SLEEP THERE.
WORKS FOR ME.
陌生人
HUH!?
跟著我
WE JUST WANT TO SLEEP HERE.
ARE YOU *JAPANESE?*
JA-PAN -EEZ?
HE SAID HE'S JAPANESE!
中國
WHO'S *THAT?*
WHERE'D SHE COME FROM?
THEY'RE *CHINESE!*
WE'RE *SAFE!*
FOR THE *NIGHT,* ANYWAY.

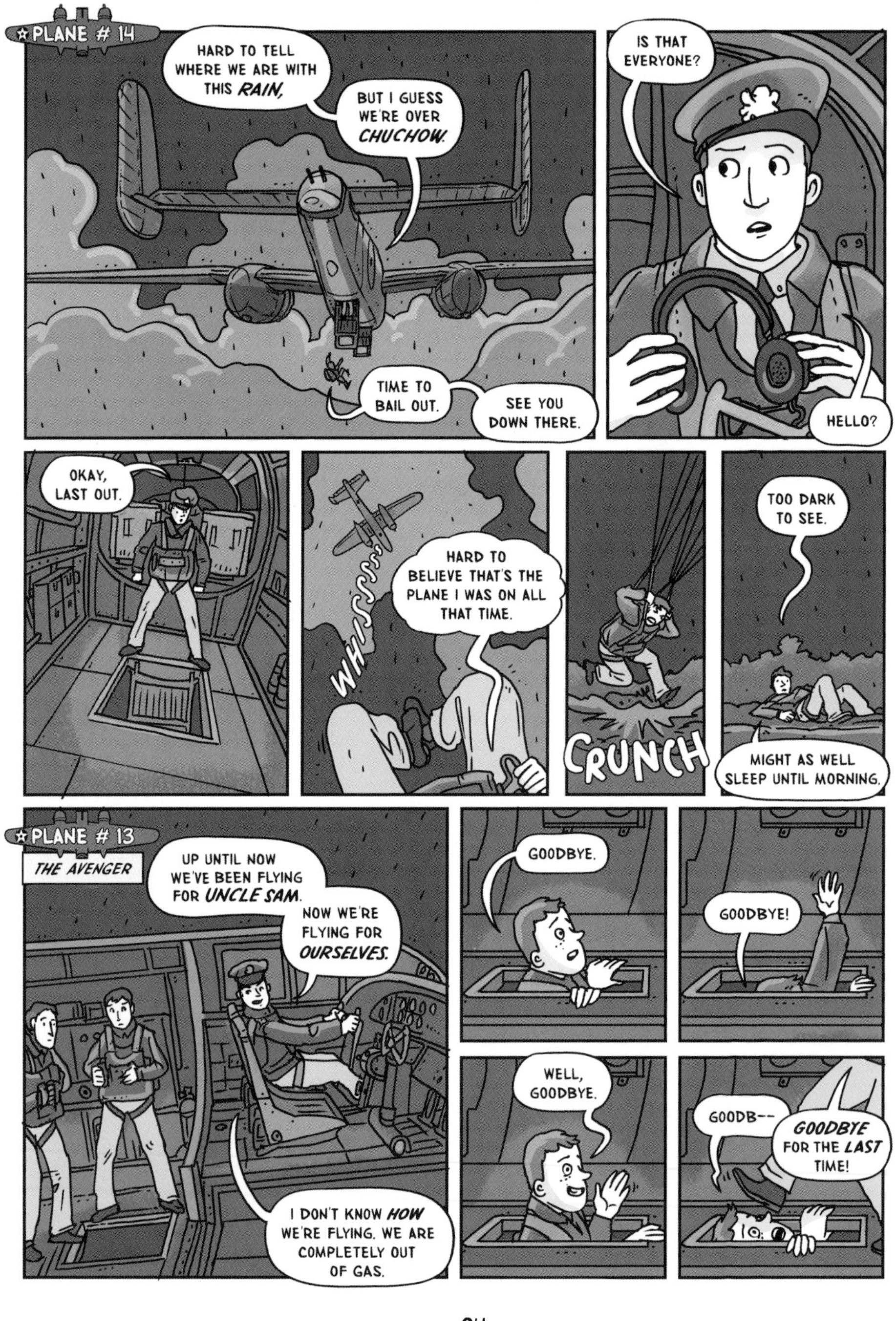
PLANE # 14
HARD TO TELL WHERE WE ARE WITH THIS RAIN,
BUT I GUESS WE'RE OVER CHUCHOW.
TIME TO BAIL OUT.
SEE YOU DOWN THERE.
IS THAT EVERYONE?
HELLO?
OKAY, LAST OUT.
WHISSSS
HARD TO BELIEVE THAT'S THE PLANE I WAS ON ALL THAT TIME.
CRUNCH
TOO DARK TO SEE.
MIGHT AS WELL SLEEP UNTIL MORNING.
PLANE # 13
THE AVENGER
UP UNTIL NOW WE'VE BEEN FLYING FOR UNCLE SAM.
NOW WE'RE FLYING FOR OURSELVES.
I DON'T KNOW HOW WE'RE FLYING. WE ARE COMPLETELY OUT OF GAS.
GOODBYE.
GOODBYE!
WELL, GOODBYE.
GOODB--
GOODBYE FOR THE LAST TIME!

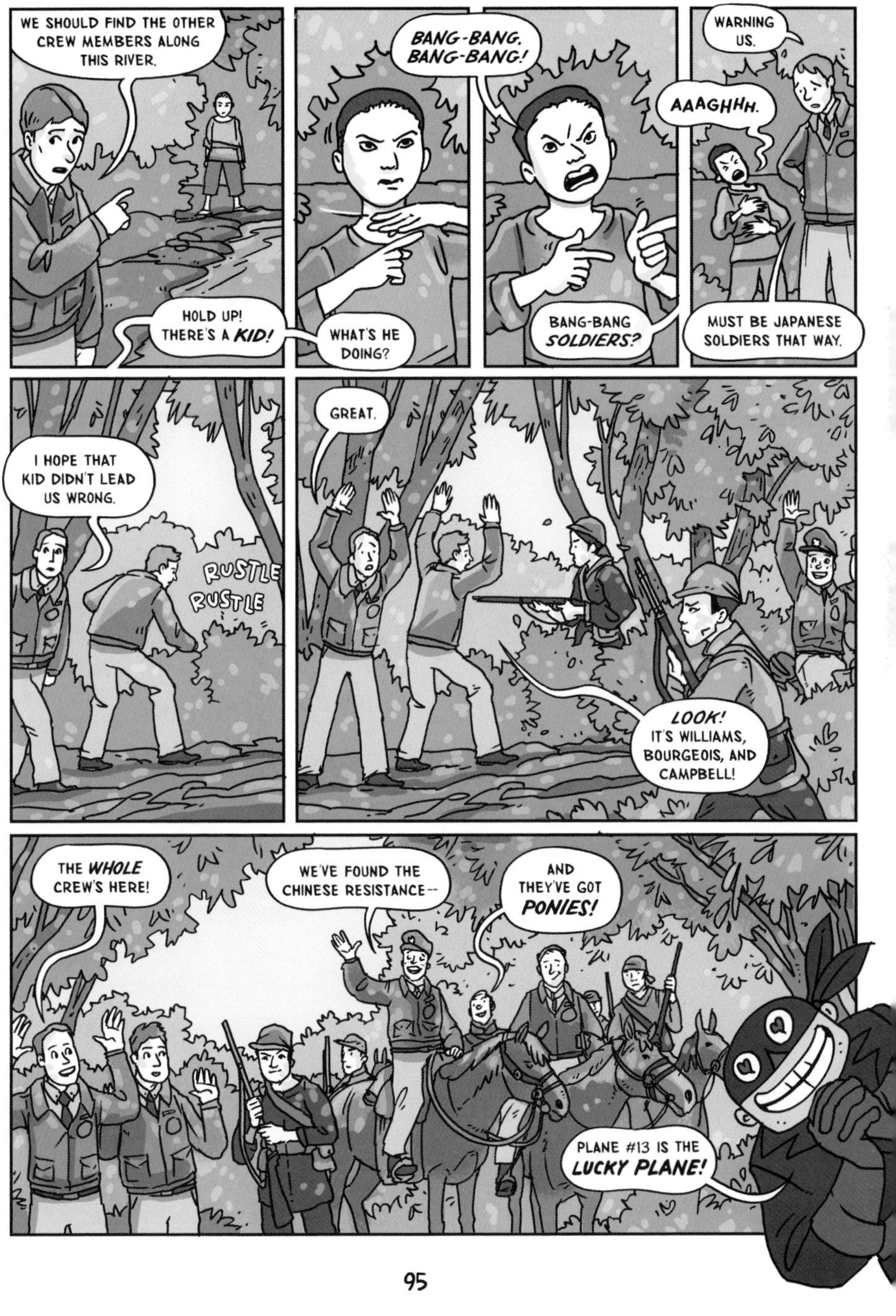

WE SHOULD FIND THE OTHER CREW MEMBERS ALONG THIS RIVER.
HOLD UP! THERE'S A KID!
WHAT'S HE DOING?
BANG-BANG. BANG-BANG!
BANG-BANG SOLDIERS?
WARNING US.
AAAGHHH.
MUST BE JAPANESE SOLDIERS THAT WAY.
I HOPE THAT KID DIDN'T LEAD US WRONG.
RUSTLE
RUSTLE
GREAT.
LOOK! IT'S WILLIAMS, BOURGEOIS, AND CAMPBELL!
THE WHOLE CREW'S HERE!
WE'VE FOUND THE CHINESE RESISTANCE--
AND THEY'VE GOT PONIES!
PLANE #13 IS THE LUCKY PLANE!

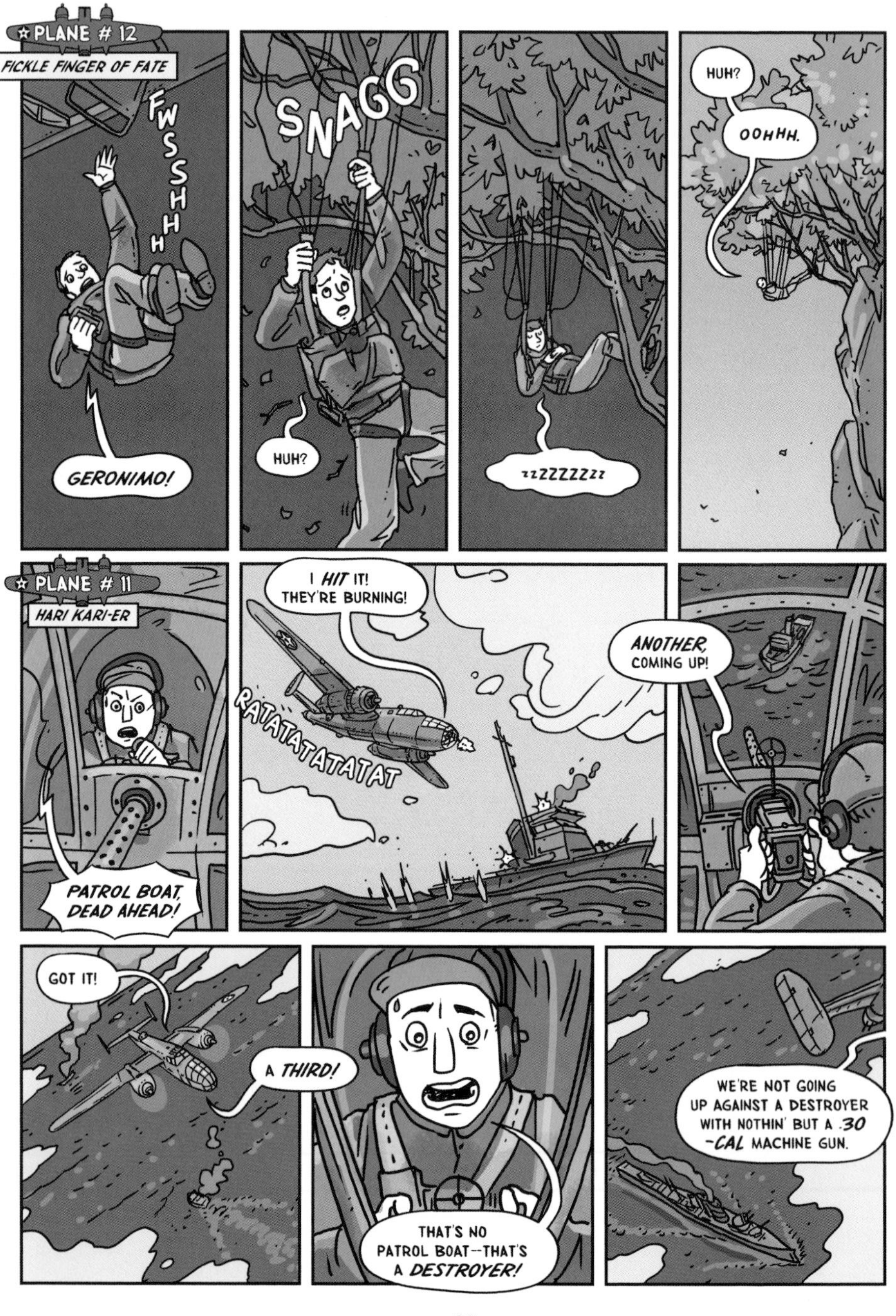
PLANE # 12
FICKLE FINGER OF FATE
FWSSHHH
GERONIMO!
SNAGG
HUH?
zzZZZZZzz
HUH?
OOHHH.
PLANE # 11
HARI KARI-ER
PATROL BOAT, DEAD AHEAD!
I HIT IT! THEY'RE BURNING!
RATATATATATATAT
ANOTHER, COMING UP!
GOT IT!
A THIRD!
THAT'S NO PATROL BOAT--THAT'S A DESTROYER!
WE'RE NOT GOING UP AGAINST A DESTROYER WITH NOTHIN' BUT A .30 -CAL MACHINE GUN.

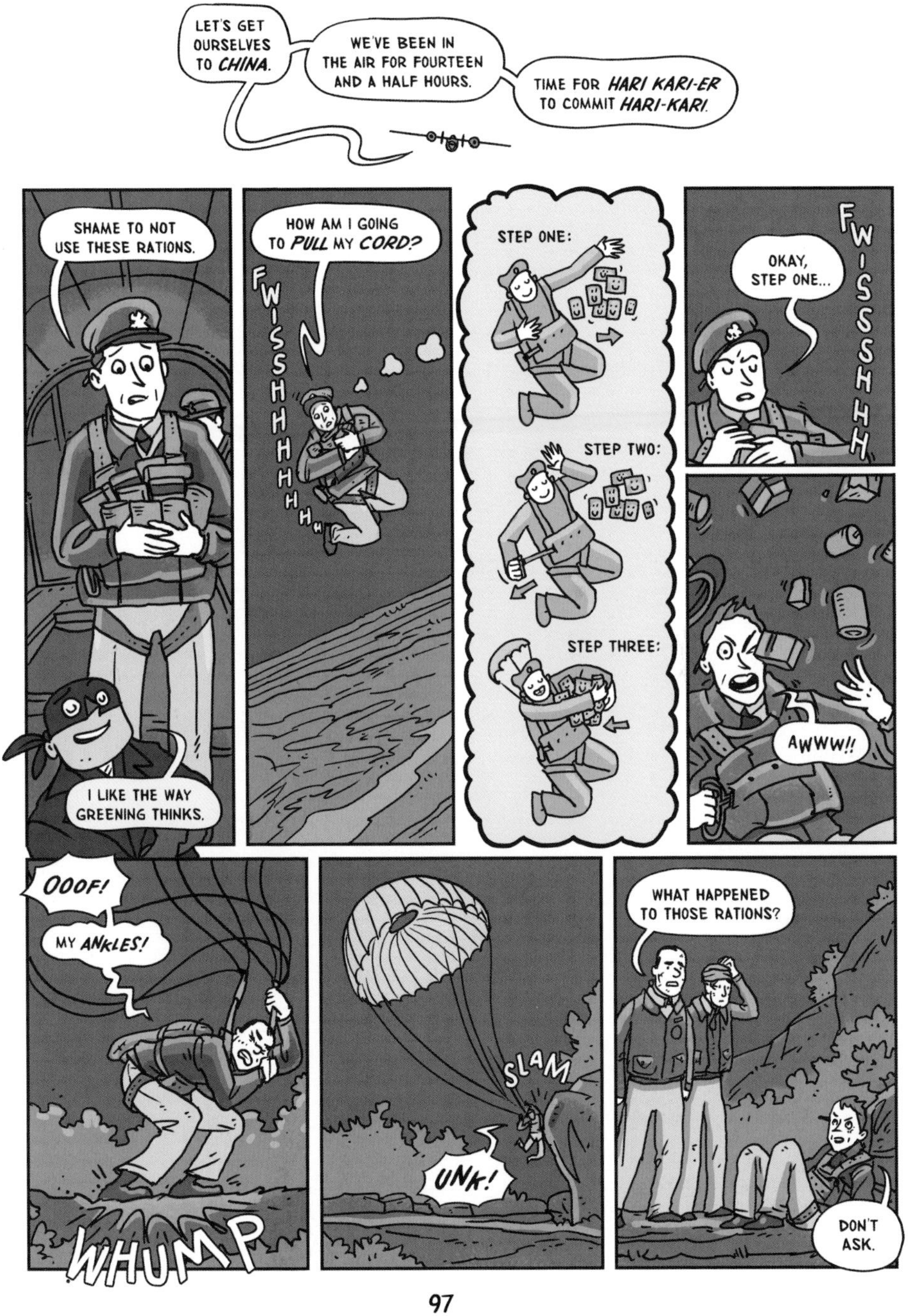
LET'S GET OURSELVES TO CHINA.
WE'VE BEEN IN THE AIR FOR FOURTEEN AND A HALF HOURS.
TIME FOR HARI KARI-ER TO COMMIT HARI-KARI.
SHAME TO NOT USE THESE RATIONS.
I LIKE THE WAY GREENING THINKS.
HOW AM I GOING TO PULL MY CORD?
FWISSHHHHHHH
STEP ONE:
STEP TWO:
STEP THREE:
FWISSSHHH
OKAY, STEP ONE...
AWWW!!
OOOF!
MY ANKLES!
WHUMP
SLAM
UNK!
WHAT HAPPENED TO THOSE RATIONS?
DON'T ASK.

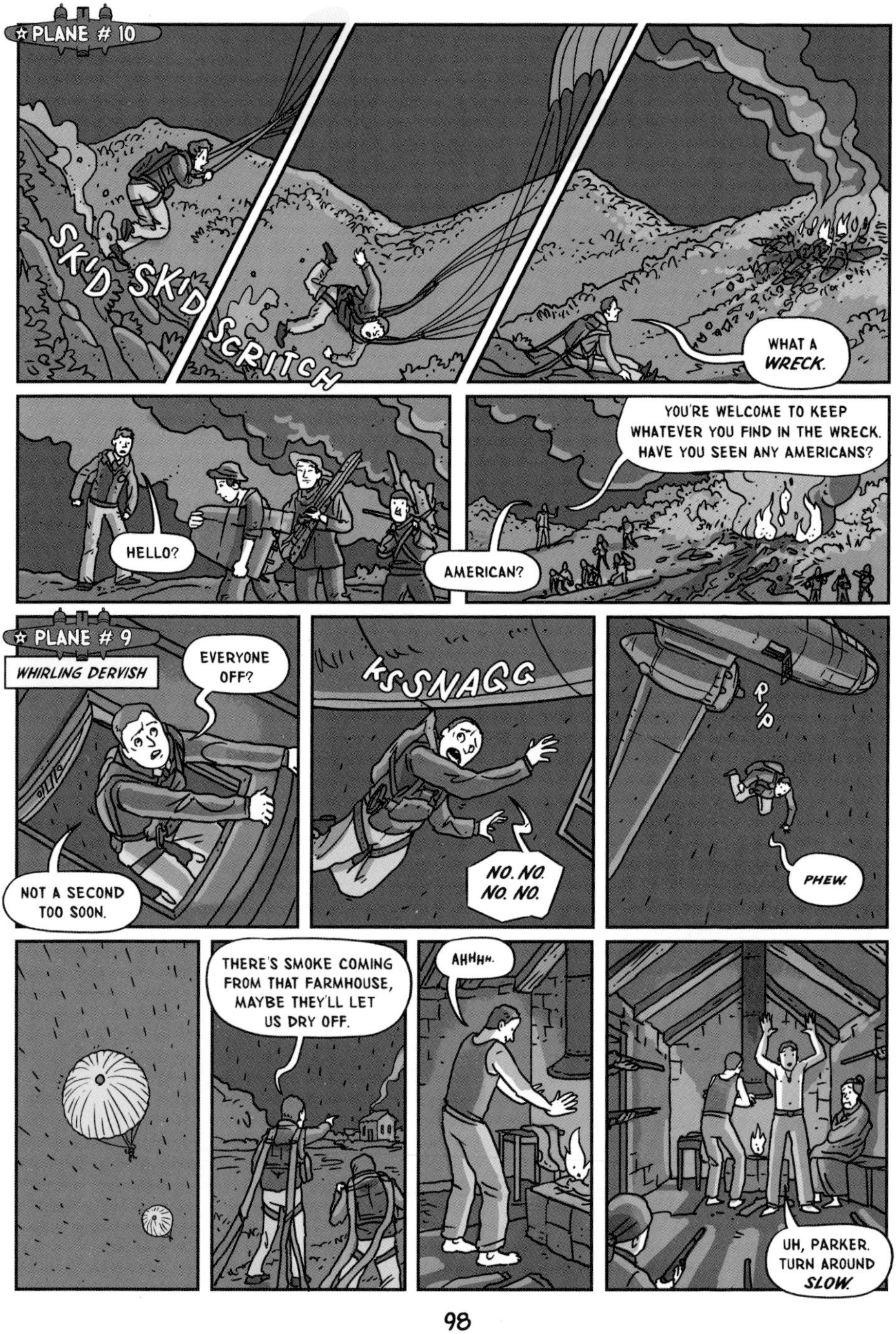

PLANE # 10
SK'D SK'D SCRITCH
WHAT A WRECK.
HELLO?
YOU'RE WELCOME TO KEEP WHATEVER YOU FIND IN THE WRECK. HAVE YOU SEEN ANY AMERICANS?
AMERICAN?
PLANE # 9
WHIRLING DERVISH
EVERYONE OFF?
NOT A SECOND TOO SOON.
KSSNAGG
NO. NO. NO. NO.
RIP
PHEW.
THERE'S SMOKE COMING FROM THAT FARMHOUSE, MAYBE THEY'LL LET US DRY OFF.
AHHHH.
UH, PARKER. TURN AROUND SLOW.

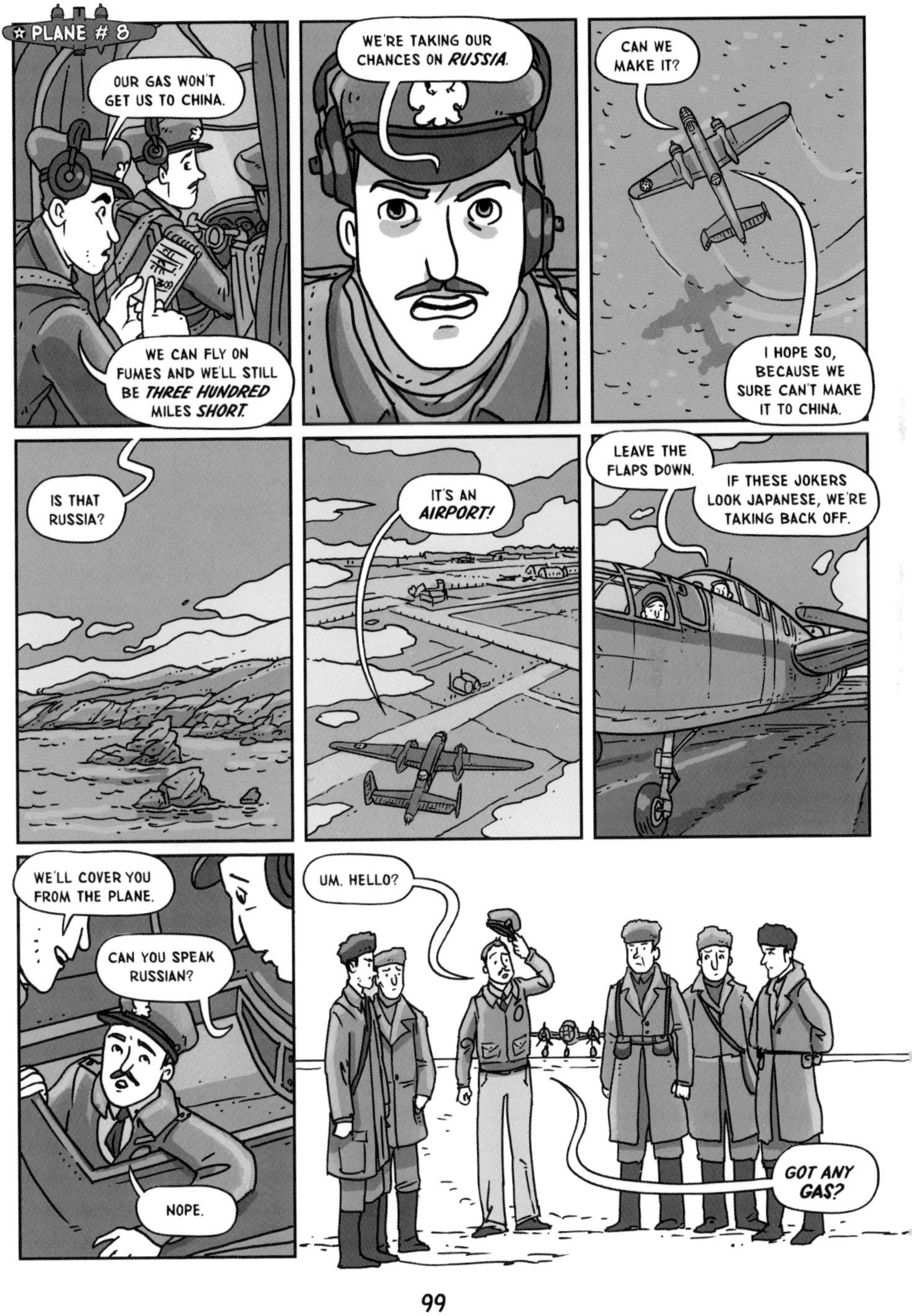
PLANE # 8
OUR GAS WON'T GET US TO CHINA.
WE CAN FLY ON FUMES AND WE'LL STILL BE THREE HUNDRED MILES SHORT.
WE'RE TAKING OUR CHANCES ON RUSSIA.
CAN WE MAKE IT?
I HOPE SO, BECAUSE WE SURE CAN'T MAKE IT TO CHINA.
IS THAT RUSSIA?
IT'S AN AIRPORT!
LEAVE THE FLAPS DOWN.
IF THESE JOKERS LOOK JAPANESE, WE'RE TAKING BACK OFF.
WE'LL COVER YOU FROM THE PLANE.
CAN YOU SPEAK RUSSIAN?
NOPE.
UM. HELLO?
GOT ANY GAS?

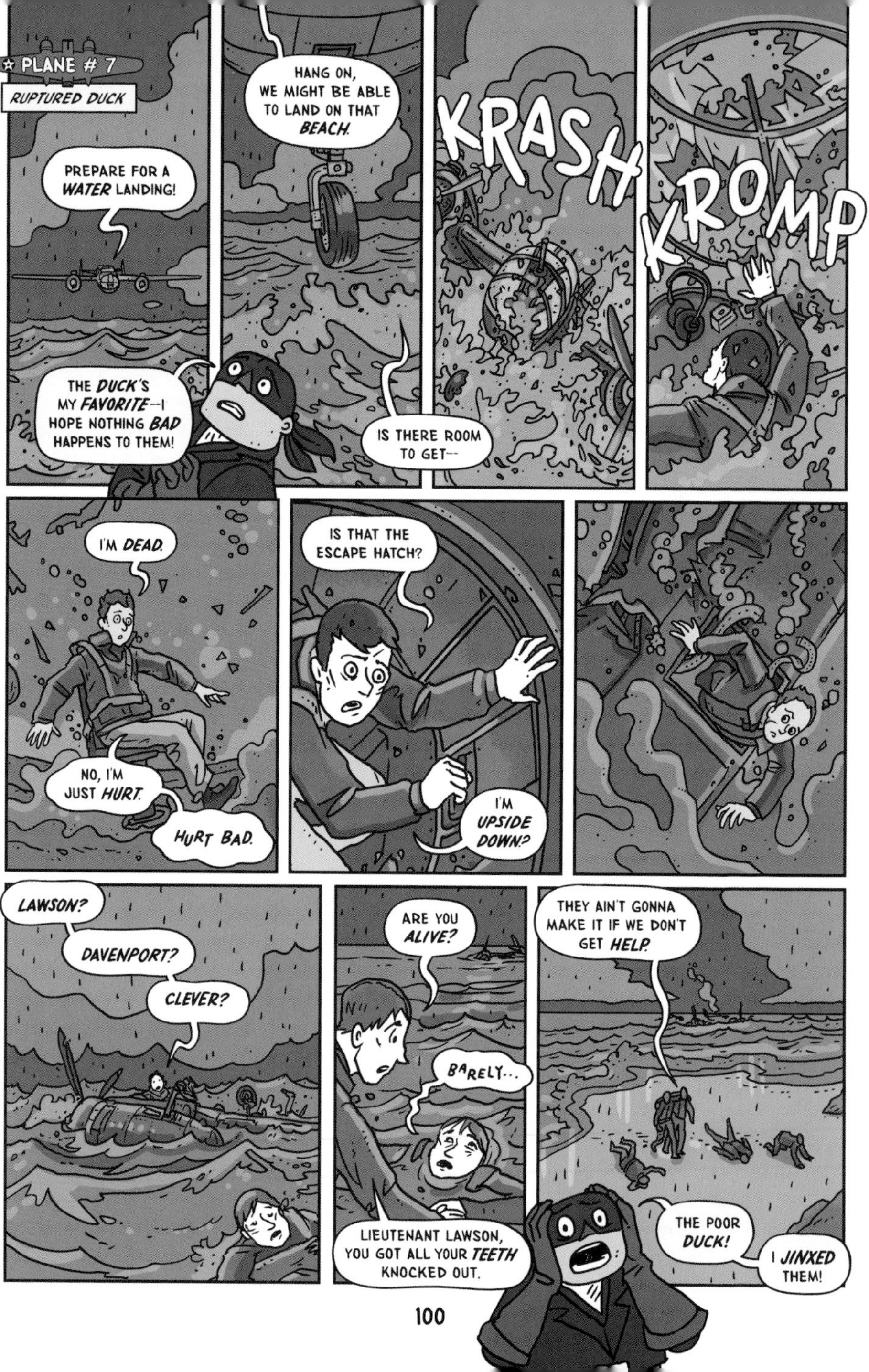
PLANE # 7
RUPTURED DUCK
PREPARE FOR A WATER LANDING!
HANG ON, WE MIGHT BE ABLE TO LAND ON THAT BEACH.
THE DUCK'S MY FAVORITE--I HOPE NOTHING BAD HAPPENS TO THEM!
IS THERE ROOM TO GET--
KRASH
KROMP
I'M DEAD.
NO, I'M JUST HURT.
HURT BAD.
IS THAT THE ESCAPE HATCH?
I'M UPSIDE DOWN?
LAWSON?
DAVENPORT?
CLEVER?
ARE YOU ALIVE?
BARELY...
LIEUTENANT LAWSON, YOU GOT ALL YOUR TEETH KNOCKED OUT.
THEY AIN'T GONNA MAKE IT IF WE DON'T GET HELP.
THE POOR DUCK!
I JINXED THEM!

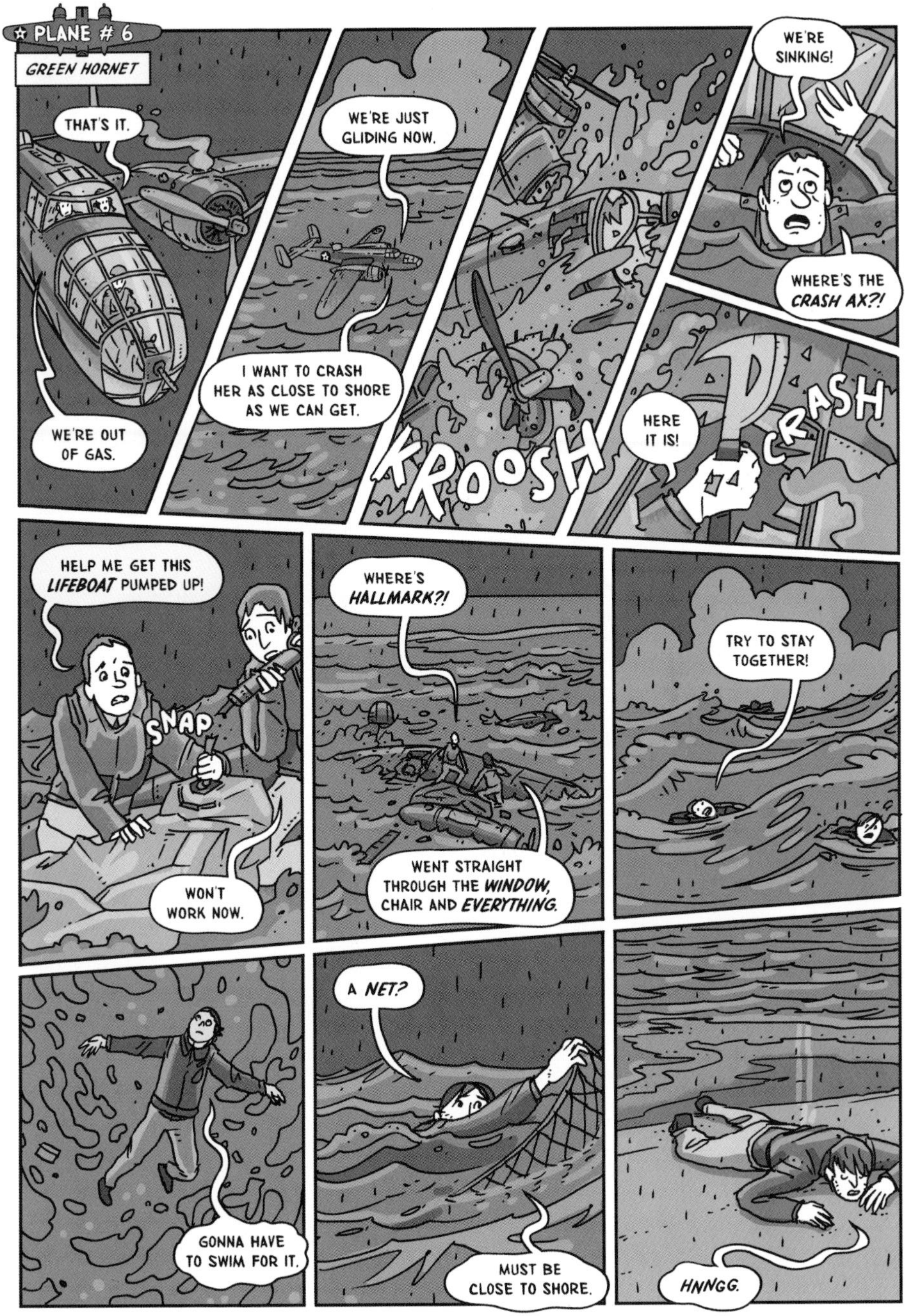

PLANE # 6
GREEN HORNET
THAT'S IT.
WE'RE OUT OF GAS.
WE'RE JUST GLIDING NOW.
I WANT TO CRASH HER AS CLOSE TO SHORE AS WE CAN GET.
KROOSH
WE'RE SINKING!
WHERE'S THE CRASH AX?!
HERE IT IS!
CRASH
HELP ME GET THIS LIFEBOAT PUMPED UP!
SNAP
WON'T WORK NOW.
WHERE'S HALLMARK?!
WENT STRAIGHT THROUGH THE WINDOW, CHAIR AND EVERYTHING.
TRY TO STAY TOGETHER!
GONNA HAVE TO SWIM FOR IT.
A NET?
MUST BE CLOSE TO SHORE.
HNNGG.

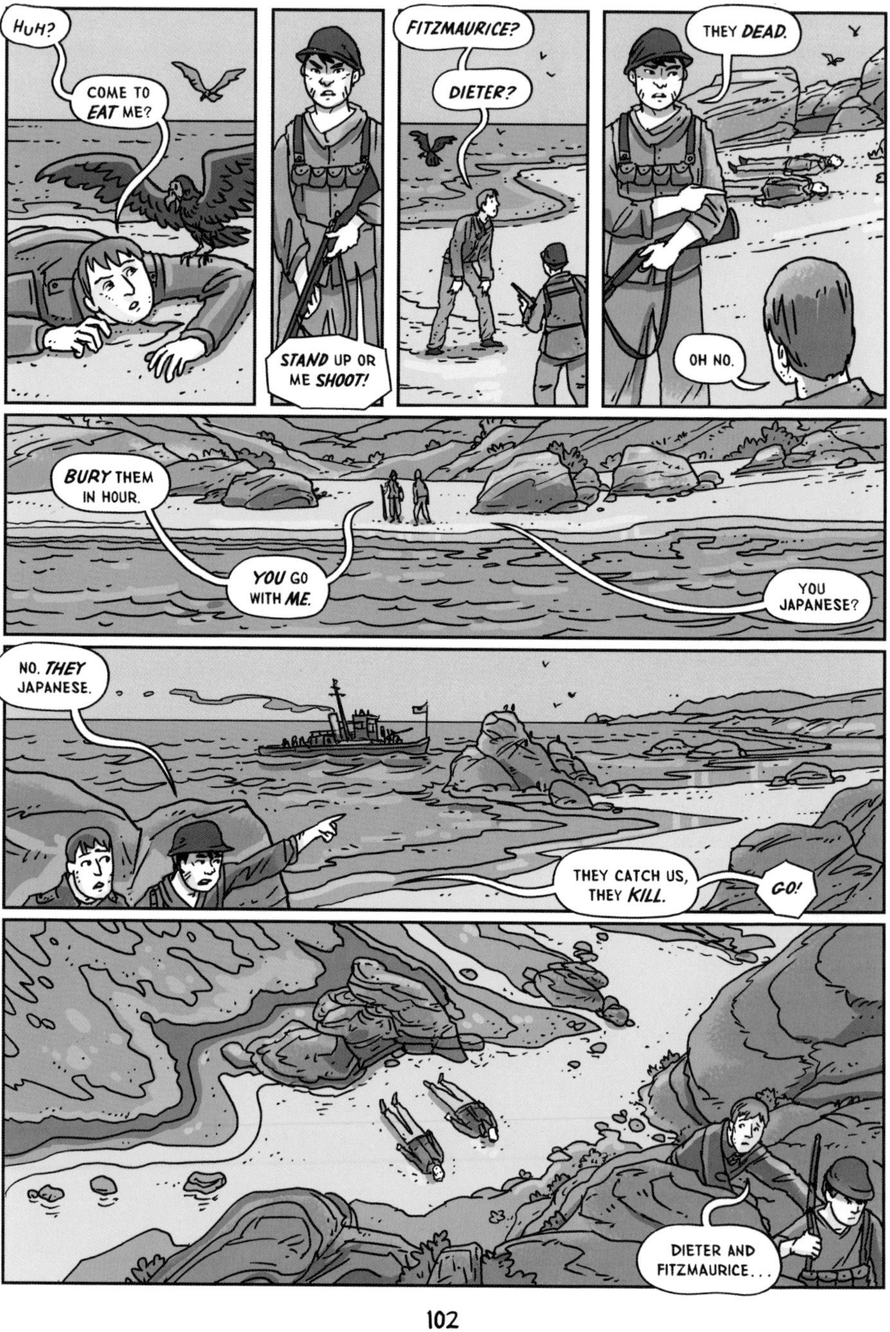

HUH?
COME TO *EAT* ME?
STAND UP OR ME *SHOOT!*
FITZMAURICE?
DIETER?
THEY *DEAD.*
OH NO.
BURY THEM IN HOUR.
YOU GO WITH *ME.*
YOU JAPANESE?
NO. *THEY* JAPANESE.
THEY CATCH US, THEY *KILL.*
GO!
DIETER AND FITZMAURICE...

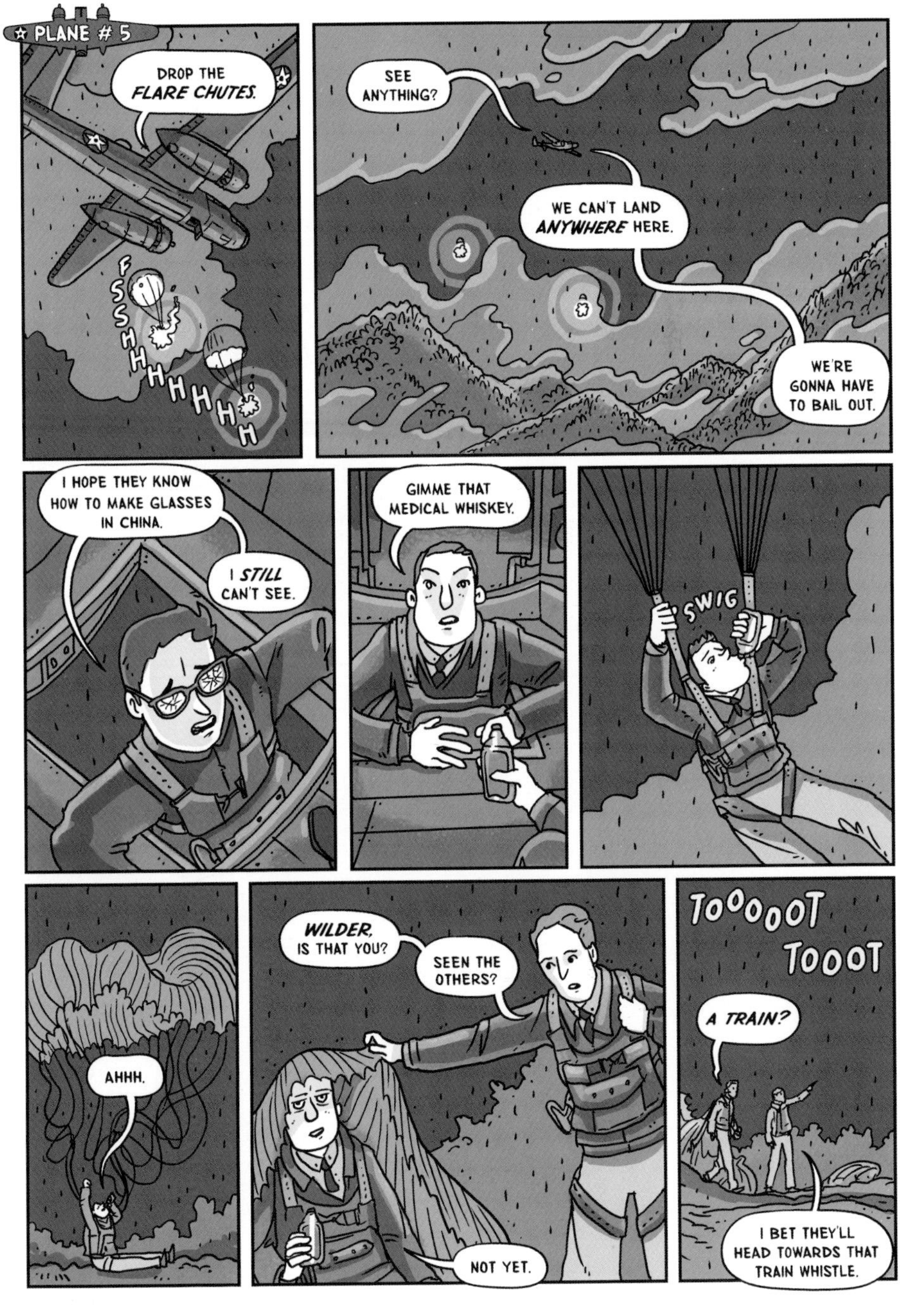
PLANE # 5
DROP THE FLARE CHUTES.
FSSHHHHHHHH
SEE ANYTHING?
WE CAN'T LAND ANYWHERE HERE.
WE'RE GONNA HAVE TO BAIL OUT.
I HOPE THEY KNOW HOW TO MAKE GLASSES IN CHINA.
I STILL CAN'T SEE.
GIMME THAT MEDICAL WHISKEY.
SWIG
AHHH.
WILDER, IS THAT YOU?
SEEN THE OTHERS?
NOT YET.
TOOOOOT TOOOT
A TRAIN?
I BET THEY'LL HEAD TOWARDS THAT TRAIN WHISTLE.

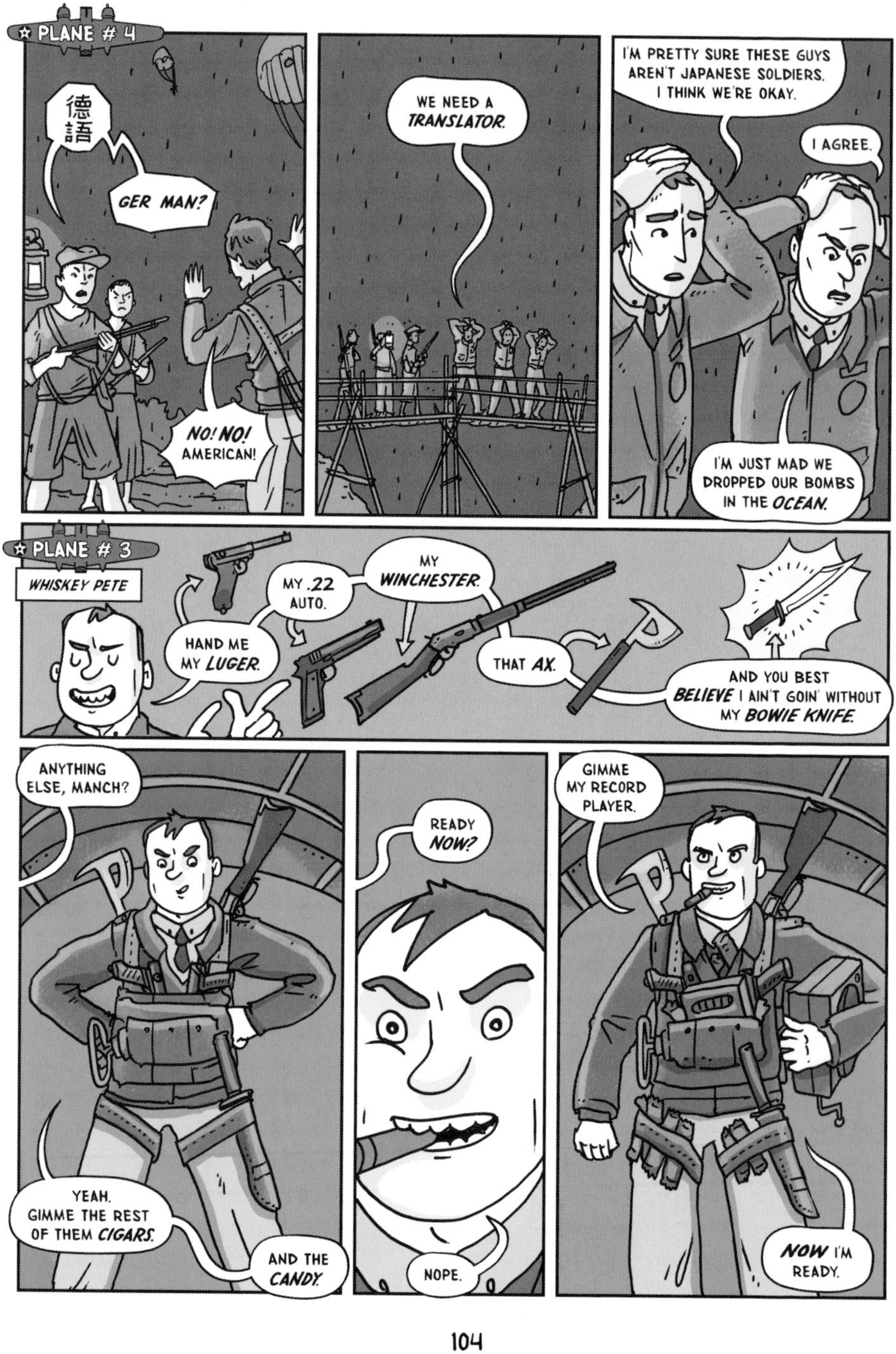
PLANE # 4
德語
GER MAN?
NO! NO! AMERICAN!
WE NEED A TRANSLATOR.
I'M PRETTY SURE THESE GUYS AREN'T JAPANESE SOLDIERS. I THINK WE'RE OKAY.
I AGREE.
I'M JUST MAD WE DROPPED OUR BOMBS IN THE OCEAN.
PLANE # 3
WHISKEY PETE
HAND ME MY LUGER.
MY .22 AUTO.
MY WINCHESTER.
THAT AX.
AND YOU BEST BELIEVE I AIN'T GOIN' WITHOUT MY BOWIE KNIFE.
ANYTHING ELSE, MANCH?
YEAH. GIMME THE REST OF THEM CIGARS.
AND THE CANDY.
READY NOW?
NOPE.
GIMME MY RECORD PLAYER.
NOW I'M READY.

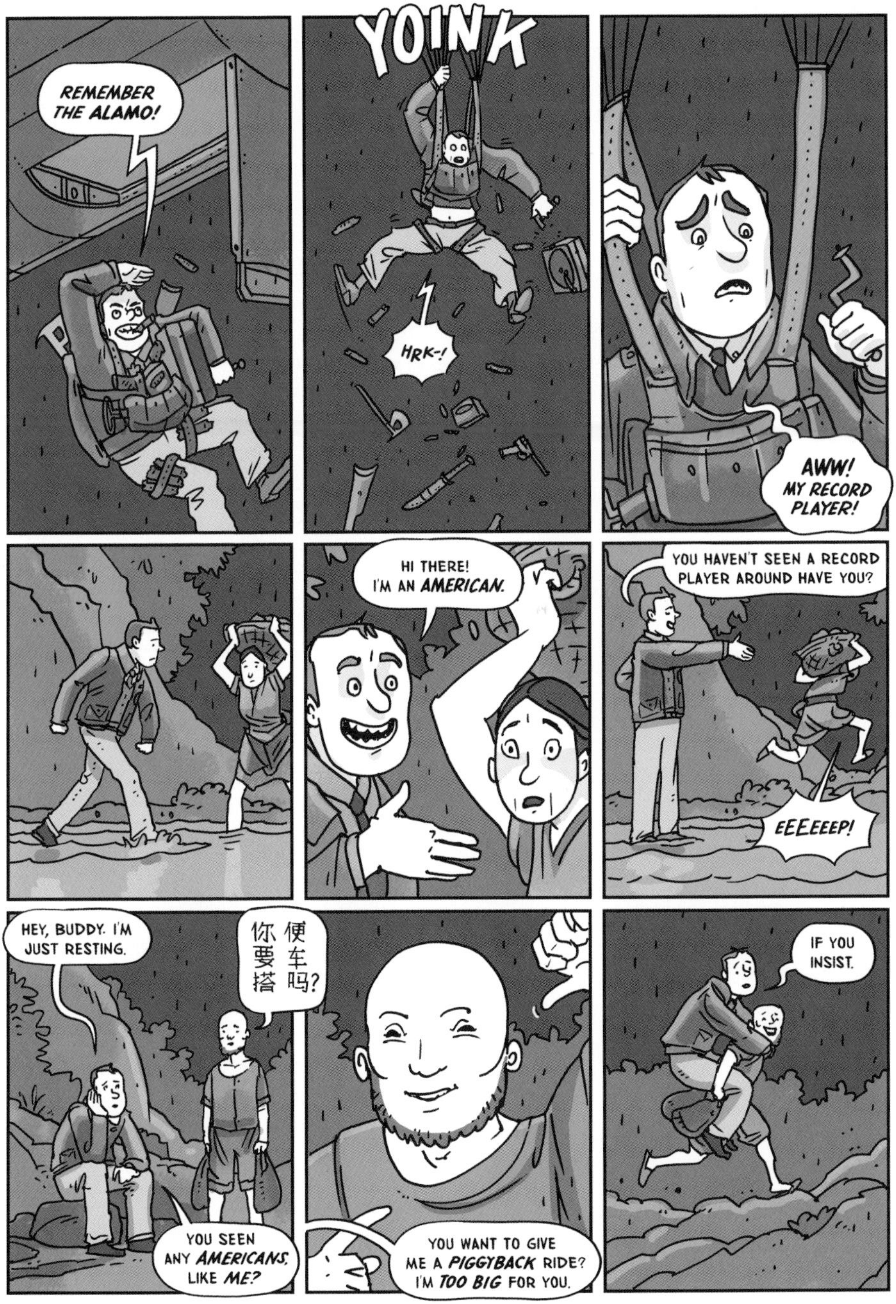
REMEMBER THE ALAMO!
YOINK
HRK-!
AWW! MY RECORD PLAYER!
HI THERE! I'M AN AMERICAN.
YOU HAVEN'T SEEN A RECORD PLAYER AROUND HAVE YOU?
EEEEEEP!
HEY, BUDDY. I'M JUST RESTING.
你要搭便车吗?
YOU SEEN ANY AMERICANS, LIKE ME?
YOU WANT TO GIVE ME A PIGGYBACK RIDE? I'M TOO BIG FOR YOU.
IF YOU INSIST.

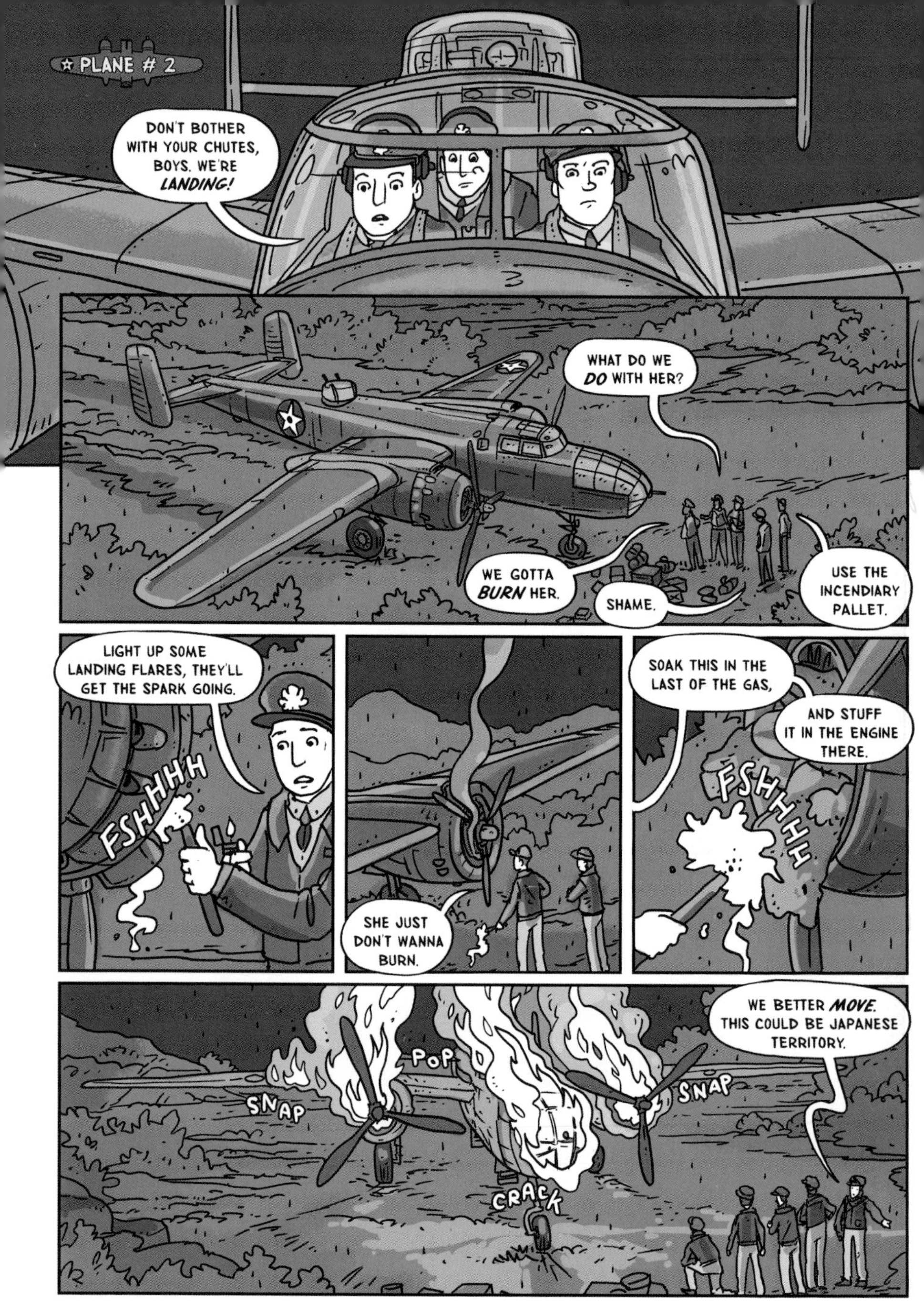
PLANE # 2
DON'T BOTHER WITH YOUR CHUTES, BOYS. WE'RE *LANDING!*
WHAT DO WE *DO* WITH HER?
WE GOTTA *BURN* HER.
SHAME.
USE THE INCENDIARY PALLET.
LIGHT UP SOME LANDING FLARES, THEY'LL GET THE SPARK GOING.
FSHHHH
SHE JUST DON'T WANNA BURN.
SOAK THIS IN THE LAST OF THE GAS,
AND STUFF IT IN THE ENGINE THERE.
FSHHHH
WE BETTER *MOVE.* THIS COULD BE JAPANESE TERRITORY.
POP
SNAP
SNAP
CRACK

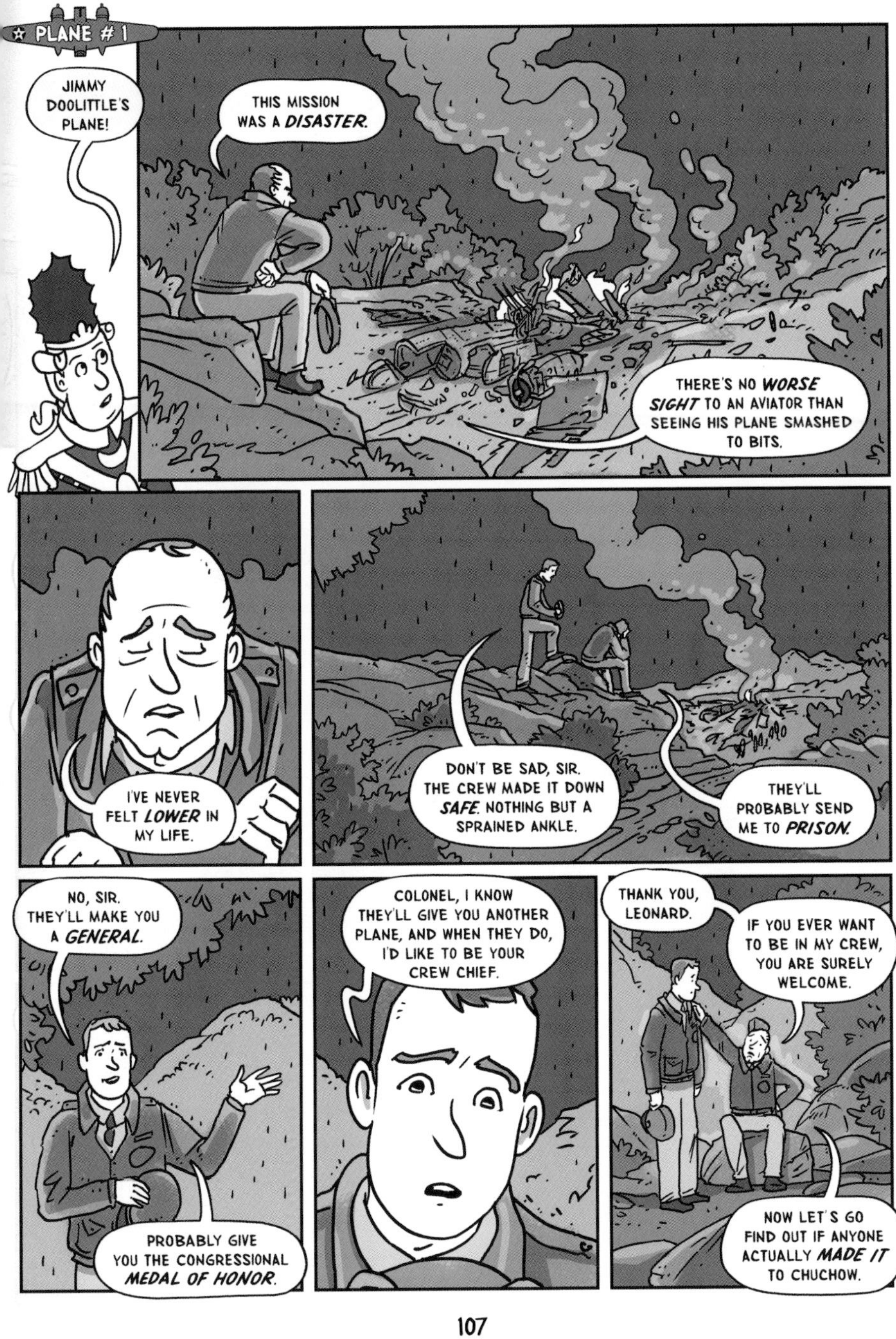
PLANE # 1
JIMMY DOOLITTLE'S PLANE!
THIS MISSION WAS A *DISASTER.*
THERE'S NO *WORSE SIGHT* TO AN AVIATOR THAN SEEING HIS PLANE SMASHED TO BITS.
I'VE NEVER FELT *LOWER* IN MY LIFE.
DON'T BE SAD, SIR. THE CREW MADE IT DOWN *SAFE.* NOTHING BUT A SPRAINED ANKLE.
THEY'LL PROBABLY SEND ME TO *PRISON.*
NO, SIR. THEY'LL MAKE YOU A *GENERAL.*
PROBABLY GIVE YOU THE CONGRESSIONAL *MEDAL OF HONOR.*
COLONEL, I KNOW THEY'LL GIVE YOU ANOTHER PLANE, AND WHEN THEY DO, I'D LIKE TO BE YOUR CREW CHIEF.
THANK YOU, LEONARD.
IF YOU EVER WANT TO BE IN MY CREW, YOU ARE SURELY WELCOME.
NOW LET'S GO FIND OUT IF ANYONE ACTUALLY *MADE IT* TO CHUCHOW.

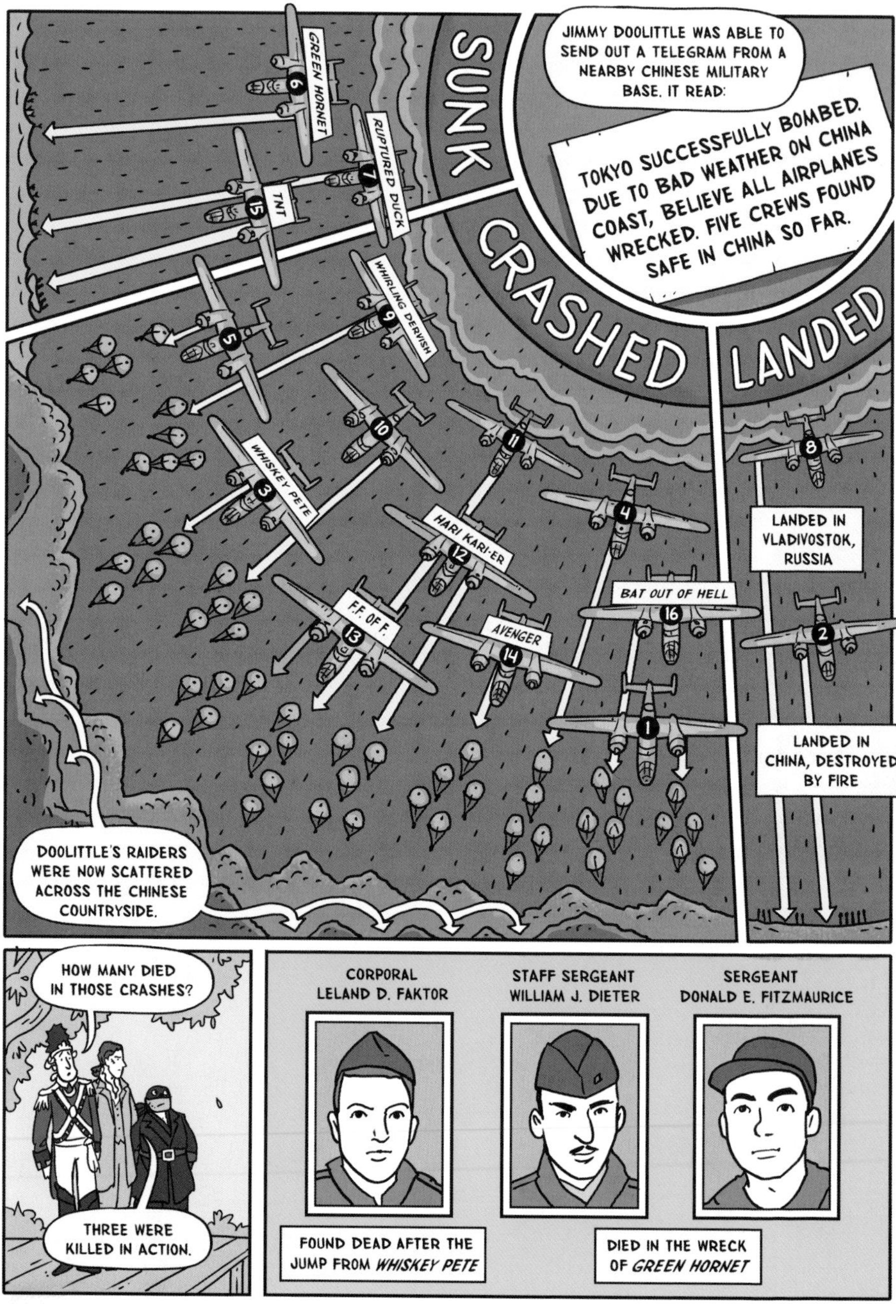
JIMMY DOOLITTLE WAS ABLE TO SEND OUT A TELEGRAM FROM A NEARBY CHINESE MILITARY BASE. IT READ:
TOKYO SUCCESSFULLY BOMBED. DUE TO BAD WEATHER ON CHINA COAST, BELIEVE ALL AIRPLANES WRECKED. FIVE CREWS FOUND SAFE IN CHINA SO FAR.
SUNK
CRASHED
LANDED
GREEN HORNET
RUPTURED DUCK
TNT
WHIRLING DERVISH
WHISKEY PETE
HARI KARI-ER
BAT OUT OF HELL
F.F. OF F.
AVENGER
LANDED IN VLADIVOSTOK, RUSSIA
LANDED IN CHINA, DESTROYED BY FIRE
DOOLITTLE'S RAIDERS WERE NOW SCATTERED ACROSS THE CHINESE COUNTRYSIDE.
HOW MANY DIED IN THOSE CRASHES?
THREE WERE KILLED IN ACTION.
CORPORAL LELAND D. FAKTOR
STAFF SERGEANT WILLIAM J. DIETER
SERGEANT DONALD E. FITZMAURICE
FOUND DEAD AFTER THE JUMP FROM WHISKEY PETE
DIED IN THE WRECK OF GREEN HORNET

RUPTURED DUCK

THE RAIDERS' LIVES WERE NOW IN THE HANDS OF THE LOCAL CHINESE CIVILIANS.

MANY RAIDERS WERE SERIOUSLY WOUNDED.

ONLY ONE OF THE CREW FROM *RUPTURED DUCK* COULD WALK.

THEY SAY A JAPANESE PATROL IS *CLOSE.*

WE HAVE TO MOVE *AGAIN.*

HANG IN THERE, LAWSON.

HNNGGG.

SSHHH.

WHERE ARE THE VILLAGERS GOING?

SO WE JUST STAY *HERE?*

JAPANESE SOLDIERS?

I DON'T KNOW.

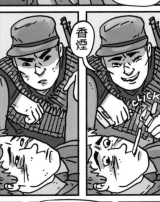

香煙

CLICK

I THINK THEY'RE ON OUR SIDE.

LAWSON AIN'T LOOKIN' TOO GOOD. WE NEED TO FIND A DOCTOR.

WE MUST BE *HALFWAY ACROSS* CHINA BY NOW.

YOU MEAN WE AREN'T EVEN ON THE *MAINLAND* YET?

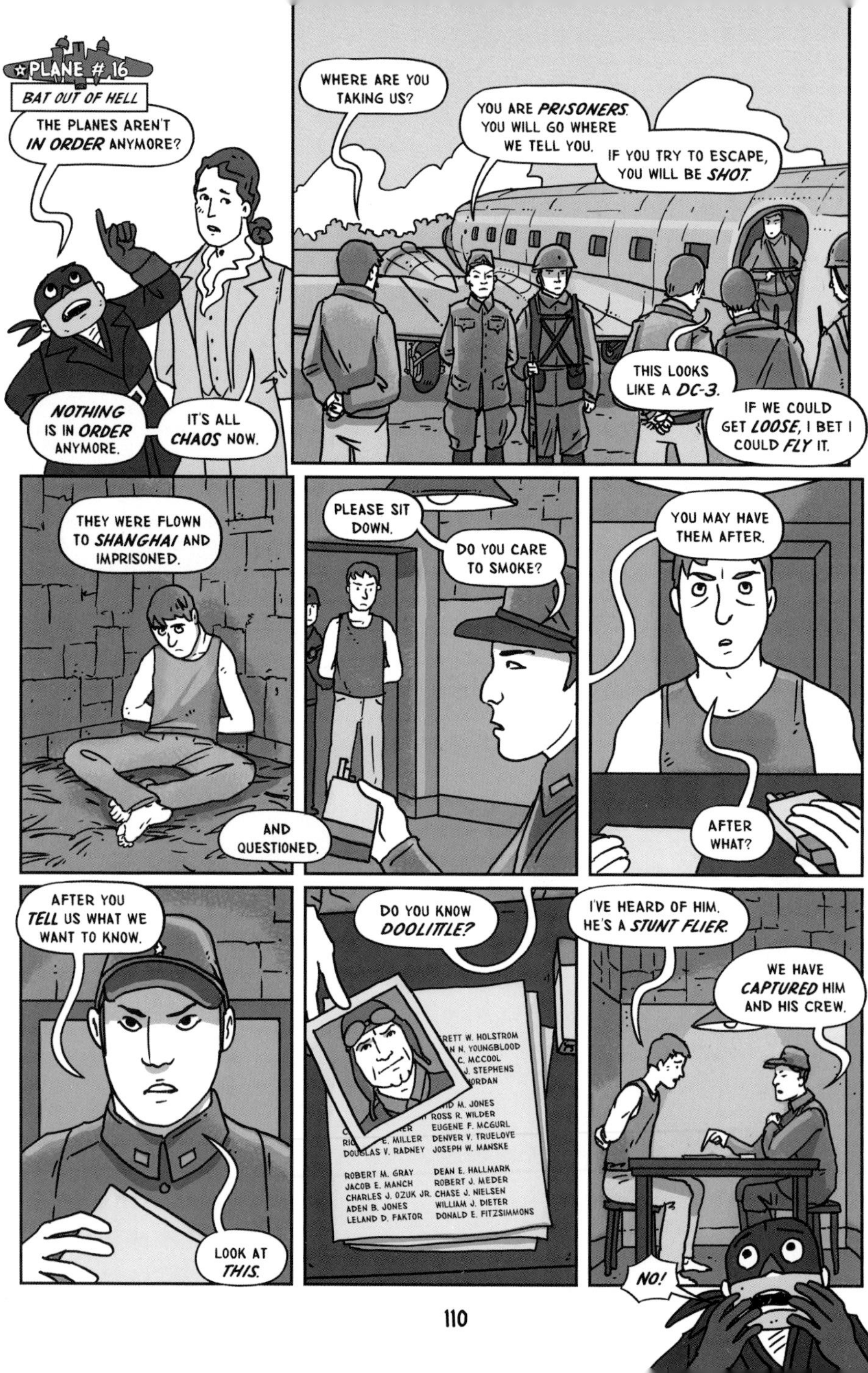
PLANE #16
BAT OUT OF HELL
THE PLANES AREN'T IN ORDER ANYMORE?
NOTHING IS IN ORDER ANYMORE.
IT'S ALL CHAOS NOW.
WHERE ARE YOU TAKING US?
YOU ARE PRISONERS. YOU WILL GO WHERE WE TELL YOU.
IF YOU TRY TO ESCAPE, YOU WILL BE SHOT.
THIS LOOKS LIKE A DC-3.
IF WE COULD GET LOOSE, I BET I COULD FLY IT.
THEY WERE FLOWN TO SHANGHAI AND IMPRISONED.
AND QUESTIONED.
PLEASE SIT DOWN.
DO YOU CARE TO SMOKE?
YOU MAY HAVE THEM AFTER.
AFTER WHAT?
AFTER YOU TELL US WHAT WE WANT TO KNOW.
LOOK AT THIS.
DO YOU KNOW DOOLITTLE?
ROSS R. WILDER
EUGENE F. MCGURL
DENVER V. TRUELOVE
JOSEPH W. MANSKE
ROBERT M. GRAY
JACOB E. MANCH
CHARLES J. OZUK JR.
ADEN B. JONES
LELAND D. FAKTOR
DEAN E. HALLMARK
ROBERT J. MEDER
CHASE J. NIELSEN
WILLIAM J. DIETER
DONALD E. FITZSIMMONS
I'VE HEARD OF HIM. HE'S A STUNT FLIER.
WE HAVE CAPTURED HIM AND HIS CREW.
NO!

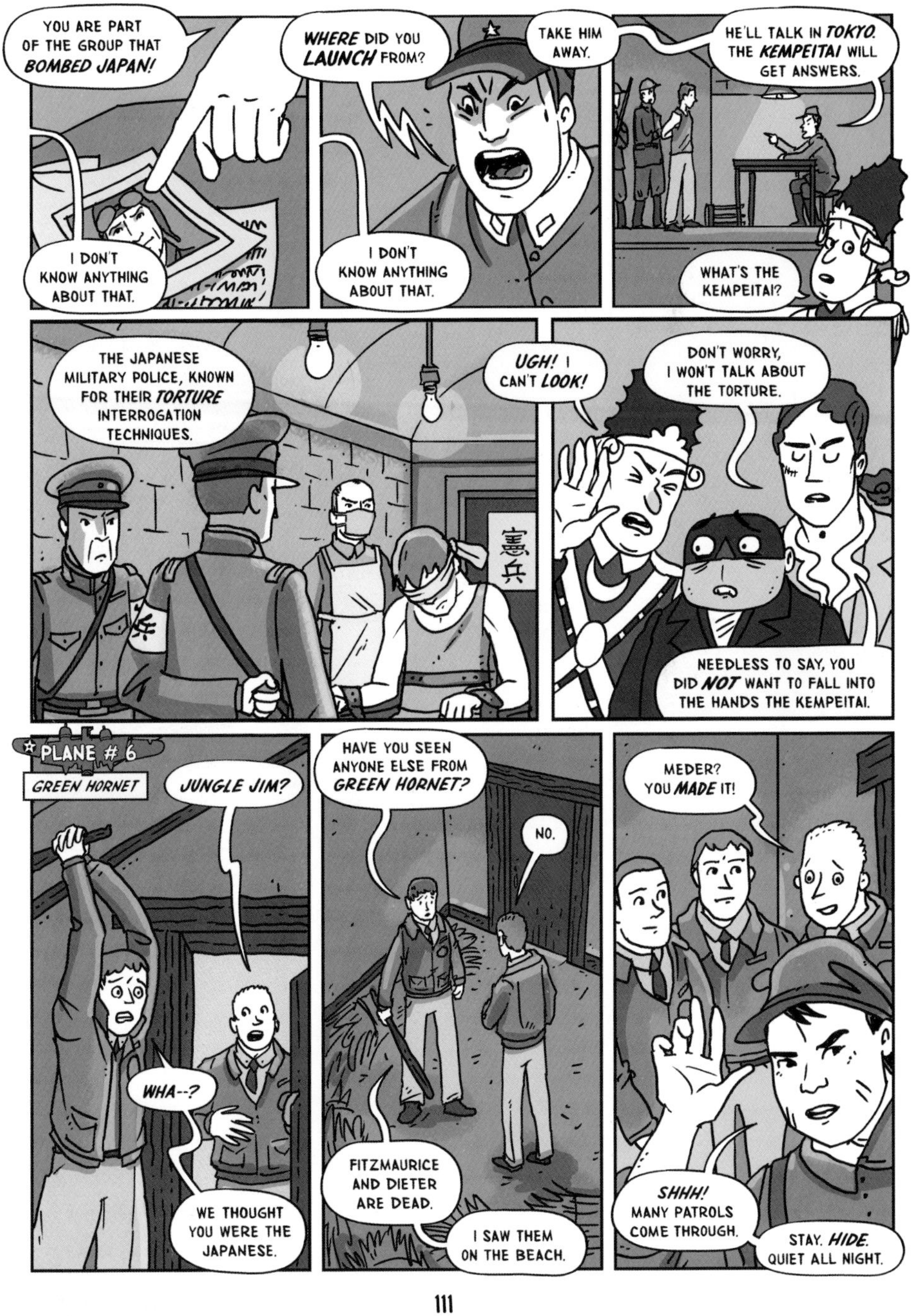
YOU ARE PART OF THE GROUP THAT BOMBED JAPAN!
I DON'T KNOW ANYTHING ABOUT THAT.
WHERE DID YOU LAUNCH FROM?
I DON'T KNOW ANYTHING ABOUT THAT.
TAKE HIM AWAY.
HE'LL TALK IN TOKYO. THE KEMPEITAI WILL GET ANSWERS.
WHAT'S THE KEMPEITAI?
THE JAPANESE MILITARY POLICE, KNOWN FOR THEIR TORTURE INTERROGATION TECHNIQUES.
憲兵
UGH! I CAN'T LOOK!
DON'T WORRY, I WON'T TALK ABOUT THE TORTURE.
NEEDLESS TO SAY, YOU DID NOT WANT TO FALL INTO THE HANDS THE KEMPEITAI.
PLANE # 6
GREEN HORNET
JUNGLE JIM?
WHA--?
WE THOUGHT YOU WERE THE JAPANESE.
HAVE YOU SEEN ANYONE ELSE FROM GREEN HORNET?
NO.
FITZMAURICE AND DIETER ARE DEAD.
I SAW THEM ON THE BEACH.
MEDER? YOU MADE IT!
SHHH! MANY PATROLS COME THROUGH.
STAY. HIDE. QUIET ALL NIGHT.

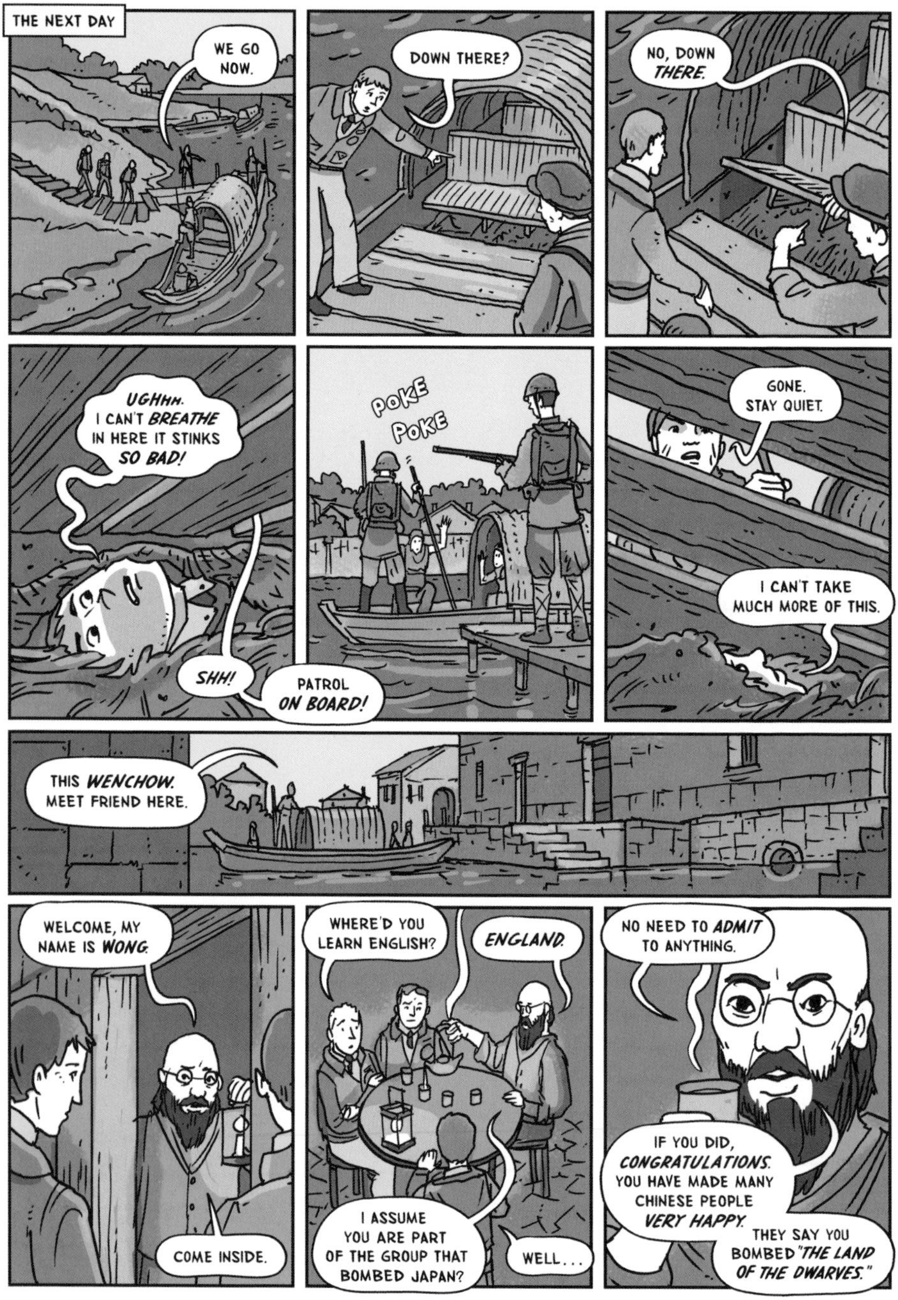
THE NEXT DAY
WE GO NOW.
DOWN THERE?
NO, DOWN *THERE.*
UGHHH. I CAN'T *BREATHE* IN HERE IT STINKS *SO BAD!*
SHH!
PATROL *ON BOARD!*
POKE POKE
GONE. STAY QUIET.
I CAN'T TAKE MUCH MORE OF THIS.
THIS *WENCHOW.* MEET FRIEND HERE.
WELCOME, MY NAME IS *WONG.*
COME INSIDE.
WHERE'D YOU LEARN ENGLISH?
ENGLAND.
I ASSUME YOU ARE PART OF THE GROUP THAT BOMBED JAPAN?
WELL...
NO NEED TO *ADMIT* TO ANYTHING.
IF YOU DID, *CONGRATULATIONS.* YOU HAVE MADE MANY CHINESE PEOPLE *VERY HAPPY.*
THEY SAY YOU BOMBED *"THE LAND OF THE DWARVES."*

THE CHINESE REALLY *HATE* THEM, HUH?

YOU HAVE *NO* IDEA. THE *HORRIBLE* THINGS I'VE SEEN,

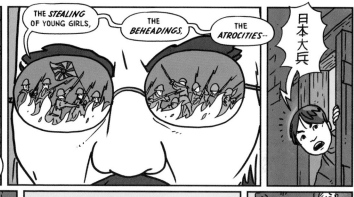

THE *STEALING* OF YOUNG GIRLS,

THE *BEHEADINGS*,

THE *ATROCITIES*--

日本大兵

THE JAPANESE ARE *HERE*,

SEARCHING THE CITY.

WE MUST LEAVE *NOW!*

THERE ARE SOLDIERS EVERYWHERE--WE'RE *TRAPPED!*

WE WILL TRY TO GET YOU OUT THE EAST GATE.

THEY MEAN BUSINESS.

CLICK CLICK

WE NEED TO CROSS THAT ROAD.

QUICK! CLIMB IN THERE!

THERE'S NO ESCAPE. WE'RE JUST GONNA HAVE TO HIDE.

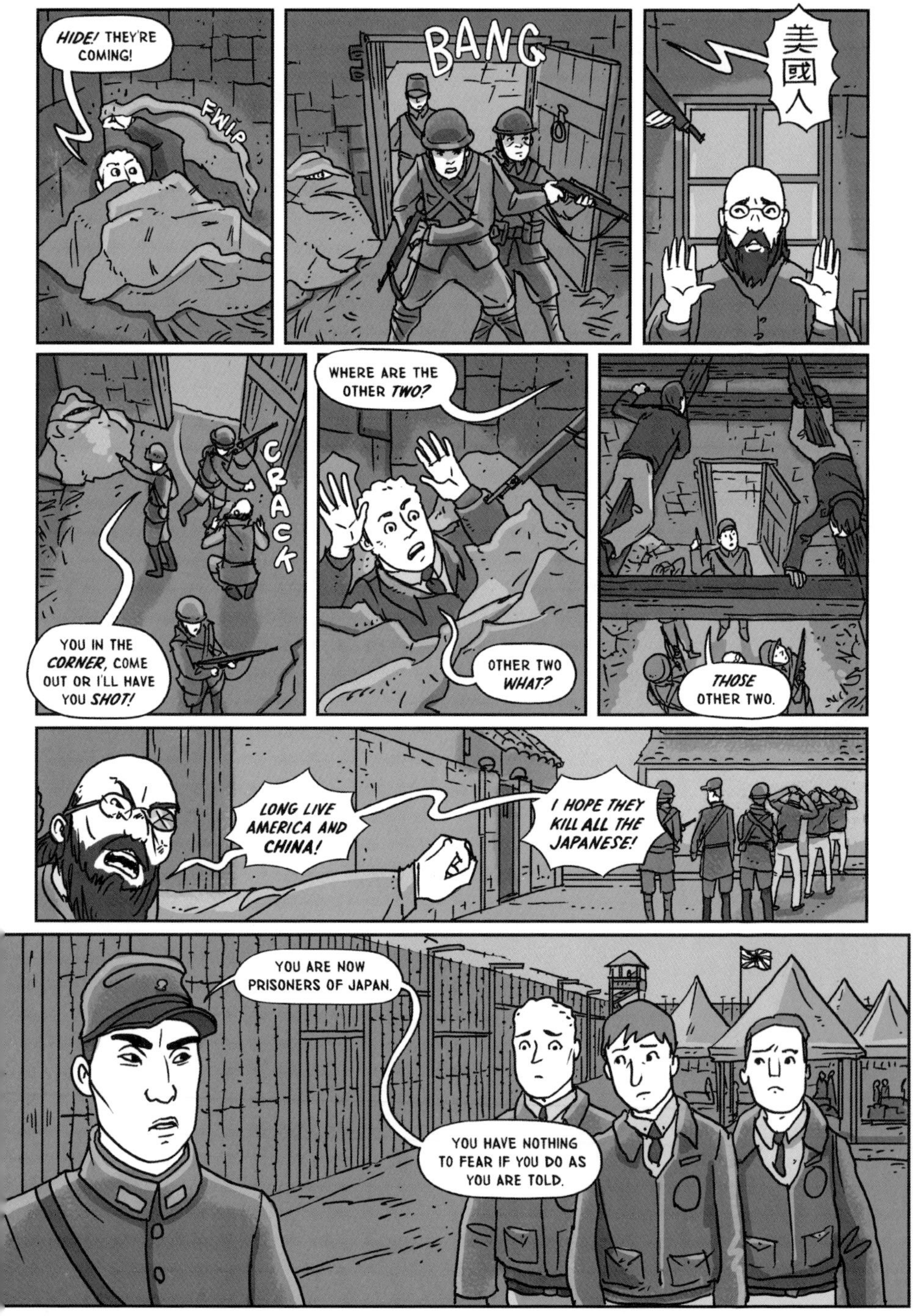
HIDE! THEY'RE COMING!
FWIP
BANG
美國人
YOU IN THE CORNER, COME OUT OR I'LL HAVE YOU SHOT!
CRACK
WHERE ARE THE OTHER TWO?
OTHER TWO WHAT?
THOSE OTHER TWO.
LONG LIVE AMERICA AND CHINA!
I HOPE THEY KILL ALL THE JAPANESE!
YOU ARE NOW PRISONERS OF JAPAN.
YOU HAVE NOTHING TO FEAR IF YOU DO AS YOU ARE TOLD.

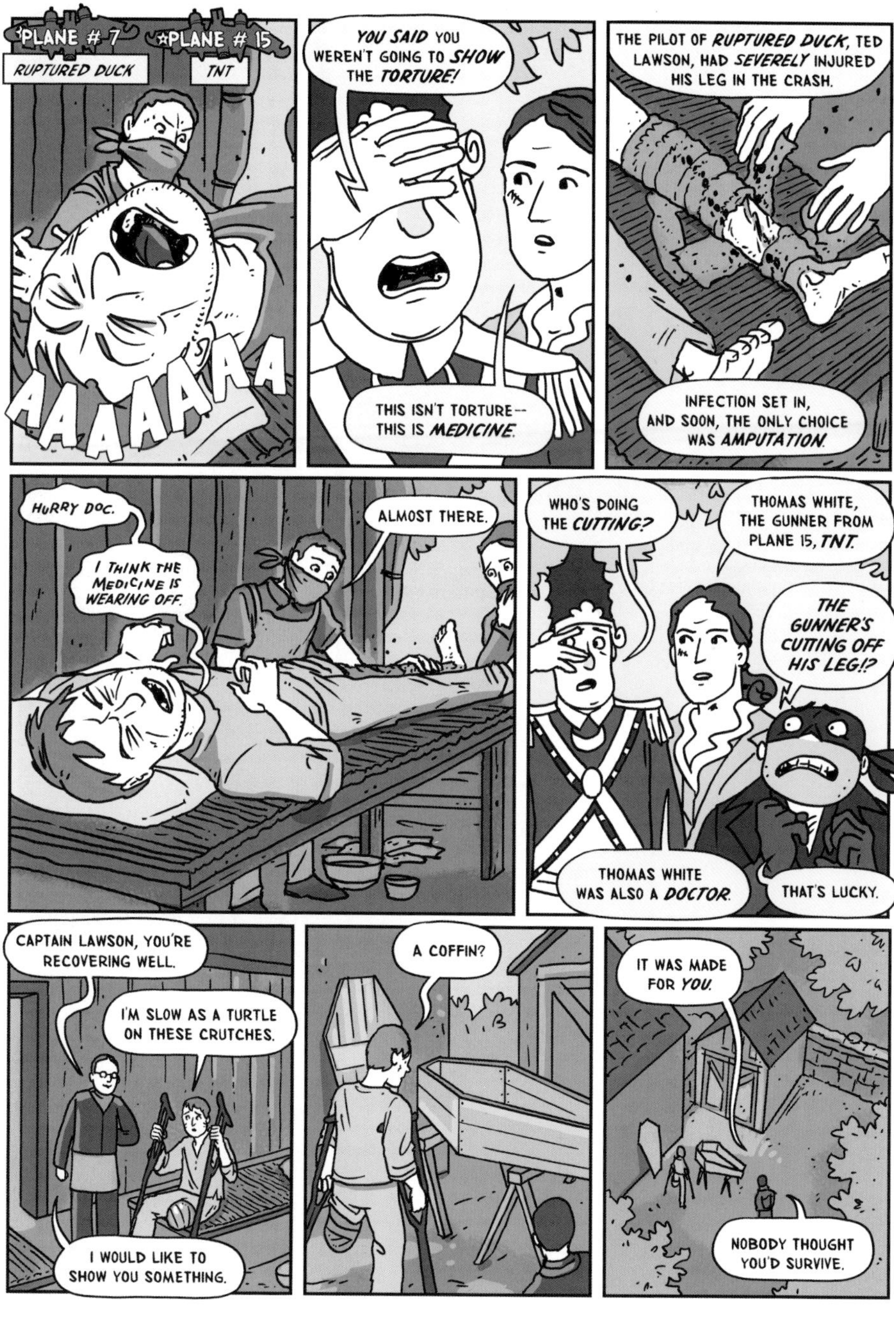
PLANE # 7
RUPTURED DUCK
PLANE # 15
TNT
AAAAAAAA
YOU SAID YOU WEREN'T GOING TO SHOW THE TORTURE!
THIS ISN'T TORTURE-- THIS IS MEDICINE.
THE PILOT OF RUPTURED DUCK, TED LAWSON, HAD SEVERELY INJURED HIS LEG IN THE CRASH.
INFECTION SET IN, AND SOON, THE ONLY CHOICE WAS AMPUTATION.
HURRY DOC.
I THINK THE MEDICINE IS WEARING OFF.
ALMOST THERE.
WHO'S DOING THE CUTTING?
THOMAS WHITE, THE GUNNER FROM PLANE 15, TNT.
THE GUNNER'S CUTTING OFF HIS LEG!?
THOMAS WHITE WAS ALSO A DOCTOR.
THAT'S LUCKY.
CAPTAIN LAWSON, YOU'RE RECOVERING WELL.
I'M SLOW AS A TURTLE ON THESE CRUTCHES.
I WOULD LIKE TO SHOW YOU SOMETHING.
A COFFIN?
IT WAS MADE FOR YOU.
NOBODY THOUGHT YOU'D SURVIVE.

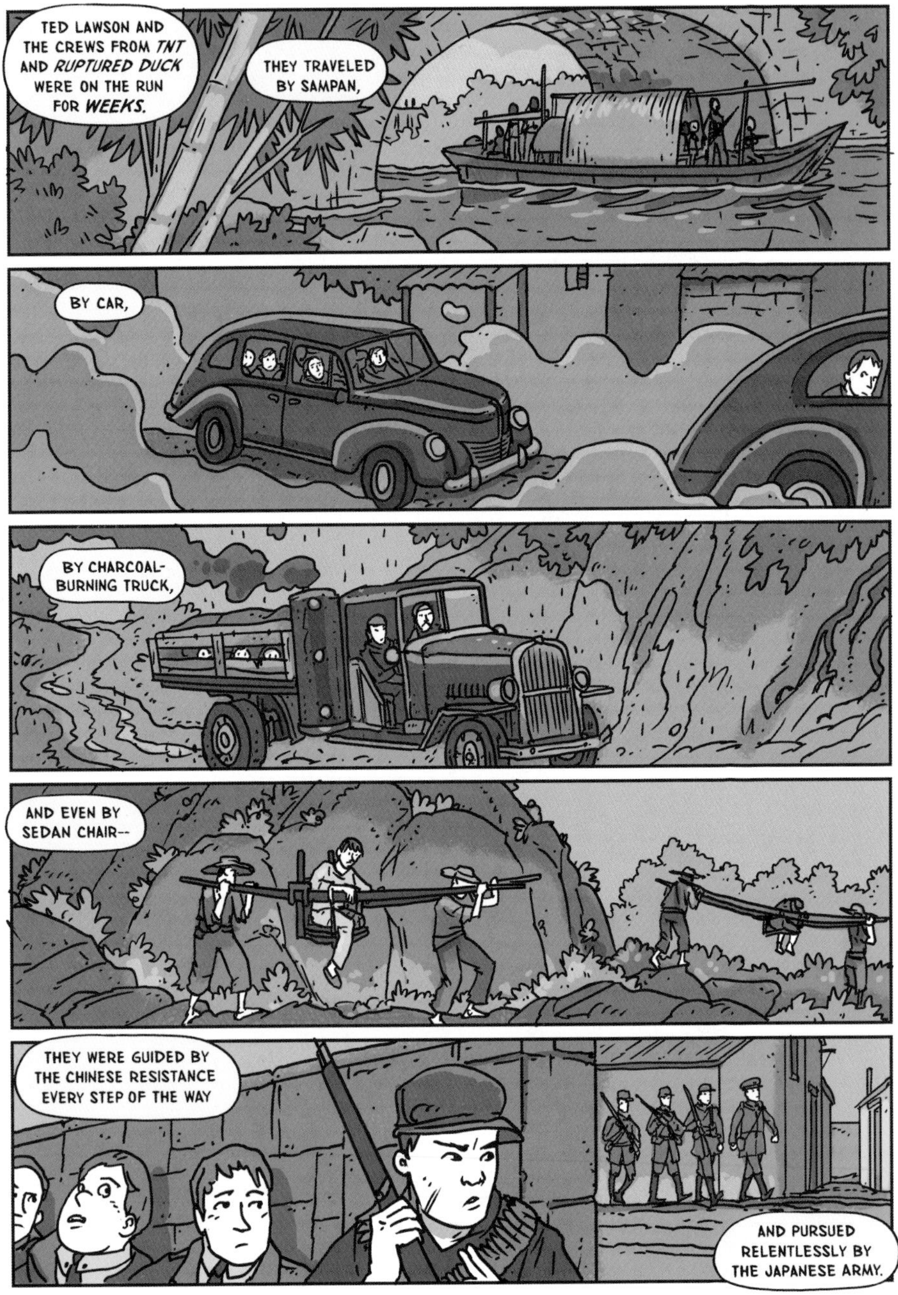
TED LAWSON AND THE CREWS FROM *TNT* AND *RUPTURED DUCK* WERE ON THE RUN FOR ***WEEKS.***
THEY TRAVELED BY SAMPAN,
BY CAR,
BY CHARCOAL-BURNING TRUCK,
AND EVEN BY SEDAN CHAIR--
THEY WERE GUIDED BY THE CHINESE RESISTANCE EVERY STEP OF THE WAY
AND PURSUED RELENTLESSLY BY THE JAPANESE ARMY.

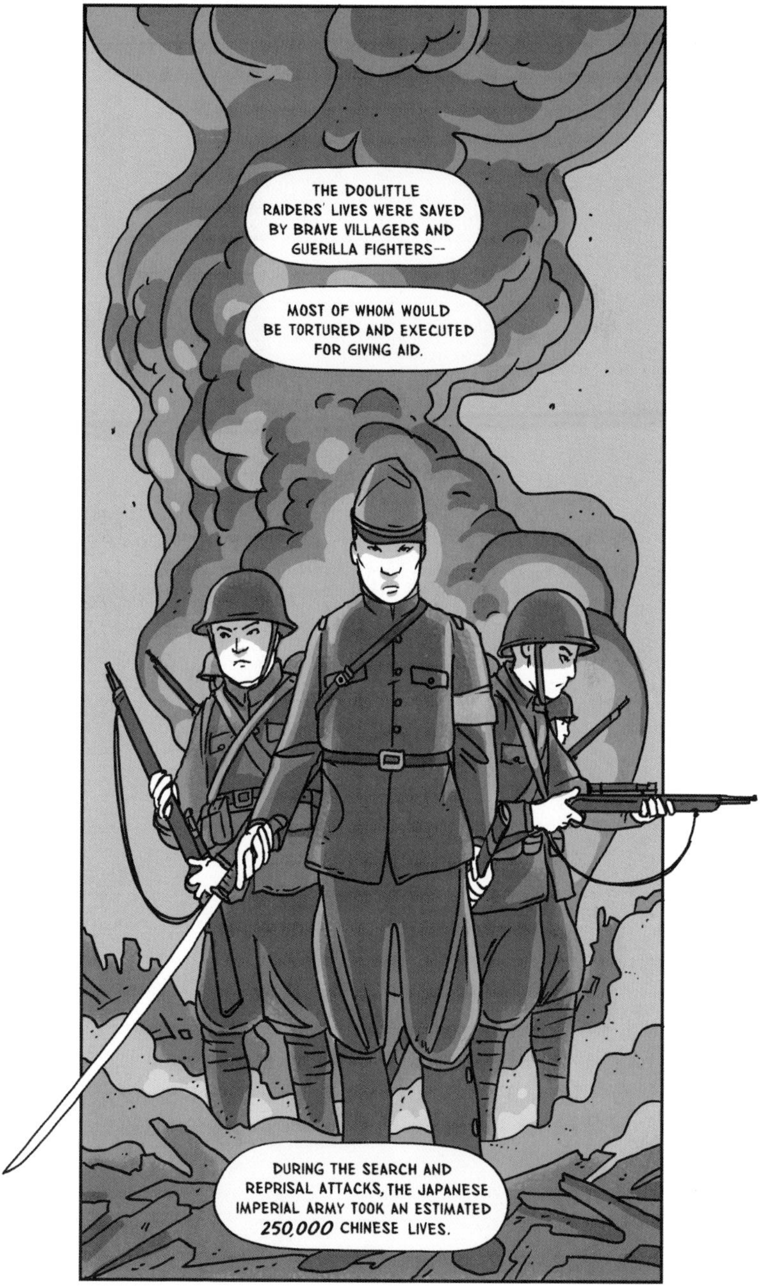
THE DOOLITTLE RAIDERS' LIVES WERE SAVED BY BRAVE VILLAGERS AND GUERILLA FIGHTERS--
MOST OF WHOM WOULD BE TORTURED AND EXECUTED FOR GIVING AID.
DURING THE SEARCH AND REPRISAL ATTACKS, THE JAPANESE IMPERIAL ARMY TOOK AN ESTIMATED *250,000* CHINESE LIVES.

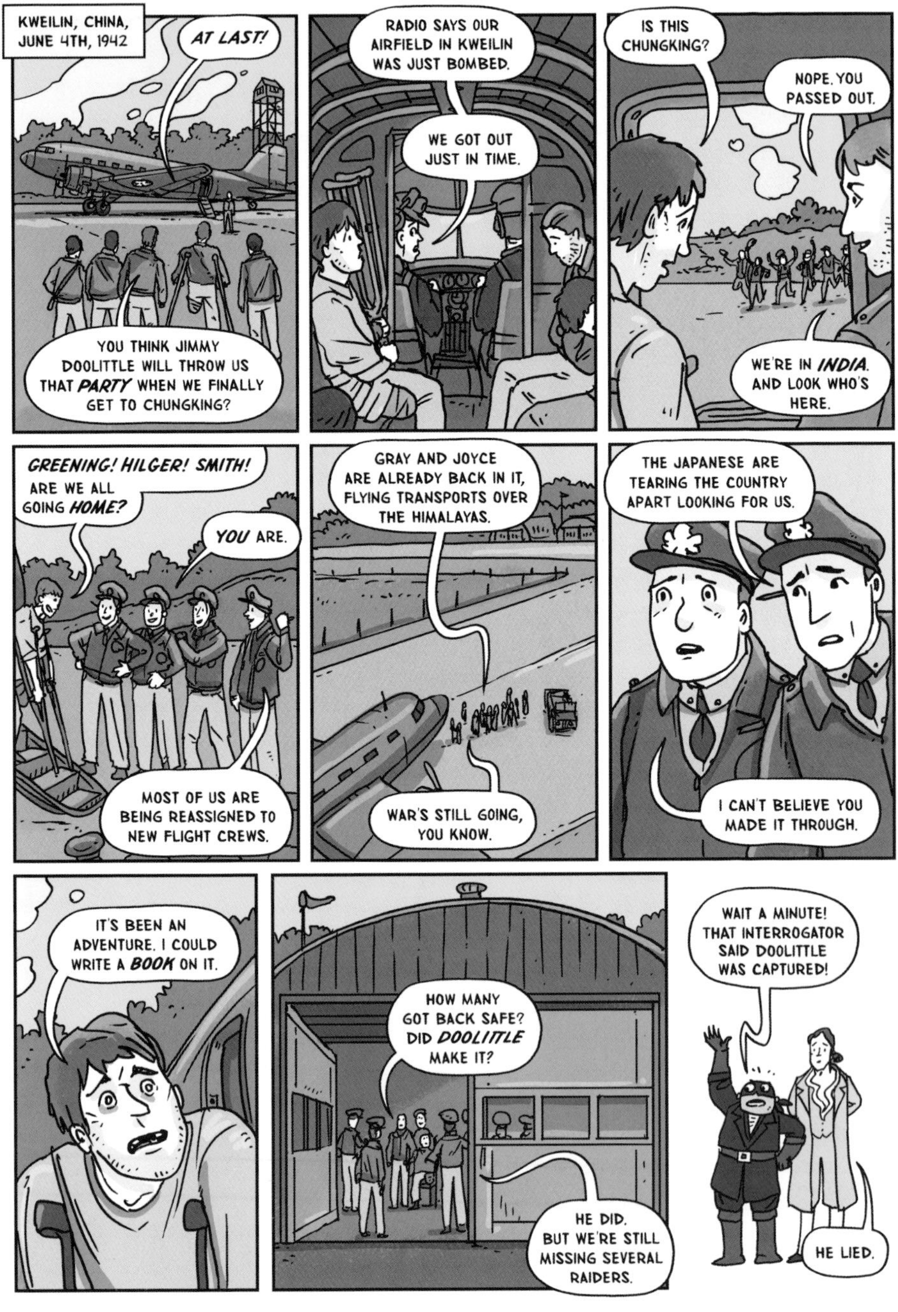
KWEILIN, CHINA, JUNE 4TH, 1942
AT LAST!
YOU THINK JIMMY DOOLITTLE WILL THROW US THAT PARTY WHEN WE FINALLY GET TO CHUNGKING?
RADIO SAYS OUR AIRFIELD IN KWEILIN WAS JUST BOMBED.
WE GOT OUT JUST IN TIME.
IS THIS CHUNGKING?
NOPE. YOU PASSED OUT.
WE'RE IN INDIA. AND LOOK WHO'S HERE.
GREENING! HILGER! SMITH! ARE WE ALL GOING HOME?
YOU ARE.
MOST OF US ARE BEING REASSIGNED TO NEW FLIGHT CREWS.
GRAY AND JOYCE ARE ALREADY BACK IN IT, FLYING TRANSPORTS OVER THE HIMALAYAS.
WAR'S STILL GOING, YOU KNOW.
THE JAPANESE ARE TEARING THE COUNTRY APART LOOKING FOR US.
I CAN'T BELIEVE YOU MADE IT THROUGH.
IT'S BEEN AN ADVENTURE. I COULD WRITE A BOOK ON IT.
HOW MANY GOT BACK SAFE? DID DOOLITTLE MAKE IT?
HE DID. BUT WE'RE STILL MISSING SEVERAL RAIDERS.
WAIT A MINUTE! THAT INTERROGATOR SAID DOOLITTLE WAS CAPTURED!
HE LIED.

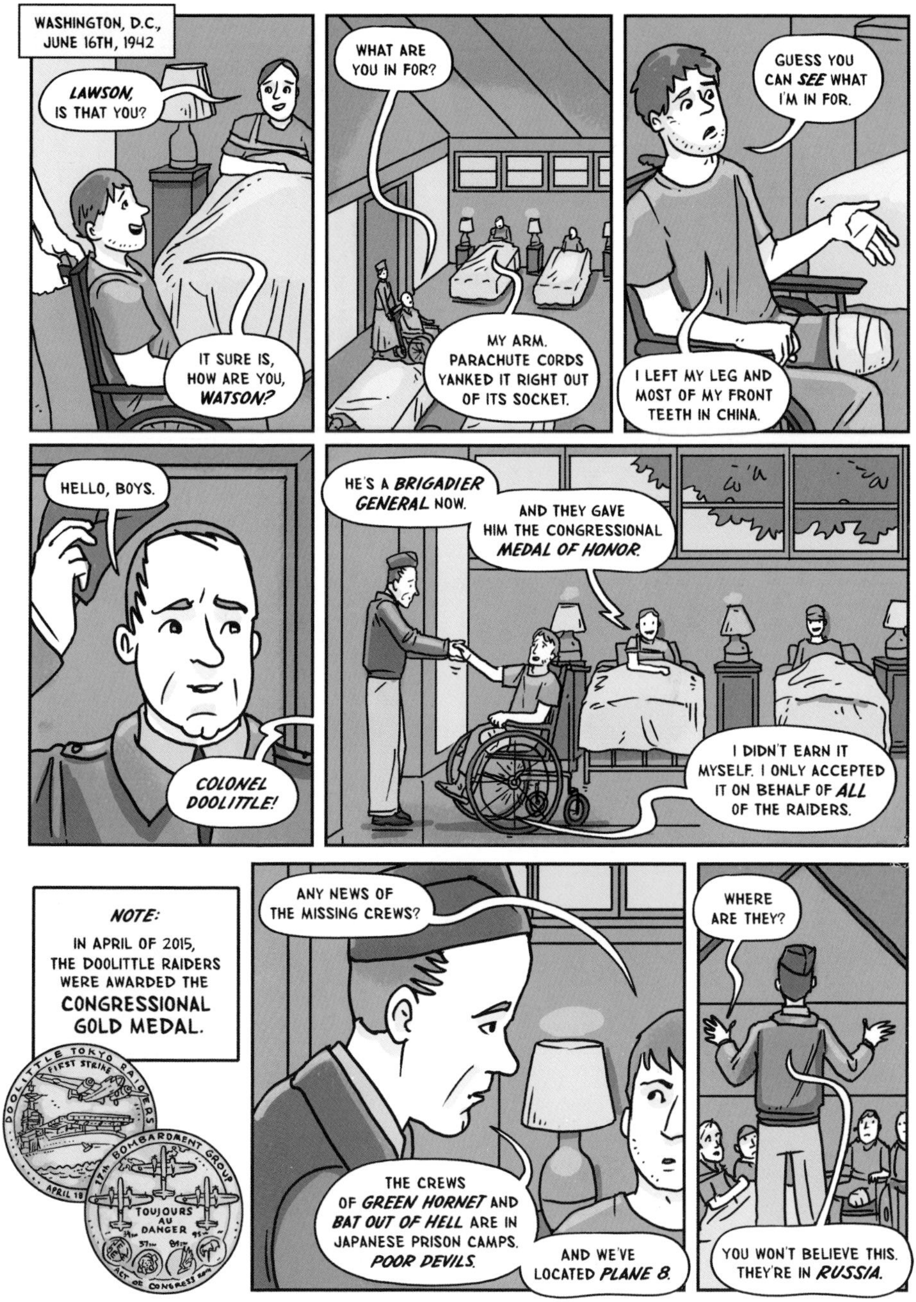
WASHINGTON, D.C., JUNE 16TH, 1942
LAWSON, IS THAT YOU?
IT SURE IS, HOW ARE YOU, WATSON?
WHAT ARE YOU IN FOR?
MY ARM. PARACHUTE CORDS YANKED IT RIGHT OUT OF ITS SOCKET.
GUESS YOU CAN SEE WHAT I'M IN FOR.
I LEFT MY LEG AND MOST OF MY FRONT TEETH IN CHINA.
HELLO, BOYS.
COLONEL DOOLITTLE!
HE'S A BRIGADIER GENERAL NOW.
AND THEY GAVE HIM THE CONGRESSIONAL MEDAL OF HONOR.
I DIDN'T EARN IT MYSELF. I ONLY ACCEPTED IT ON BEHALF OF ALL OF THE RAIDERS.
NOTE:
IN APRIL OF 2015, THE DOOLITTLE RAIDERS WERE AWARDED THE CONGRESSIONAL GOLD MEDAL.
DOOLITTLE TOKYO RAIDERS
FIRST STRIKE
APRIL 18
BOMBARDMENT GROUP
TOUJOURS AU DANGER
ACT OF CONGRESS
ANY NEWS OF THE MISSING CREWS?
THE CREWS OF GREEN HORNET AND BAT OUT OF HELL ARE IN JAPANESE PRISON CAMPS. POOR DEVILS.
AND WE'VE LOCATED PLANE 8.
WHERE ARE THEY?
YOU WON'T BELIEVE THIS. THEY'RE IN RUSSIA.

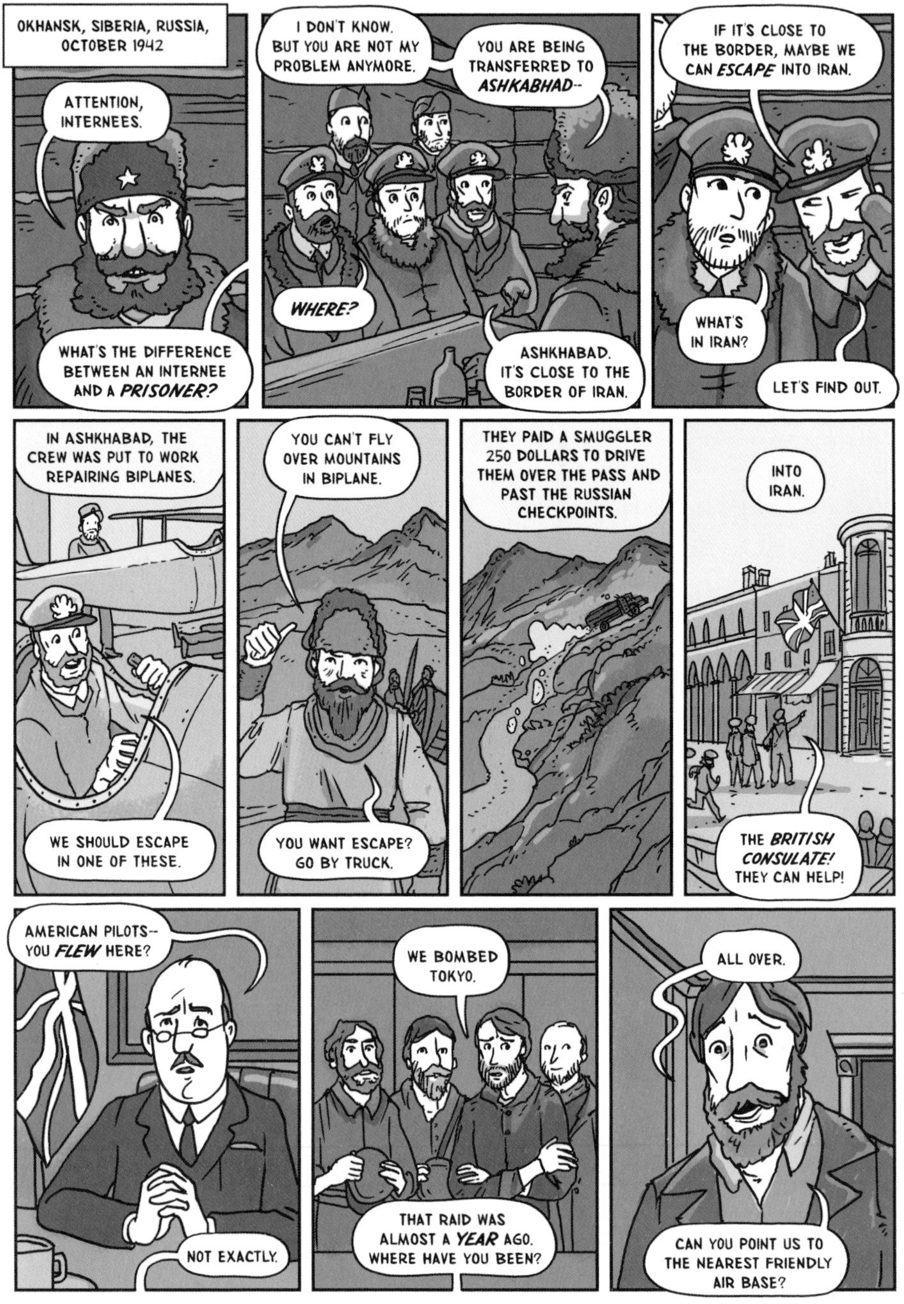
OKHANSK, SIBERIA, RUSSIA, OCTOBER 1942
ATTENTION, INTERNEES.
WHAT'S THE DIFFERENCE BETWEEN AN INTERNEE AND A *PRISONER?*
I DON'T KNOW. BUT YOU ARE NOT MY PROBLEM ANYMORE.
YOU ARE BEING TRANSFERRED TO *ASHKABHAD*--
WHERE?
ASHKHABAD. IT'S CLOSE TO THE BORDER OF IRAN.
IF IT'S CLOSE TO THE BORDER, MAYBE WE CAN *ESCAPE* INTO IRAN.
WHAT'S IN IRAN?
LET'S FIND OUT.
IN ASHKHABAD, THE CREW WAS PUT TO WORK REPAIRING BIPLANES.
WE SHOULD ESCAPE IN ONE OF THESE.
YOU CAN'T FLY OVER MOUNTAINS IN BIPLANE.
YOU WANT ESCAPE? GO BY TRUCK.
THEY PAID A SMUGGLER 250 DOLLARS TO DRIVE THEM OVER THE PASS AND PAST THE RUSSIAN CHECKPOINTS.
INTO IRAN.
THE *BRITISH CONSULATE!* THEY CAN HELP!
AMERICAN PILOTS-- YOU *FLEW* HERE?
NOT EXACTLY.
WE BOMBED TOKYO.
THAT RAID WAS ALMOST A *YEAR* AGO. WHERE HAVE YOU BEEN?
ALL OVER.
CAN YOU POINT US TO THE NEAREST FRIENDLY AIR BASE?

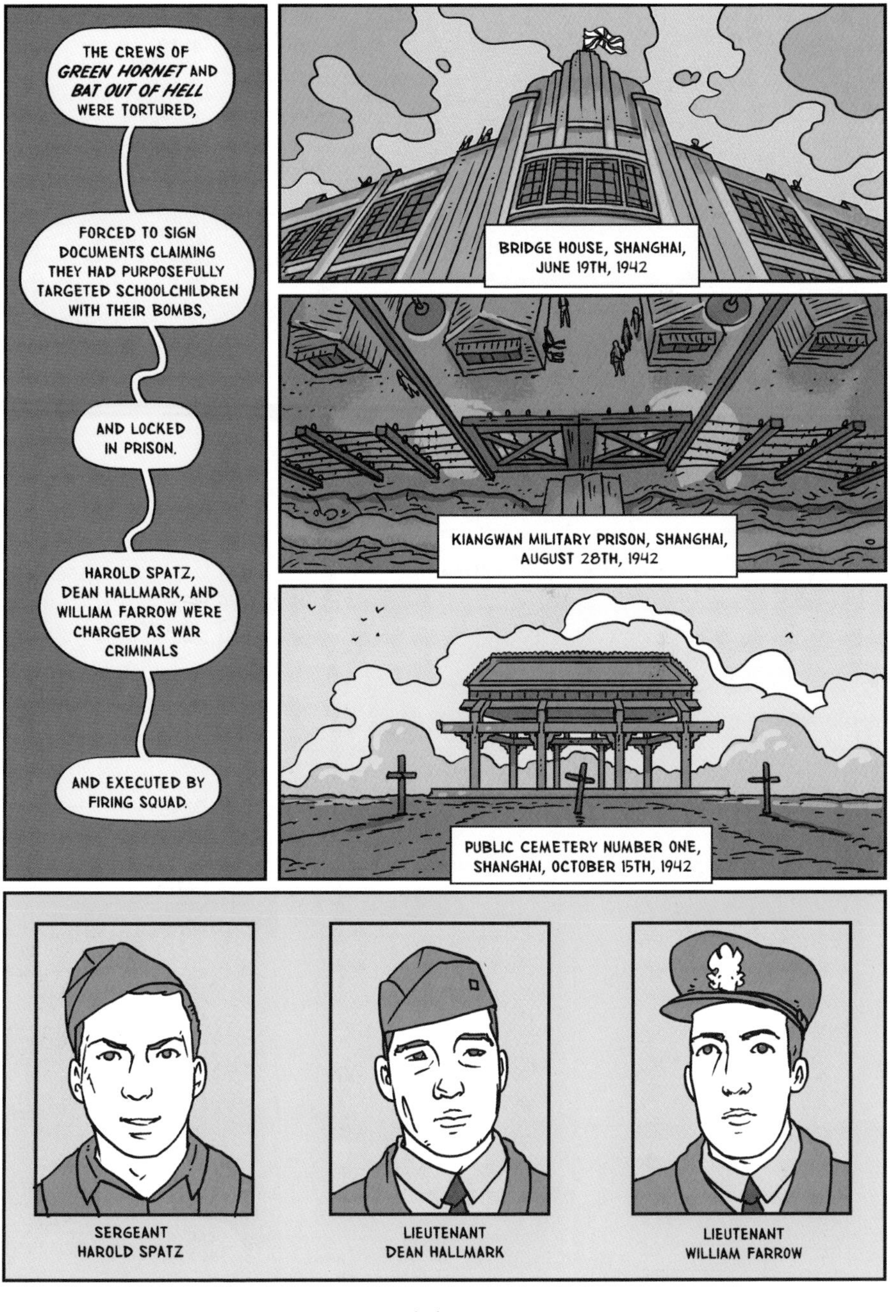
THE CREWS OF *GREEN HORNET* AND *BAT OUT OF HELL* WERE TORTURED,
FORCED TO SIGN DOCUMENTS CLAIMING THEY HAD PURPOSEFULLY TARGETED SCHOOLCHILDREN WITH THEIR BOMBS,
AND LOCKED IN PRISON.
HAROLD SPATZ, DEAN HALLMARK, AND WILLIAM FARROW WERE CHARGED AS WAR CRIMINALS
AND EXECUTED BY FIRING SQUAD.
BRIDGE HOUSE, SHANGHAI, JUNE 19TH, 1942
KIANGWAN MILITARY PRISON, SHANGHAI, AUGUST 28TH, 1942
PUBLIC CEMETERY NUMBER ONE, SHANGHAI, OCTOBER 15TH, 1942
SERGEANT HAROLD SPATZ
LIEUTENANT DEAN HALLMARK
LIEUTENANT WILLIAM FARROW

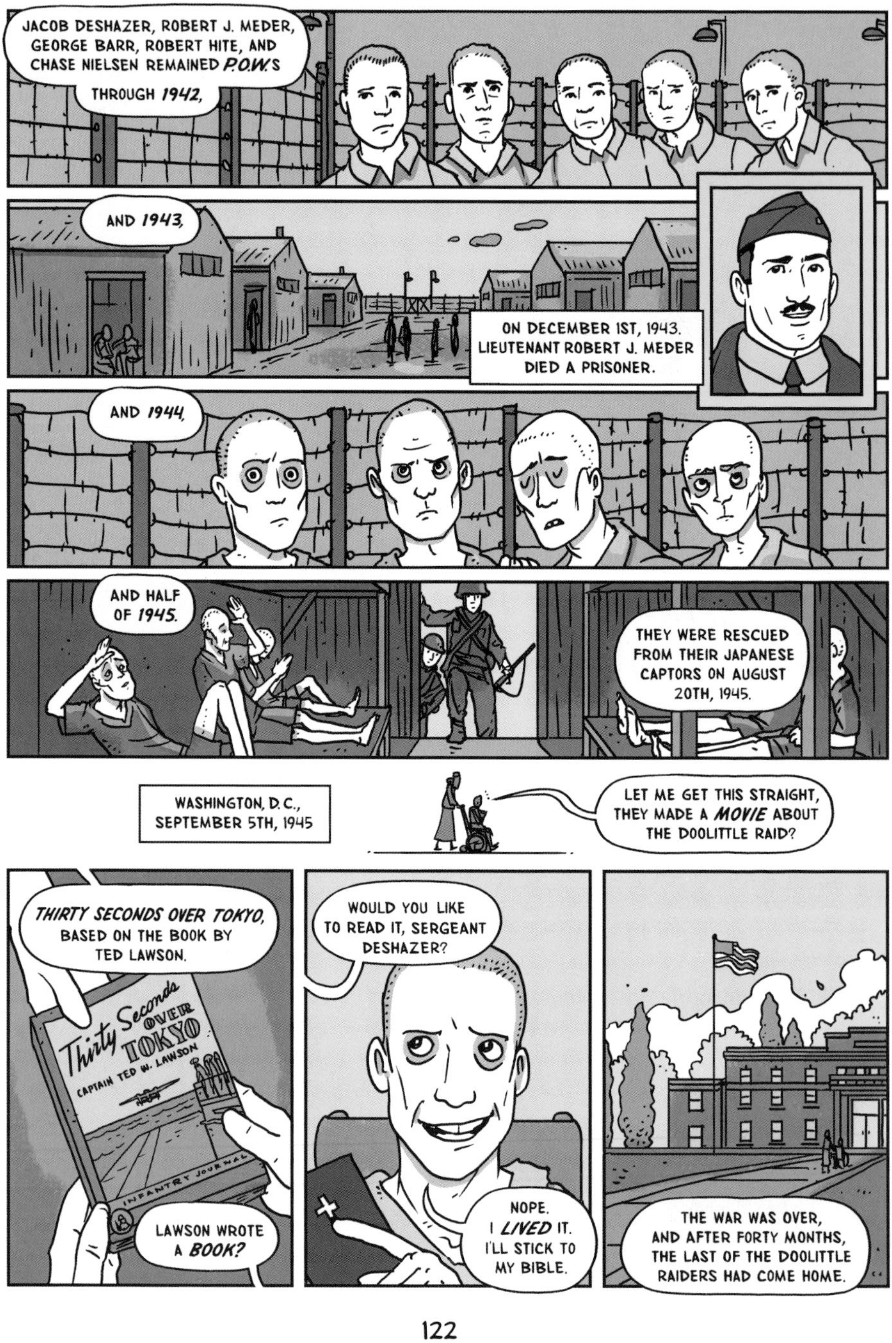
JACOB DESHAZER, ROBERT J. MEDER, GEORGE BARR, ROBERT HITE, AND CHASE NIELSEN REMAINED P.O.W.S
THROUGH 1942,
AND 1943,
ON DECEMBER 1ST, 1943. LIEUTENANT ROBERT J. MEDER DIED A PRISONER.
AND 1944,
AND HALF OF 1945.
THEY WERE RESCUED FROM THEIR JAPANESE CAPTORS ON AUGUST 20TH, 1945.
WASHINGTON, D.C., SEPTEMBER 5TH, 1945
LET ME GET THIS STRAIGHT, THEY MADE A MOVIE ABOUT THE DOOLITTLE RAID?
THIRTY SECONDS OVER TOKYO, BASED ON THE BOOK BY TED LAWSON.
Thirty Seconds OVER TOKYO
CAPTAIN TED W. LAWSON
INFANTRY JOURNAL
LAWSON WROTE A BOOK?
WOULD YOU LIKE TO READ IT, SERGEANT DESHAZER?
NOPE. I LIVED IT. I'LL STICK TO MY BIBLE.
THE WAR WAS OVER, AND AFTER FORTY MONTHS, THE LAST OF THE DOOLITTLE RAIDERS HAD COME HOME.

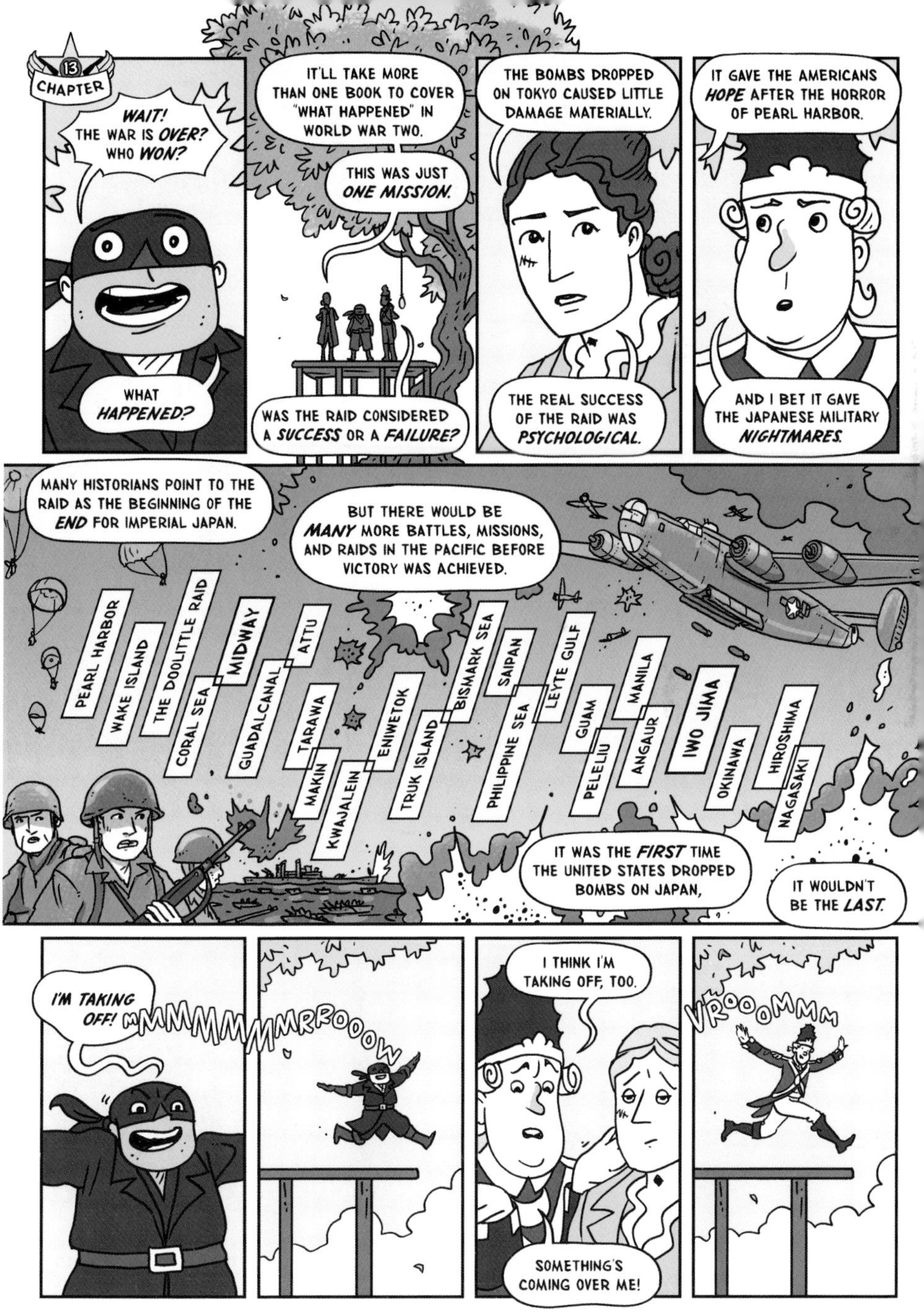
CHAPTER 13
WAIT! THE WAR IS OVER? WHO WON?
WHAT HAPPENED?
IT'LL TAKE MORE THAN ONE BOOK TO COVER "WHAT HAPPENED" IN WORLD WAR TWO.
THIS WAS JUST ONE MISSION.
WAS THE RAID CONSIDERED A SUCCESS OR A FAILURE?
THE BOMBS DROPPED ON TOKYO CAUSED LITTLE DAMAGE MATERIALLY.
THE REAL SUCCESS OF THE RAID WAS PSYCHOLOGICAL.
IT GAVE THE AMERICANS HOPE AFTER THE HORROR OF PEARL HARBOR.
AND I BET IT GAVE THE JAPANESE MILITARY NIGHTMARES.
MANY HISTORIANS POINT TO THE RAID AS THE BEGINNING OF THE END FOR IMPERIAL JAPAN.
BUT THERE WOULD BE MANY MORE BATTLES, MISSIONS, AND RAIDS IN THE PACIFIC BEFORE VICTORY WAS ACHIEVED.
PEARL HARBOR
WAKE ISLAND
THE DOOLITTLE RAID
CORAL SEA
MIDWAY
GUADALCANAL
ATTU
TARAWA
MAKIN
KWAJALEIN
ENIWETOK
TRUK ISLAND
BISMARK SEA
PHILIPPINE SEA
SAIPAN
LEYTE GULF
GUAM
PELELIU
MANILA
ANGAUR
IWO JIMA
OKINAWA
HIROSHIMA
NAGASAKI
IT WAS THE FIRST TIME THE UNITED STATES DROPPED BOMBS ON JAPAN,
IT WOULDN'T BE THE LAST.
I'M TAKING OFF!
MMMMMMMMRROOOOW
I THINK I'M TAKING OFF, TOO.
SOMETHING'S COMING OVER ME!
VROOOMMM

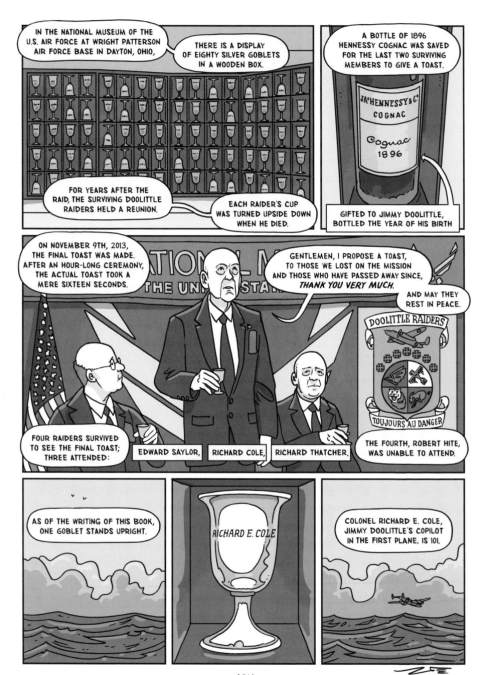

IN THE NATIONAL MUSEUM OF THE U.S. AIR FORCE AT WRIGHT PATTERSON AIR FORCE BASE IN DAYTON, OHIO,

THERE IS A DISPLAY OF EIGHTY SILVER GOBLETS IN A WOODEN BOX.

A BOTTLE OF 1896 HENNESSY COGNAC WAS SAVED FOR THE LAST TWO SURVIVING MEMBERS TO GIVE A TOAST.

JA'HENNESSY & C.
COGNAC
Cognac
1896

FOR YEARS AFTER THE RAID, THE SURVIVING DOOLITTLE RAIDERS HELD A REUNION.

EACH RAIDER'S CUP WAS TURNED UPSIDE DOWN WHEN HE DIED.

GIFTED TO JIMMY DOOLITTLE, BOTTLED THE YEAR OF HIS BIRTH

ON NOVEMBER 9TH, 2013, THE FINAL TOAST WAS MADE. AFTER AN HOUR-LONG CEREMONY, THE ACTUAL TOAST TOOK A MERE SIXTEEN SECONDS.

GENTLEMEN, I PROPOSE A TOAST, TO THOSE WE LOST ON THE MISSION AND THOSE WHO HAVE PASSED AWAY SINCE, *THANK YOU VERY MUCH.*

AND MAY THEY REST IN PEACE.

DOOLITTLE RAIDERS
TOUJOURS AU DANGER

FOUR RAIDERS SURVIVED TO SEE THE FINAL TOAST; THREE ATTENDED:

EDWARD SAYLOR,   RICHARD COLE,   RICHARD THATCHER.

THE FOURTH, ROBERT HITE, WAS UNABLE TO ATTEND.

AS OF THE WRITING OF THIS BOOK, ONE GOBLET STANDS UPRIGHT.

RICHARD E. COLE

COLONEL RICHARD E. COLE, JIMMY DOOLITTLE'S COPILOT IN THE FIRST PLANE, IS 101.

NH
HT

NATHAN HALE'S HAZARDOUS TALES

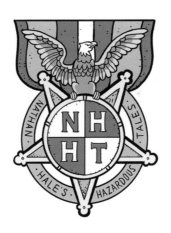

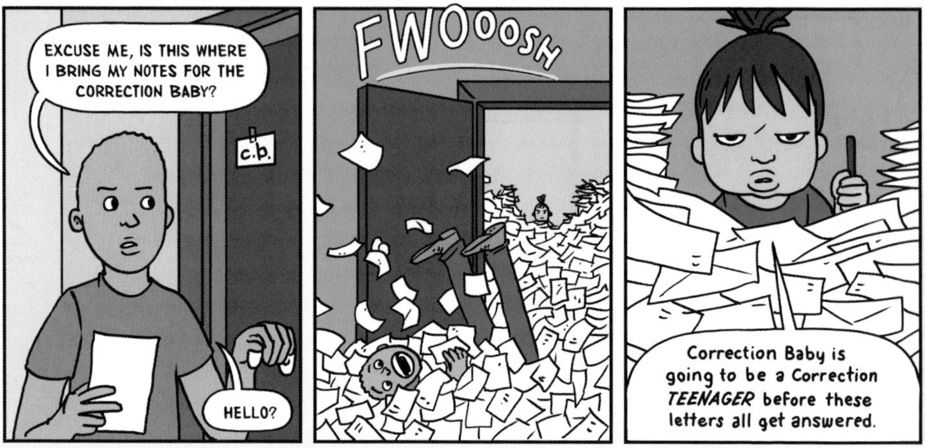
EXCUSE ME, IS THIS WHERE I BRING MY NOTES FOR THE CORRECTION BABY?
c.b.
HELLO?
FWOooSH
Correction Baby is going to be a Correction *TEENAGER* before these letters all get answered.

IF YOU DON'T MIND A LONG WAIT, SEND YOUR COMMENTS AND CORRECTIONS TO: CORRECTIONBABY@HAZARDOUSTALES.COM

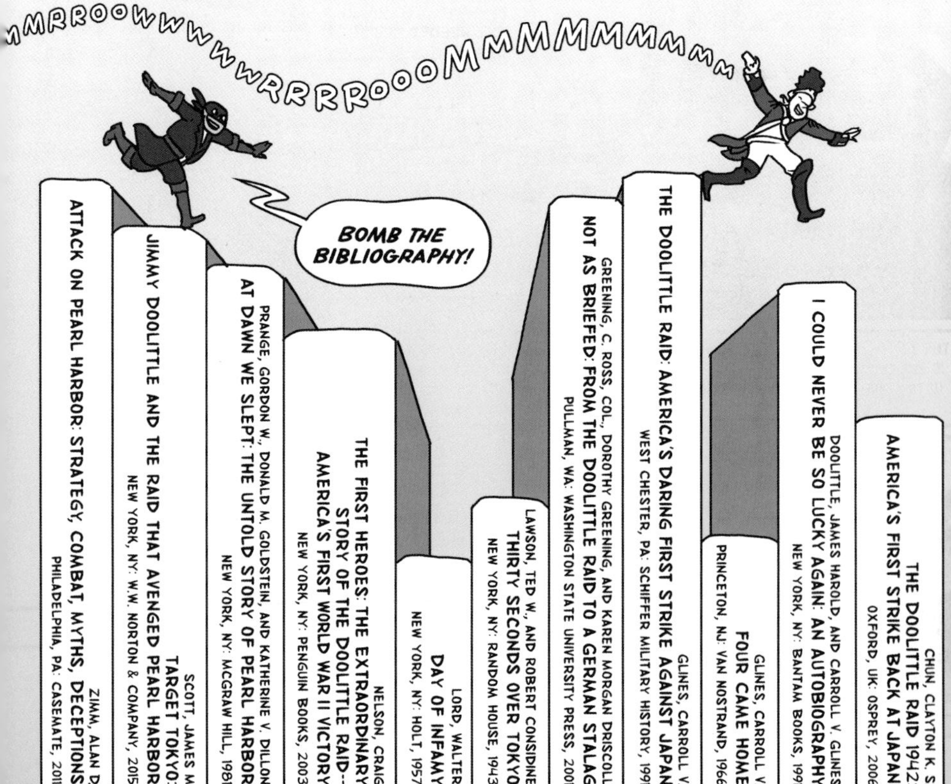
MMRROOWWWWWRRRRROOOOMMMMMMMMMMM
BOMB THE BIBLIOGRAPHY!
ZIMM, ALAN D. ATTACK ON PEARL HARBOR: STRATEGY, COMBAT, MYTHS, DECEPTIONS PHILADELPHIA, PA: CASEMATE, 2011
SCOTT, JAMES M. TARGET TOKYO: JIMMY DOOLITTLE AND THE RAID THAT AVENGED PEARL HARBOR NEW YORK, NY: W.W. NORTON & COMPANY, 2015
PRANGE, GORDON W., DONALD M. GOLDSTEIN, AND KATHERINE V. DILLON AT DAWN WE SLEPT: THE UNTOLD STORY OF PEARL HARBOR NEW YORK, NY: MCGRAW HILL, 1981
NELSON, CRAIG THE FIRST HEROES: THE EXTRAORDINARY STORY OF THE DOOLITTLE RAID-- AMERICA'S FIRST WORLD WAR II VICTORY NEW YORK, NY: PENGUIN BOOKS, 2003
LORD, WALTER DAY OF INFAMY NEW YORK, NY: HOLT, 1957
LAWSON, TED W., AND ROBERT CONSIDINE THIRTY SECONDS OVER TOKYO NEW YORK, NY: RANDOM HOUSE, 1943
GREENING, C. ROSS, COL., DOROTHY GREENING, AND KAREN MORGAN DRISCOLL NOT AS BRIEFED: FROM THE DOOLITTLE RAID TO A GERMAN STALAG PULLMAN, WA: WASHINGTON STATE UNIVERSITY PRESS, 2001
GLINES, CARROLL V. THE DOOLITTLE RAID: AMERICA'S DARING FIRST STRIKE AGAINST JAPAN WEST CHESTER, PA: SCHIFFER MILITARY HISTORY, 1991
GLINES, CARROLL V. FOUR CAME HOME PRINCETON, NJ: VAN NOSTRAND, 1966
DOOLITTLE, JAMES HAROLD, AND CARROLL V. GLINES I COULD NEVER BE SO LUCKY AGAIN: AN AUTOBIOGRAPHY NEW YORK, NY: BANTAM BOOKS, 1991
CHUN, CLAYTON K. S. THE DOOLITTLE RAID 1942: AMERICA'S FIRST STRIKE BACK AT JAPAN OXFORD, UK: OSPREY, 2006

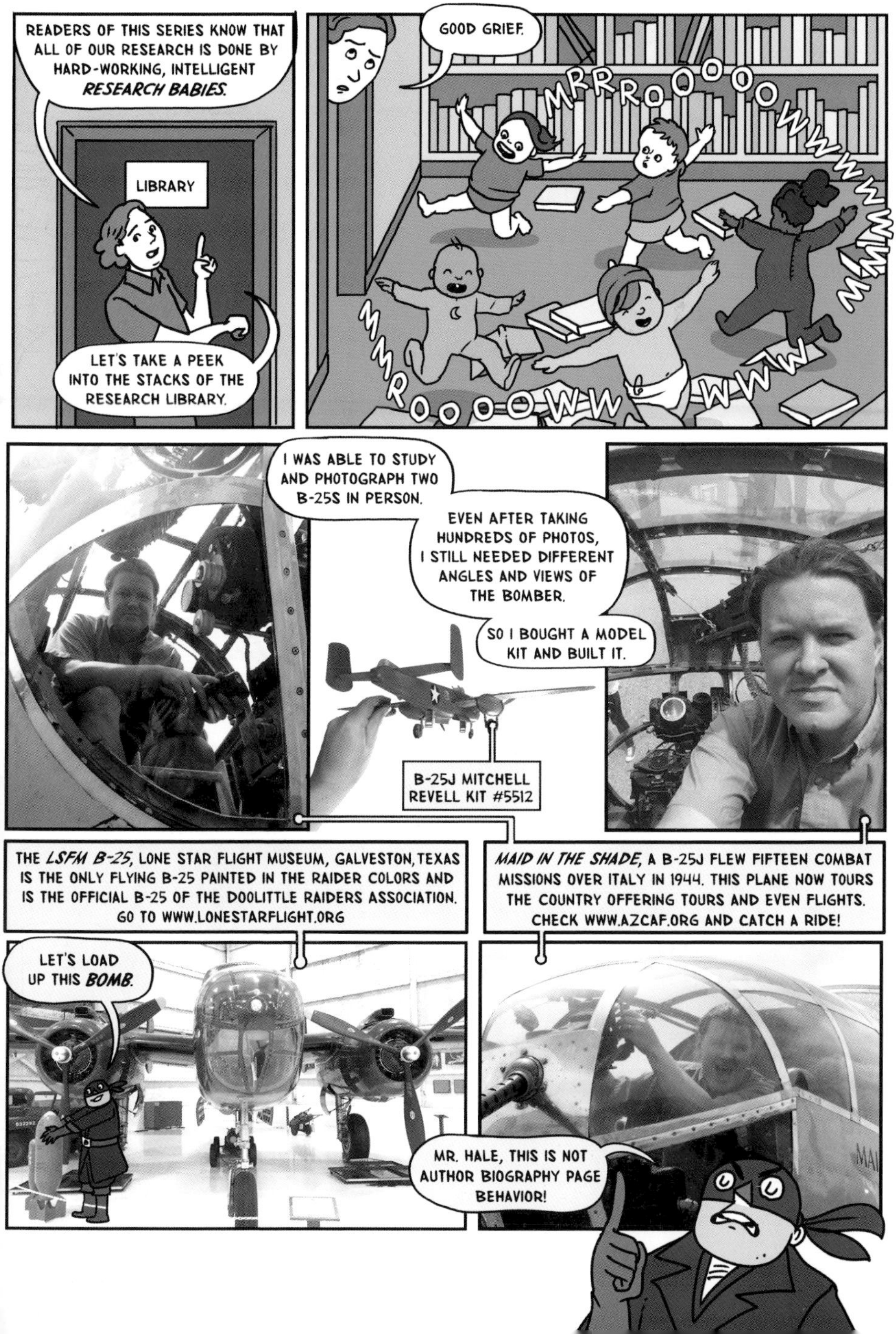
READERS OF THIS SERIES KNOW THAT ALL OF OUR RESEARCH IS DONE BY HARD-WORKING, INTELLIGENT *RESEARCH BABIES.*
LIBRARY
LET'S TAKE A PEEK INTO THE STACKS OF THE RESEARCH LIBRARY.
GOOD GRIEF.
MRRROOOOOOWWWWWWMMMMMM
MMROOOOOOWW
WWWW
I WAS ABLE TO STUDY AND PHOTOGRAPH TWO B-25S IN PERSON.
EVEN AFTER TAKING HUNDREDS OF PHOTOS, I STILL NEEDED DIFFERENT ANGLES AND VIEWS OF THE BOMBER.
SO I BOUGHT A MODEL KIT AND BUILT IT.
B-25J MITCHELL REVELL KIT #5512
THE *LSFM B-25*, LONE STAR FLIGHT MUSEUM, GALVESTON, TEXAS IS THE ONLY FLYING B-25 PAINTED IN THE RAIDER COLORS AND IS THE OFFICIAL B-25 OF THE DOOLITTLE RAIDERS ASSOCIATION. GO TO WWW.LONESTARFLIGHT.ORG
MAID IN THE SHADE, A B-25J FLEW FIFTEEN COMBAT MISSIONS OVER ITALY IN 1944. THIS PLANE NOW TOURS THE COUNTRY OFFERING TOURS AND EVEN FLIGHTS. CHECK WWW.AZCAF.ORG AND CATCH A RIDE!
LET'S LOAD UP THIS *BOMB*.
MR. HALE, THIS IS NOT AUTHOR BIOGRAPHY PAGE BEHAVIOR!

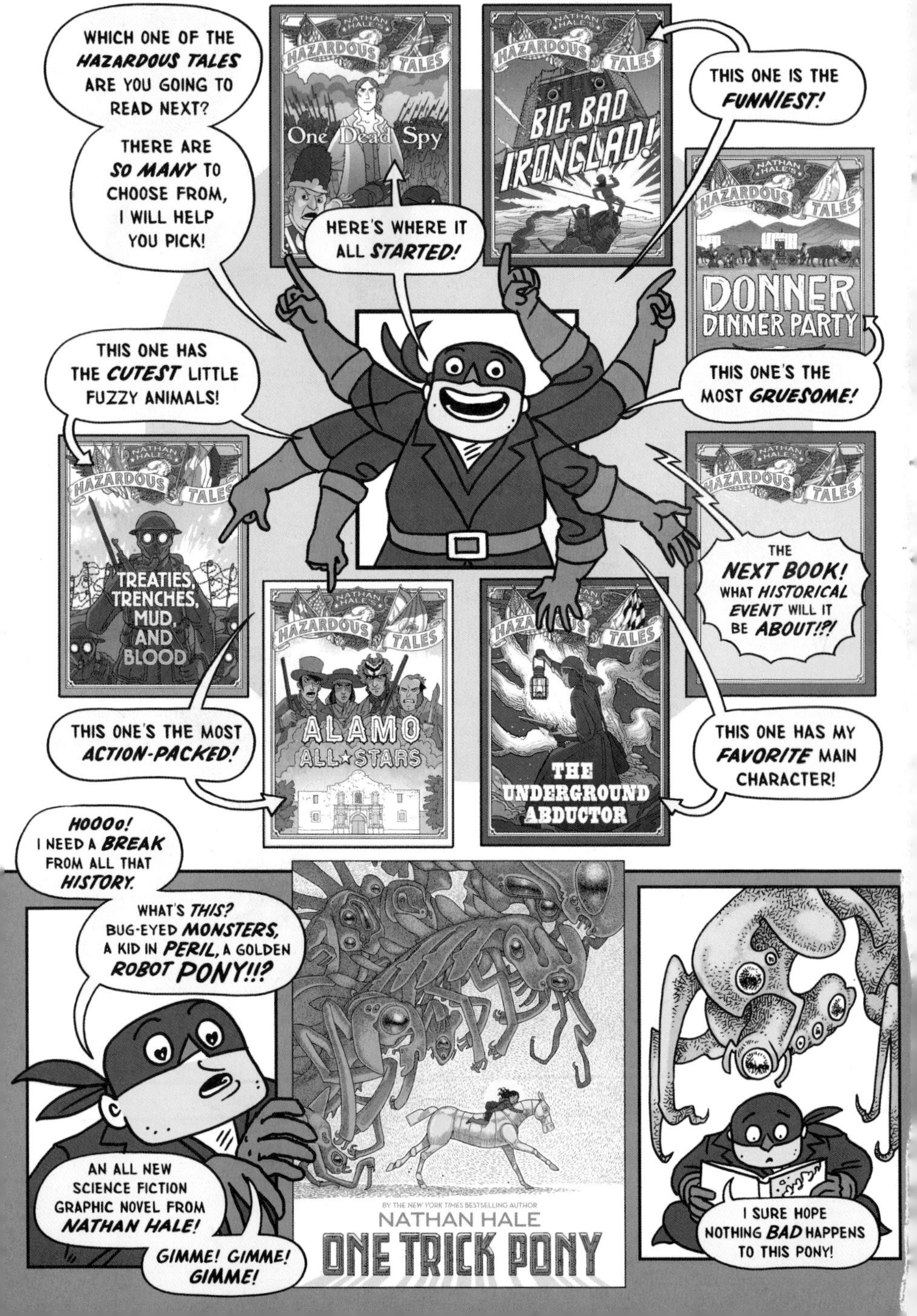

WHICH ONE OF THE HAZARDOUS TALES ARE YOU GOING TO READ NEXT?
THERE ARE SO MANY TO CHOOSE FROM, I WILL HELP YOU PICK!
NATHAN HALE'S HAZARDOUS TALES
One Dead Spy
HERE'S WHERE IT ALL STARTED!
NATHAN HALE'S HAZARDOUS TALES
BIG BAD IRONCLAD!
THIS ONE IS THE FUNNIEST!
NATHAN HALE'S HAZARDOUS TALES
DONNER DINNER PARTY
THIS ONE'S THE MOST GRUESOME!
THIS ONE HAS THE CUTEST LITTLE FUZZY ANIMALS!
NATHAN HALE'S HAZARDOUS TALES
TREATIES, TRENCHES, MUD, AND BLOOD
NATHAN HALE'S HAZARDOUS TALES
THE NEXT BOOK! WHAT HISTORICAL EVENT WILL IT BE ABOUT!?!
NATHAN HALE'S HAZARDOUS TALES
ALAMO ALL★STARS
THIS ONE'S THE MOST ACTION-PACKED!
HAZARDOUS TALES
THE UNDERGROUND ABDUCTOR
THIS ONE HAS MY FAVORITE MAIN CHARACTER!
HOOOo! I NEED A BREAK FROM ALL THAT HISTORY.
WHAT'S THIS? BUG-EYED MONSTERS, A KID IN PERIL, A GOLDEN ROBOT PONY!!!?
BY THE NEW YORK TIMES BESTSELLING AUTHOR
NATHAN HALE
ONE TRICK PONY
AN ALL NEW SCIENCE FICTION GRAPHIC NOVEL FROM NATHAN HALE!
GIMME! GIMME! GIMME!
I SURE HOPE NOTHING BAD HAPPENS TO THIS PONY!

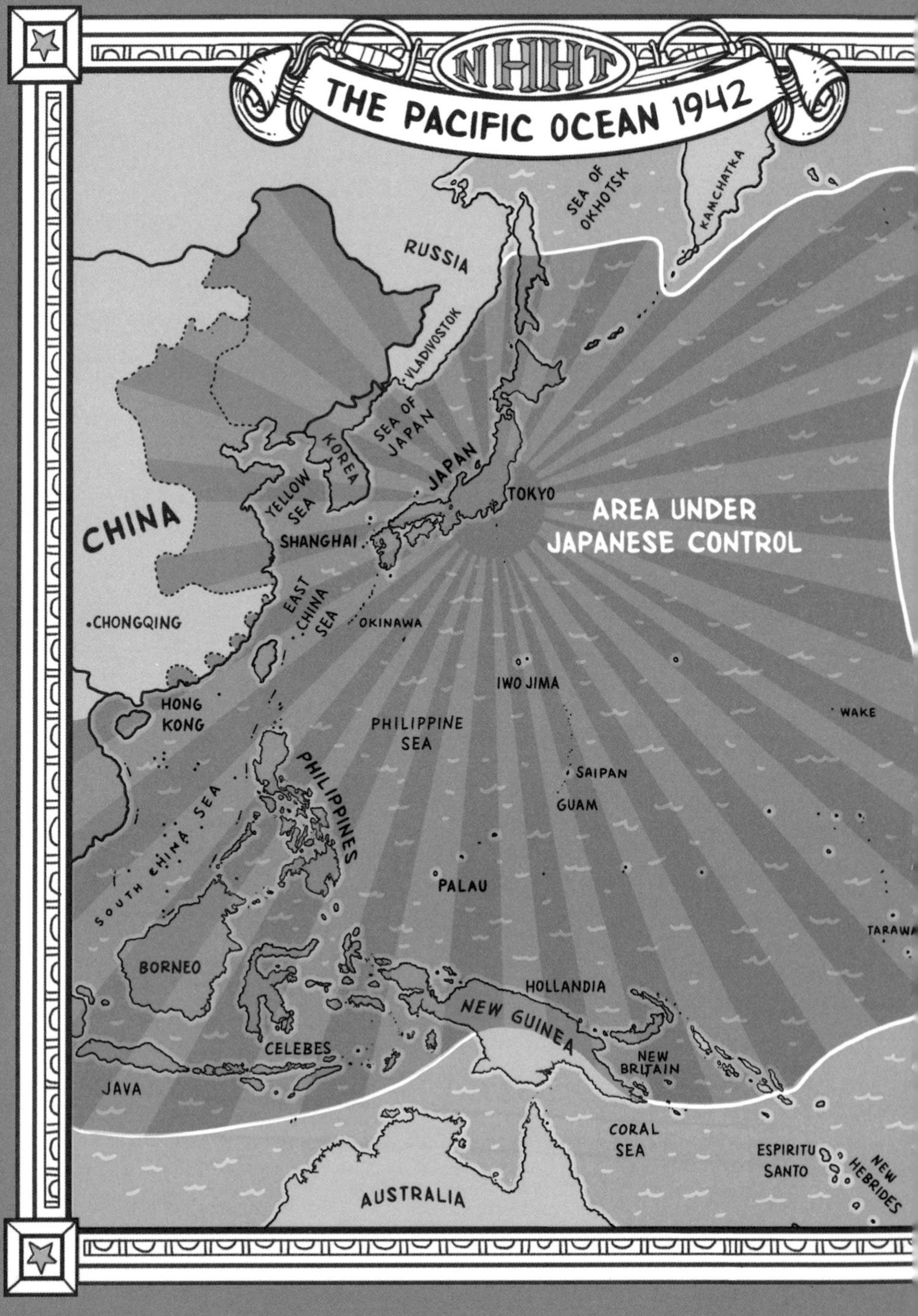

NHHT
THE PACIFIC OCEAN 1942
SEA OF OKHOTSK
KAMCHATKA
RUSSIA
VLADIVOSTOK
SEA OF JAPAN
KOREA
JAPAN
TOKYO
YELLOW SEA
CHINA
SHANGHAI
AREA UNDER JAPANESE CONTROL
EAST CHINA SEA
OKINAWA
CHONGQING
IWO JIMA
HONG KONG
PHILIPPINE SEA
WAKE
PHILIPPINES
SAIPAN
GUAM
SOUTH CHINA SEA
PALAU
TARAWA
BORNEO
HOLLANDIA
NEW GUINEA
CELEBES
NEW BRITAIN
JAVA
CORAL SEA
ESPIRITU SANTO
NEW HEBRIDES
AUSTRALIA